Electronic Voting and Democracy

Also by Norbert Kersting

REFORMING LOCAL GOVERNMENT IN EUROPE: Closing the Gap between Democracy and Efficiency (*editor with Angelika Vetter*)

POVERTY AND DEMOCRACY: Political Participation and Self-Help in Third World Cities (*editor with Dirk Berg Schlosser*)

DEMOCRATIZATION AND POLITICAL CULTURE IN COMPARATIVE PERSPECTIVE (*editor with Lasse Cronqvist*)

Also by Harald Baldersheim

THE SELF-REGULATING MUNICIPALITY (*editor with Krister Ståhlberg*)

Electronic Voting and Democracy

A Comparative Analysis

Edited by

Norbert Kersting
Senior Lecturer in Political Science, University of Marburg, Germany

and

Harald Baldersheim
Professor of Political Science, University of Oslo, Norway

First published 2004 by
PALGRAVE MACMILLAN
Houndmills, Basingstoke, Hampshire RG21 6XS and
175 Fifth Avenue, New York, N. Y. 10010
Companies and representatives throughout the world

PALGRAVE MACMILLAN is the global academic imprint of the Palgrave Macmillan division of St. Martin's Press, LLC and of Palgrave Macmillan Ltd. Macmillan® is a registered trademark in the United States, United Kingdom and other countries. Palgrave is a registered trademark in the European Union and other countries.

ISBN 978-1-349-51891-3   ISBN 978-0-230-52353-1 (eBook)
DOI 10.1057/9780230523531

This book is printed on paper suitable for recycling and made from fully managed and sustained forest sources. Logging, pulping and manufacturing processes are expected to conform to the environmental regulations of the country of origin.

A catalogue record for this book is available from the British Library.

Library of Congress Cataloging-in-Publication Data
Electronic voting and democracy: a comparative analysis/edited by Norbert Kersting and Harald Baldersheim.
    p. cm.
  Includes bibliographical references and index.
    1. Internet voting–Cross-culture studies. 2. Electronic voting–Cross-culture studies. 3. Internet–Political aspects. 4. Political participation–Computer network resources. 5. Comparative government. I. Kersting, Norbert. II. Baldersheim, Harald, 1944–
    JF1032.E43 2004
    324.6'5–dc22   2004045077

Contents

List of Figures and Tables

Figures

Tables

Notes on the Contributors

Joachim Åström, Department of Social Sciences, University of Örebro, Sweden.

Harald Baldersheim, Professor, Department of Political Science, University of Oslo, Norway.

Hubertus Buchstein, Professor, Institute of Political Science, University of Greifswald, Germany.

Wolfgang Drechsler, Professor, Department of Public Administration, University of Tartu, Estonia.

Hans Geser, Professor, Department of Political Science, University of Zürich, Switzerland.

Kimmo Grönlund, Department of Political Science, Abo Akademi University, Turku, Finland.

Pia Karger, Federal Ministry of the Interior, Berlin, Germany.

Norbert Kersting, Institute for Political Science, Philipps University Marburg, Germany.

Robert Kofler, Institute for Information Economics, Vienna University of Economics.

Robert Krimmer, Institute for Information Economics, Vienna University of Economics.

Ronald Leenes, Department of Law, Twente University, Enschede, Netherlands.

Ülle Madise, Executive Secretary and Advisor, Constitutional Committee, Estonian Parliament, Estonia.

Ramona S. McNeal, Department of Political Science, Kent State University, Ohio, USA.

Pippa Norris, Professor, John F. Kennedy School of Government, Harvard University, USA.

Jan Olsson, Professor, Department of Social Sciences, University of Örebro, Sweden.

Lawrence Pratchett, Department of Public Policy, De Montfort University, Leicester, United Kingdom.

Alexander Prosser, Professor, Institute for Information Economics, Vienna University of Economics.

Maija Setälä, Department of Political Science, University of Turku, Finland.

Fred Solop, Professor, Department of Political Science, University of Northern Arizona, USA.

Jörgen S. Svensson, Department of Sociology, Twente University, Enschede, Netherlands.

Caroline J. Tolbert, Professor, Department of Political Science, Kent State University, Ohio, USA.

Melvin Wingfield, Department of Public Policy, De Montfort University, Leicester, United Kingdom.

Preface

In 2001, the first German online election took place during the direct election for the head of county executive. During research on this pilot project it became quite clear that there is a lack of both theoretical reflection and empirical data on the subject. This situation sparked the idea to initiate a team of political scientists concerned with Internet voting and e-democracy in order to build a research agenda and to foster comparative research.

The Internet Voting Workshop, which took place in June 2002, provided an overview of the pilot projects and strategies regarding Internet voting in various local and national elections. The workshop focused primarily on social, political and legal aspects of Internet voting and less on technical matters. Survey data as well as the results of qualitative research in focus groups were presented. The workshop was financed by the Fritz-Thyssen foundation, which also financed empirical research on the Internet election project in Marburg. The workshop was organized by the Research Committee 05 (Comparative Studies on Local Government and Politics) of the International Political Science Association (IPSA) and the Institute of Political Science at Philipps University in Marburg.

At times, the implementation of online voting seems to be a horse-race. Which country will be the first to implement this instrument? For some years now, a number of countries have developed expertise in order to investigate Internet voting, and a number of book projects underway, mostly national case studies, came to our knowledge during the planning of the workshop. The workshop aimed to bring together prominent experts working in this field, including representatives of groups from national administrations (mostly the ministry of the interior). Participants came from many countries, while colleagues who were unable to attend were kept informed about its progress and its results.

The lively discussions in the workshop highlighted variations with regard to national administrative and legal settings as well as political-cultural diversity. One of the discoveries of the workshop was how such diversity may lead to context-bound and nationally specific paths towards e-democracy. Nevertheless, some generalizations also emerged.

We would like to thank all participants involved. Together with the helping hands of Kym Turner, David Bosold and Anna Maria Mischkowsky the workshop was made into a wonderful and stimulating event, and we hope that there will be further fruitful cooperation. Interested colleagues are warmly welcome to join us in further efforts in this field.

NORBERT KERSTING
HARALD BALDERSHEIM

Part I

Issues and Theoretical Frameworks

1
Electronic Voting and Democratic Issues: An Introduction

Norbert Kersting and Harald Baldersheim

The rapid spread of the Internet since the 1990s has led to high expectations for democracy. The Internet has been presented as a means to more transparency in political life and new forms of political communication. Especially with regard to elections, the core process of modern democracies, the Internet has promised concrete and speedy advantages (Slaton 1992). Online elections may simplify and speed up the electoral process and also reduce costs, and the counting of votes and presentation of results may be carried out faster and more reliably. The falling rates of electoral participation that have been observed in many Western democracies since the 1980s have triggered a search for new ways of stimulating voter interest in elections and politics, and the Internet has naturally been a focus of hope in this respect. Some even claim that electronic voting and other uses of the Internet may fundamentally change the nature of the democratic process as we have known it. Lower costs of political communication could, for example, herald a new dawn for direct democracy (Coleman 2001; Gibson 2001), and perhaps the ideals of discursive democracy may finally be realized in cyberspace. Public Man (Sennet 1977) may rise again. Through Internet participation and Internet protest, as was the idea of some protagonists, a new form of strong democracy may emerge (see Barber 1989, 1999; Tsagarousianu 1998). However, there are also skeptical voices to be heard in the discussions on digital democracy and Internet voting.

This book explores two set of issues: (1) the potentials, problems and experiences associated with electronic voting and other steps towards e-democracy, and (2) why some countries seem more willing than others to take such steps, especially the introduction of electronic voting.

E-democracy: a definition

Since the publication of Karl Deutsch's classic *The Nerves of Government* (1965), the functions of and capacities with regard to information processing and communication have been considered vital for political systems. Steps towards electronic democracy are taken when these functions are supported or enhanced by electronic devices (machines and software) of various types (see Engstöm 2000; Jansen and Priddat 2001; West 2002; Cap Gemini and Young 2003). Electronic devices may also facilitate transactions between governments and citizens, such as service delivery or voting. The growing literature on e-democracy is focusing on the new opportunities for democratic participation presented by electronic channels of information processing, communication and transaction (Hague and Loader 2002; Karmack and Nye 2002), as indicated in Figure 1.1. Through electronic devices these features are also becoming increasingly integrated, which is indicated by double-ended arrows in the figure. From the PC in the parlour, for example, the citizen may get information about local politics, discuss political matters with fellow citizens or with council members, and, when his/her mind is made up, (perhaps) cast a vote for the party or candidate of his/her choice.

- *Information.* The possibility for citizens to consult political information is the most widespread function delivered by the new information and communication technologies. Information can be disseminated more effectively, and the democratic objectives of transparency, for example, can be achieved more easily. Policy documents, the structures and procedures of institutions, the programmes of political parties and candidates and other information

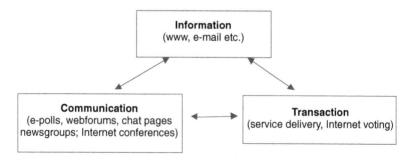

Figure 1.1   Features of e-democracy

can be rapidly disseminated to citizens. This kind of information normally reflects the broadcasting characteristics of e-citizen information systems since there is one authority delivering information to many citizens (www-pages).

- *Communication.* The Internet facilitates the exchange of information between individuals and groups. This may take place as individual consultation where the authorities address citizens individually and receive individual responses; the individual form of communication via e-mail is a fast and cheap way to contact the administration for individual citizens. The Internet also opens up the possibility of collective consultations, when, in a two-way information system for example, authorities might address citizens with questionnaires (e-polls). Collective communication is also possible in a less standardized way (web forums, newsgroups, chat pages, online conferences), where citizens may also enter into discussions with other citizens and also with elected officials or members of the bureaucracy.
- *Transaction.* Empowered by new information and by deliberations of the discursive community citizens may participate in decision-making processes, for example e-referenda or Internet voting. Such forms of participation go beyond citizen consultation and amount to opportunities for influencing government and parliamentary decisions (see Budge 1996).

However, it is still open to discussion whether Internet voting is to be seen as an important step in a chain of citizen empowerment and deliberation (Hague and Loader 2002), or as a deplorable debasement of the democratic process. This is the issue around which the contributions to this volume revolve.

What is electronic voting?

Electronic voting is voting supported by electronic devices. The range of devices may include electronic registration of votes, electronic counting of votes and, lately, channels for remote voting, especially the Internet. In this book, we focus in particular on the potential for remote voting over the Internet, but other means of electronic voting are also considered. Below, a typology of electronic voting devices and procedures is developed (Table 1.1). First, electronic voting procedures may be characterized by the type of channel of communication offered to the voter with regard to the act of casting the vote. Here, the main distinction is between the Internet and other types of devices. Furthermore, the level of control exercised by the electoral authorities is taken into account (see Kersting 2002a). In some cases, electoral computers are located in the polling station and can thus be completely controlled by the electoral authorities. Identification and authentication are carried out by the officials in the polling station through existing voter registers. External manipulation, for example by computer viruses, Trojan horses or other service attacks is not possible because there is no external communication and the data are stored on the polling machine.

Modern electoral machines in use in United States elections and in some European cities were often introduced as pilot projects in order to test voting via a computer. In the USA, electronic voting devices have a long tradition. Beside the traditional ballot voting in some states and counties mechanical lever-machines, electronic punch-card systems, direct recording electronic systems or optical scan-ballots have been introduced (see Caltech/MIT voting technology project 2001). The complications experienced with the punch-card and the butterfly-ballot systems during the 2000 presidential elections are well-known. With the exception of the Netherlands and Belgium, in most of the European pilots the electronic vote had to be confirmed by casting a traditional ballot paper as well (Buchstein 2000). The electronic vote was therefore just a simulation of the real vote.

Voting by the Internet can be divided into three types:

- *Intranet voting in the polling station.* Here the Internet is used to transfer the data from the polling station to the local, regional or central electoral authority. This kind of voting is performed at a public

Table 1.1 A typology of electronic voting procedures*

Level of infrastructure control by electoral authority	Internet	Other electronic devices
High	Intranet poll site voting	Voting machines
Medium	Kiosk voting	
Low	Internet voting	SMS text voting
		Telephone voting
		Interactive digital television voting

*See also Gibson 2001; Pratchett *et al.* 2002; Gritzalis 2003.

computer and is similar to a system of electronic voting machines. The connection from the polling station to the headquarters is for the most part by Intranet. External manipulation, for example by computer viruses or external service attacks, is in principle still possible but can be prevented more easily.

- *Kiosk voting.* Here, voters have the opportunity to use special computers situated in public rooms such as libraries, schools or shopping malls. Because the electoral process cannot be controlled by public authorities, special instruments for electronic authentication are necessary, for example a digital signature or smart card, finger prints, and so on.
- *Internet voting.* Remote Internet voting at home or from the workplace entails further technical risks. Here, software programs or other instruments such as smart cards are required for identification and authentication. However, the social context cannot be readily controlled and problems regarding the secrecy of the vote may arise.

Online elections have been tried out in variety of arenas and institutional settings. Such experiments are more numerous in voluntary associations and large private companies, such as elections to student bodies in universities or elections of shareholder representatives to company boards. Many countries have been more reluctant to introduce online procedures for political elections, for example parliamentary or local elections; there are usually constitutional and other legal hurdles that have to be overcome. The legal issues often revolve around problems of secrecy of the vote and the security of the electoral process. Other skeptics have pointed to the so-called digital divide that may prevent certain groups of citizen from making use of electronic voting channels.

Voter turnout and the digital divide

Is Internet voting an instrument that may serve to enhance voter turnout? Since the 1980s in a number of countries voter turnout has been decreasing dramatically, so that low voter turnout is becoming more than a marginal phenomenon. The greater volatility of electorates affects the established parties which are experiencing problems mobilizing their core partisan groups. Low voter turnout is seen as a symbol of diminishing legitimacy of the political system as well. Some argue that the spread of negative attitudes towards politicians and parties represents a crisis of the political system (see Lijphart 1997):

widespread participation in free and fair elections is postulated as a constitutional goal and is seen as an important element in the definition of democracy (Dahl 1989).

Table 1.2 presents an overview of the development of voter turnout in national elections in nine countries since 1970. Most of the countries have experienced a decline in turnout. Sweden is largely an exception to this trend while France has seen the most dramatic decline. In local and European elections levels of participation are even lower than in national elections. In the latest European elections, for example, only 40 per cent of the German electorate turned out and between 50 and 60 per cent of Germans voted in local elections. In the UK, levels of European and local participation have become even lower than those of Germany.

The growth of non-voting is a complex phenomenon that is far from fully explained. Post-materialist values among the younger generation may be part of the explanation, leading to a preference for unconventional channels of participation (demonstrations, NGOs, referenda, single-issue politics, and so on). The decline of traditional social and concomitant political ties (class, church) may be another factor. The feeling of civic obligation that has so far characterized the voting habits among the older generations is on the wane in other groups (Wolfinger and Rosenstone 1980; Renz 1997; DETR 1998, 2000).

Is Internet voting likely to amend this situation? The existence of a *digital divide* is an argument that may be levelled against hopes placed in the Internet. Is the spread of information and communication technologies (ICT) so fast and access to the Internet actually so ubiquitous that by now talk about its advent has a realistic foundation? Despite the rapid spread of the Internet, use of or access to ICT is still far from universal. Deborah Philipps characterizes this situation in claiming that, 'Some voters are more equal than others' (see Gibson 2001). The variations in access to ICT and the Internet are explored further in Chapter 2 by Kimmo Grönlund. Although there are methodological problems in ascertaining levels of Internet access, it is also obvious that the Internet is spreading fast. Access and use are typically lower among the older generation, people with low education and in peripheral districts. However, since voting is lower precisely among those groups that seem to be most disaffected with or uninterested in traditional politics (young, educated urbanites), who are also at the same time those that represent the digital generation, there may in fact be reasons to expect that Internet voting might be an attractive channel for groups who would not otherwise bother to go to the polling station.

Table 1.2   National Parliamentary Elections: Voter Turnout since 1970 (percentages)

Year	USA	Switzerland	Austria	Estonia	Finland	France	Germany	United Kingdom	Sweden
1970	70.3		91.8		82.2			72.2	88.3
1971		56.4	92.4						
1972	79.9				81.4		91.1		
1973						81.3			90.8
1974	58.2							78.9/72.9	
1975		52.4	92.9		73.8				
1976	77.6						90.7		91.8
1977									
1978	57.0					71.6			
1979		48.1	92.9		75.3			76.0	90.7
1980	76.5						88.6		
1981						70.9			
1982	61.1								91.4
1983		48.9			75.7		89.1	72.8	
1984	74.6								
1985									89.9
1986	54.9		90.5			78.5			
1987		47.5			72.1		84.3	75.4	
1988	72.5					66.2			86.0
1989									
1990	56.0		90.5	78.0			77.8		
1991		46.0			68.4				86.7
1992	78.0			67.8				77.8	
1993						68.9			
1994	57.6		91.9				79.0		88.1
1995		42.2	85.9	68.9	68.6				

Table 1.2 National Parliamentary Elections: Voter Turnout since 1970 (percentages) continued

Year	USA	Switzerland	Austria	Estonia	Finland	France	Germany	United Kingdom	Sweden
1996	66.0								
1997	51.5					68.0		71.5	
1998							82.2		81.4
1999	48.5	43.2	80.4	57.4	65.3				
2000									
2001								59.4	
2002			84.3			60.3	79.1		
2003		45.6							

Source: IDEA (2002).

Problems of secrecy, security and privacy

Problems regarding security and privacy are core issues in discussions on electronic voting, and solutions to these issues are central to the notions of free and fair elections. The issue of secrecy and security is addressed in Table 1.3, which presents an overview of the extent to which safeguards of a 'free vote' and 'fair elections' are explicitly mentioned in the constitution of a sample of countries.

In most of these countries, general, direct, free and equal elections that maintain the secrecy of the vote are protected by constitutional stipulations and safeguards. A free vote is characterized by the absence of manipulation in the voting process. When secrecy and privacy are guaranteed through physical measures in the polling station and in registration and counting procedures, ballots can be cast without fear of manipulation or pressure from others. The question is if this secrecy is controlled by the state or if it is the responsibility of the voter. In traditional polling-station voting it is normally the public authorities that take responsibility for secrecy and security. With Internet voting from home or 'on the run' the citizen will have to take such responsibility. Furthermore, the secrecy defines the relation of the voter to the state and its agencies. The voting decision is expected to be anonymous, which is to say that public authorities should not be able to ascertain who has voted for whom. To what extent voter anonymity can be guaranteed in online elections is still a matter of debate.

This debate has led to doubts about online elections, based on the normative points of view outlined above. The argument is that if secrecy and anonymity of the vote cannot be guaranteed, this may jeopardize the legitimacy of the election with potential repercussions for the entire political system. These arguments are developed into serious objections to online elections in Chapter 3 by Hubertus Buchstein.

However, electoral systems and voting procedures are not static elements of a political order, they change and evolve over time in response to changing circumstances. We argue below that it is reasonable to see the debate on online elections as part of a wider process of political evolution.

Changing electoral procedures: adapting to the new voter, an evolutionary perspective

Table 1.3 outlines how electoral systems may vary across countries, and also identifies certain trends in the development of electoral systems.

Table 1.3 Constitutional stipulations regarding free and fair elections

	Constitutional clauses	Secrecy mandated	General enfranchisement	Norms of free elections	Equality of voters stipulated	Direct elections mandatory
United States	Am. 15/19/24/26	No	No	No	No	No
Switzerland	Art. 34II/136I/149II	No	No	Yes	Yes	Yes
Austria	Art. 26	Yes	Yes	Yes	Yes	Yes
Estonia	§60	Yes	Yes	Yes	Yes	Yes
Finland	Sect. 25	Yes	Yes	No	Yes	Yes
France	Art. 3 III	Yes	Yes	No	Yes	Yes
Germany	Art. 38	Yes	Yes	Yes	Yes	Yes
United Kingdom						
Sweden	Chap. 3 §1	Yes	No	Yes	Yes	Yes

Source: Schweizerische Bundeskanzlei (2002a).

These trends represent responses to new social conditions and lifestyles among the electorates. We will argue that the introduction of online elections represents a further step in this process of adaptation that has already been under way for some time.

Recent reforms in electoral legislation in many countries listed in Table 1.3 show that as a reaction to the decreasing voter turnout two reform trajectories (Table 1.4) are being pursued. One trajectory leads to a growing focus on the situation of the individual citizen in the electoral process. This is often accompanied by a certain anti-party attitude, and so citizens are given more influence in the recruitment of political candidates and incumbents. Personalized electoral systems such as direct election of mayors and special forms of the personal vote, for example transferable votes (cumulative voting, panache), are implemented or dis-

Table 1.4 Electoral rules and infrastructure

Electoral rules	*Electoral infrastructure*
Electoral systems (proportional/majority)	Voter registration
Size of the electoral districts	Voting on a rest day
Electoral counting system (Hare-Niemeyer/d'Hondt)	More days of voting
Quora (5 per cent, etc.)	Early voting
Enfranchisement of foreigners	Proxy voting
Lower age of voting	Postal voting
Length of legislative period (frequency of elections)	Electronic voting machines
Conjunction of elections	Cross linking of the polling stations
Personal vote (direct election of mayors; transferable vote (cumulative vote, panache), etc.	Alternative polling booth
Referenda	Electronic voting by telephone, sms text messages, digital TV, etc.)
	Remote Internet voting

(left margin, with downward arrow): Individualization
(right margin, with downward arrow): Automatization

Towards the digital voter?

Sources: See Kersting (2002b); Norris (2002).

cussed. The voice of the citizen is also strengthened by new forms of direct democracy such as the introduction of referenda. The growing popularity of user surveys may be seen as an expression of the same trend emerging at the output side of the political system.

The second trajectory is found in various initiatives intended to make the process of voting more convenient to the voter, such as the introduction of postal voting, early voting, polling machines, automatic registration of voters, and a cross-linking of polling stations in order to build up a centralized voter register. Remote online voting and voting by telephone or sms text voting belong to this second type of reform. The common denominator of such innovations is the liberalization and automatization of the voting process, that is the voter may vote at his/her convenience without having to go to a specific polling station in a specific place on a specific day. This trajectory may have profound effects on the voting process, to some extent breaking with the traditional idea of the symbol-laden ballot in the polling station.

If these two trajectories are manifestations of deeper social trends, Internet voting may be hard to resist in the long run. Individualization and automatization may be intertwined processes that drive wider changes of political systems. What are the long-run implications for the democratic process? Is the digital voter Public Man in a new form, or is a semi-privatized consumer democracy the best we may hope for?

Implications for the democratic process: varieties of e-democracy

There is no lack of speculations as to the implications of ICT for democratic developments. As mentioned above, some implications are seen as being of a benign nature, others as more threatening. It is, first of all, evident that electronic channels and devices may support many features of existing *representative* democracy. ICT is a powerful tool for facilitating communication between governmental agencies and citizens and is increasingly applied in this manner by a multitude of governmental bodies, including national parliaments and local councils. An impressive array of applications could be listed in this respect, for example electronic information and retrieval systems that ease the electoral scrutiny of the decision-making process of representative bodies. Furthermore, as political parties increasingly seek to establish a presence on the net, political competition may intensify, especially if the Internet makes it easier for new parties to become established. During election campaigns various types of online 'voter compasses' are presented, intended to help voters get a more accurate picture of party positions on various issues. Arguably, such devices may make the choice process easier for a number of voters. So it is not unreasonable to argue that ICT in general and the Internet more specifically may serve to deepen representative democracy and to reduce some feelings of distance and alienation among certain groups of citizens.

It may also be argued, however, that the Internet and online voting may open up for plebescitarian or cesarist types of democracy. The Internet may reduce the cost of elections greatly and also the time it takes to go to the polls for governments and voters alike. The temptation to submit more and more issues to the polls may be hard to resist. Referenda will become substitutes for political leadership, especially in issues that cut across party lines and therefore split parties. Or political leaders may seek to circumvent parliamentary processes of decision-making and go directly to the people with issues, framed in such a way as to make certain that the outcome will be convenient to the powers-that-be.

One of the attractive visions engendered by ICT and Internet potential is that of *deliberative* democracy: more informed and sincere political debates made possible through easier access to information and the establishment of debate pages on the net. Here the free and open exchange of views and information may take place, less restricted by the asymmetries caused by unequal access to traditional mass media and the 'censorship' exercised by the columns of 'letters to the editor'.

The Internet has also turned out to be a channel for *activists* and *protesters* of all kinds. The potential of the Internet in this respect has been vividly demonstrated in connection with various international summits, such as the WTO meeting in Seattle or the EU meeting in Gothenburg. At the local level municipalities increasingly use the Internet to encourage citizens to make constructive contributions to decisions on various local issues, but activists may also use the Internet to thwart or block municipal initiatives. Protests may be coordinated through local chat pages or electronic actions encouraged, for example e-mail bombardment of public agencies or elected representatives with the 'wrong' view. The latter type of occurrences demonstrates the destructive and disruptive potential of the new media.

It has also been argued that more *communitarian* ideals may be realized with the assistance of the Internet. A 'virtual community' may seem self-contradictory, but some leading communitarians claim that communities may be established through the Internet with the essential features of a 'real' community (Etzioni and Etzioni

1999: 241). A community is defined as affect-laden relationships – bonding – supported by a common culture. To what extent virtual communities can actually be found is not quite clear but the authors maintain that systems with the necessary features to establish and sustain such communities can be designed using existing ICT components, for example interactive broadcasting over the web.

The structure of this book

The book is divided into three parts. In Part I the main issues related to online voting are spelt out. In Chapter 2 the actual spread of online technologies and know-how is investigated, addressing the issue of how deep the digital divides run, and to what extent such gaps represent barriers to online elections. In Chapter 3 constitutional and normative issues related to online voting are debated, and the reservations with regard to Internet voting are forcefully formulated. Next, a series of articles on developments with regard to online voting in individual countries is presented in Part II. The country studies demonstrate that there is indeed much variation with regard to interest in and willingness to experiment with Internet voting. Analyses of pilot experiments with electronic voting (Germany and the USA) are presented in Part III along with a study of voter attitudes to online voting and an assessment of the extent to which online voting is actually going to change electoral habits.

An interesting pattern to emerge, when collating trends with regard to the introduction of online voting in the final chapter, is that there is no one-to-one relationship between national interest (or lack thereof) in Internet voting and spread and use of the Internet in the population: This finding suggests that other factors besides technology must be taken into account when seeking to explain the spread of online voting. A contextual model of analysis is suggested in order to account for the emergent pattern of e-democratic initiatives across countries. The evolution of e-democracy seems clearly contingent upon crises of political legitimacy as well as technological opportunities and voter sophistication.

References

Aldrich, J. (1993) 'Rational Choice and Turnout', in *American Journal of Political Science*, 37: 246–78.
Almond, G. and Verba, S. (eds) (1980) *The Civic Culture Revisited*. Boston: Little, Brown.

Alvarez, M. and Nagler, J. (2000) *The Likely Consequences of Internet Voting for Political Representation*. Los Angeles: Loyola Law School.

Baldersheim, H. (2001) *E-Government in Nordic Cities and Regions*. Canterbury: ECPR Congress.

Barber, B. (1984). *Strong Democracy*. Berkeley: Berkeley Press.

Barber, B. (1999) 'Three Scenarios for the Future of Technology and Strong Democracy', in *Political Science Quarterly*, 113: 573–90.

Barnes, S., Kaase, M. *et al.* (1979) *Political Action*. London: Sage.

Brookings Institute (2000) *The Future of Internet Voting*. Washington, DC: Brookings Institute.

Buchstein, H. (2000) 'Präsenzwahl, Briefwahl, Online-Wahl und der Grundsatz der geheimen Stimmabgabe', in *Zeitschrift für Parlamentsfragen*, 4S: 886–902.

Budge, I. (1996) *The New Challenges Old Direct Democracy*. Oxford: Polity Press.

Caltech/MIT (2000) *Voting Technology Project: Residual Votes Attributable to Technology. An Assessment of the Reliability of Existing Voting Equipment*. Cambridge, Mass.: MIT Press.

Cap Gemini and Young (2003) *Online Availability of Public Services*. Berlin: <http://www.de.cgey.com/ servlet/PB/show/1005708/eEurope.pdf>

Coleman, S. (2001) 'What Was New? Online Innovations in the 2000 US Elections', in S. Coleman (ed.), *Elections in the Age of Internet: Lessons from the United States*. London: Hansard Society: 48–64.

DETR (UK Department of the Environment, Transport and the Regions) (2000) *Turnout at Local Elections*. London.

DETR (UK Department of the Environment, Transport and the Regions) (1998) *British Social Attitudes Survey*. London.

Deutsch, K. (1965) *The Nerves of Government. The Nerves of Government: Models of Political Communication and Control*. New York: Free Press.

Elster, J. (ed.) (1998) *Deliberative Democracy*. Cambridge: Cambridge University Press.

Engström, M. (2000) *Rebooting Europe*. British Council: <http://www.network-europe.net>

Gibson, R. (2001) 'Elections Online: Assessing Internet Voting in Light of the Arizona Democratic Primary', in *Political Science Quarterly*, 116(4): 561–83.

Green, D. and Shapiro, I. (1994) *Pathologies of Rational Choice Theory. A Critique of Applications in Political Science*. New Haven: Yale University Press.

Gritzalis, D. (ed.) (2003) *Secure Electronic Voting*. Boston: Kluwer Academic Publishers.

Habermas, J. (1997) *Die Einbeziehung des Anderen*. Frankfurt: Suhrkamp.

Hague, B. and Loader, B. (eds) (1999) *Digital Democracy. Discourse and Decision Making in the Information Age*. London: Routledge.

Holznagel, B. and Hanßmann, A. (2001) 'Möglichkeiten von Wahlen und Bürgerbeteiligung per Internet', in Holznagel, B. *et al. Elektronische Demokratie. Bürgerbeteiligung per Internet zwischen Wissenschaft und Praxis*. München: Beck: 55–72.

IDEA (International Institute for Democracy and Electoral Assistance) (2002) *Voter Turnout from 1945 to 1997. A Global Report on Participation*. Stockholm: IDEA.

Jackman, R. (1987) 'Political Institutions and Voter Turnout in the Industrial Democracies', in *American Political Science Review*, 81, 2: 405–23.

Jackman, R. and Miller, R. (1995) 'Voter Turnout in the Industrial Democracies during 1980s', in *Comparative Political Studies*, 27(4): 467–92.

Jansen, S. and Pridat, B. (2001) *Electronic Government. Neue Potentiale für einen Modernen Staat.* Stuttgart: Klett Cotta.

Karmack, E. C. and Nye, J. S. (Jr) (eds) (2002) *Governance.com. Democracy in the Information Age.* Spring Hill: Brookings Institution Press.

Kersting, N. (2002a) 'Internet-Wahlen im Vergleich. Deutschland, USA und Schweiz', in A. Siedschlag *et al.* (eds), *Kursbuch Internet und Politik 2/2002.* Opladen: Leske.

Kersting, N. (2002b) 'Die Zukunft der Parteien in der Lokalpolitik', in J. Bogumil (ed.), *Kommunale Entscheidungsprozesse im Wandel – Theoretische und Empirische Analysen.* Leske und Budrich: 139–62.

Kriesi, H. (2002) *E-voting. Motivation and Information Issues Workshop on E-voting and the European Parliamentary Elections.* Florence: European University Institute, May 2002.

Lijphart, A. (1997) 'Unequal Participation, Democracy's Unresolved Dilemma', in *American Political Science Review*, 85(4):1393–406.

Milner, H. (2001) *The Institutional Context of Civic Literacy, the Missing Link Between Social Capital and Political Participation.* ECPR conference Kent.

Norris, P. (2001) *A Digital Divide: Civic Engagement, Information Poverty and the Internet and in Democratic Societies.* New York: Cambridge University Press.

Norris, P. (2002a) *Democratic Phoenix: Political Activism Worldwide.* NY: Cambridge University Press.

Ohms, B. L. and Rieser, H. (1989) 'Die Briefwahl. Eine Möglichkeit für im Ausland lebende Staatsbürger, ihre politischen Rechte auszuüben? Ein europäischer Rechtsvergleich', in *Österreichisches Jahrbuch für Politik*: 209–23.

Polsby, N. (1963) *Community Power and Political Theory.* New Haven: Yale University Press.

Powell, B. (1980) 'Voting Turnout in 30 Democracies. Partisan, Legal, and Social Economic Influences', in R. Rose (ed.), *Electoral Participation. A Comparative Analysis.* London: Sage: 5–34.

Pratchett, L. (2002) *The Implementation of Electronic Voting in the UK.* London: Local Government Association.

Przeworski, A. und Teune, H. (1970) *The Logic of Comparative Social Inquiry.* New York: Wiley.

Putnam, R. D. (2000) *Bowling Alone. The Collapse and Revival of American Community.* New York: Simon & Schuster.

Schweizerische Bundeskanzlei (2002a) *Bericht über den Vote électronique. Chancen, Risiken und Machbarkeit elektronischer Ausübung politischer Rechte.* Bern: Bundeskanzlei.

Schweizerische Bundeskanzlei (2002b) *Vote électronique. Elektronische Ausübung politischer Rechte. Chancen, Risiken, Machbarkeit. Beilage 5: Stimmgeheimnis, Stimmzwang und Volksrechte in den souveränen Staaten der Welt.* Bern: Bundeskanzlei.

Schweizerische Bundeskanzlei (2002c) *Vote électronique. Elektronische Ausübung politischer Rechte. Chancen und Risiken, Machbarkeit. Beilage 3: Das Einwohnerregister (Stimmregister).* Bern: Bundeskanzlei.

Sennet, R. (1977) *The Fall of Public Man.* New York: Knopf.

Slaton, D. C. (1992) *Televote. Expanding Citizen Participation in the Quantum Age.* New York: Praeger.

Southwell, P. and Burchett, J. (2000) 'The Effect of All Mail Elections on Voter Turnout', *Social Science Quarterly*, 28(1): 72–9.
Tolbert, C. and McNeal, R. (2001) *Does the Internet Increase Voter Participation in Elections*. San Francisco: American Political Science Association.
Tsagarousianu, R. *et al.* (eds) (1998) *Cyberdemocracy*. London: Routledge.
Weber, M. (1923) *Wirtschaft und Gesellschaft*. Tübingen: Siebeck.
West, D. (2002) *Global E.-Government. Full Report Sept. 2002*. Brown University: <http://www.insidespolitics.org/egovt02int.html>
Wolfinger, R. and Rosentone, S. (1980) *Who Votes*. New Haven: Yale University Press.

2
Cyber Citizens: Mapping Internet Access and Digital Divides in Western Europe*

Kimmo Grönlund

Access to the new information and communication technologies (ICT) and an interest among citizens in using the technologies for political purposes are preconditions for the emergence of a polity with some of the features described as 'e-democracy'. This chapter investigates use of the Internet at the individual level in Western Europe with an emphasis on democratic aspects. The spread of the Internet has been accompanied by hopes for a democratic revival. But there are also fears that a new divide is emerging – the Digital Divide. How well-founded are these hopes and fears? The chapter cannot give the full answer to these questions, but mapping the spread of the ICT across countries and in various subgroups of the population will at least provide a foundation for assessing the potential for realizing some version of e-democracy and online voting.

The present chapter addresses the spread of ICT and examines digital divides in Western Europe from three perspectives. First, I am interested in the divide between countries; that is, how equally the West European countries are wired to the web. Second, I study divides within countries; that is, how equally the access and usage of the Internet are distributed in individual countries. Third, and perhaps most importantly, I attempt to establish if people actually use the Internet for political or democratic purposes. Even possible divisions into political and non-political users amongst the Internet public are studied.

* Parts of this work were carried out at the ZA-EUROLAB at the Zentralarchiv für Empirische Sozialforschung (ZA), Cologne. The Large Scale Facility was supported by the Improving Human Potential (IHP) Programme – Access to Research Infrastructures of the European Union.

Studying user profiles of different ICTs does not leave much choice when it comes to data selection; unfortunately, there is little hard comparative evidence at hand. Luckily, there are some soft data suitable for comparative analyses. I have chosen to use recent Eurobarometers that have been gathered by the European Commission. Especially two so-called Flash Barometers are useful, since their questions pertain to Internet use in particular. The objectives of the chapter are primarily descriptive but the determinants of the digital divide are discussed in relation to the prospects of electronic democracy as well.

ICTs in democratic decision-making

Political scientists have for a long time, even before the Internet was developed, debated the possibilities of exploiting ICTs for democratic purposes (e.g. Lewin 1970; Barber 1984). Communication technology has often been seen as a means to enhance deliberation between citizens, or even reduce democratic inequalities between them. Robert Dahl (1989: 338ff), for instance, in his famous framework for a more advanced democracy, proposes that an advanced democracy needs an 'attentive public' that is equally informed of the facts related to the political agenda and its issues. Since this ideal, however, seems improbable in real life, Dahl suggests a system of special *minipopulae* for political issues. A minipopulus should be representative of the whole population, the *demos*, and consist of, for example, 1,000 randomly selected citizens. According to his suggestion, a representative minipopulus could deliberate on an issue and announce its choices thereafter. The process could take a year and the meetings could be held via 'telecommunications'. A minipopulus could have an advisory committee of scholars and specialists. It must be kept in mind that Dahl's suggestion was put forward prior to the actual information age; he could not know the real potential of interactive and even mobile ICTs.

Implementing new decision-making applications via electronic channels has raised questions about the possible democratic consequences related to information and communication technology in general and the Internet in particular. Social scientists do not share a uniform view on the possibilities. The optimists have suggested that the use of new ICTs provide solutions to the civic distrust and the new political demands in established representative democracies, and provide opportunities for more democratic governance at the international level (Lewin 1970; Barber 1984). Sceptics have raised doubts about the overall possibilities of more participatory or deliberative forms of democracy in modern societies with increasing complexity (Habermas 1996: 315ff). They have also criticized the quality of communication transferred through ICTs (Barber 1999). Moreover, Norris (2001) has argued that the access and use of ICTs may reflect existing political inequalities both at the national and international levels. According to the most pessimistic views, the new ICTs may enhance the tendencies towards commercialism, consumerism and privacy at the expense of interest and participation in politics (Barber 1999).

In the latter part of the 1990s, both scholars and politicians became interested in the democratic potential of the Internet. A debate emerged with regard to its potential on the one hand, and its limits and inequalities on the other hand. The digital divide is a widely used concept that describes the gap between those who are digitally equipped and literate and those who are not. Norris (2001) defines three separate aspects of the digital divide. First, there is a global divide that refers to the divergence of Internet access between industrialized countries and developing countries. Second, there is a divide within different societies between the information rich and the information poor. Especially blue-collar workers, the elderly and the unemployed, that is groups that do not gain access to the Internet at school or work, might be left on a sidetrack in the networked world. Third, there is a democratic divide within the online community between those who engage themselves in political life via the Internet and those who do not. This divide can, of course, merely reflect the distribution of political interest of the population in the non-digital 'real' world.

The digital divide between countries

Globally, the Internet has grown very rapidly. According to an estimate by Nua.com, a company that specialized in Internet demographics, there were 26 million Internet users worldwide in 1995. In September 2002, the estimate was over 600 million users. This fast growth corresponds to over 80 million new users annually. Relatively speaking, however, less than 10 per cent of the world's population is online. Moreover, there is a clear geographical division between the wired and the non-wired world. Approximately 400 million users live in North America, Western Europe or Japan, whilst in many poor countries such as in Africa and Southeast Asia, the Internet is practically non-existent.

First, the levels of the Internet penetration in West European countries are studied (Table 2.1). This is done with two measures.

Table 2.1   Internet access and use in Western Europe, 2001 (percentage of households and personal users with access)

	Household access	Uses personally
Austria	47	62
Belgium	36	46
Denmark	59	70
Finland	50	64
France	30	45
Germany	38	53
Greece	10	17
Iceland	70	75
Ireland	48	56
Italy	34	37
Luxembourg	43	46
Netherlands	64	69
Norway	62	68
Portugal	26	33
Spain	25	37
Sweden	61	68
United Kingdom	49	57

Source: Flash Eurobarometer 112 (2002).

Comparisons of the households' access to the Internet as well as the shares of people who personally use the Internet are made. Thus, a special Eurobarometer (EB) survey on the new ICTs is used. For comparative reasons, this particular EB was conducted not only in EU countries but also in Iceland and Norway. The data were collected in November 2001. In the text some comparisons are also made with an earlier EB, conducted in October 2000.

In the first data column it can be seen that Iceland is the most wired country in Europe; altogether 70 per cent of Icelandic households are connected to the Internet. It is followed closely by a group of four countries, the Netherlands, Norway, Sweden and Denmark, in which almost two-thirds of households have a connection to the WWW. In Finland, the UK, Ireland and Austria almost half of households seem to be wired to the web. Within the EU, the average has risen from 28 per cent in 2000 to 38 per cent in November 2001. A digital divide between countries does seem to exist in Western Europe; in Greece, for example, only one household in ten claims to have access to the Internet.

Measuring access to the Internet from home is one way of looking at the possibilities to exploit the information highway. Other ways, however, are needed in order to get the whole picture. Accessibility can be obtained through several channels, at work or via terminals placed in Internet cafés or kiosks, schools and libraries. Therefore, the second data column reveals how European nations place themselves according to the question: 'Do you personally use the Internet?'

As may be expected, the pattern of Internet use at the individual level is similar to the households' access figures. Naturally, the shares of people using the Internet exceed the shares of households with an access to the Internet. Two-thirds of the adult population use the Internet in the Nordic countries and the Netherlands. Moreover, at least one-third of individuals use the Internet in all the Western European countries. There is one exception, however; in Greece, only 17 per cent of people use the Internet. Since all the Mediterranean countries show more modest usage shares than the other countries, it is legitimate to talk of a north–south division even within Western Europe.

The European countries have different strategies when it comes to public funding of ICT infrastructure and accessibility, and this is partly reflected in citizens' use of the Internet. Some countries offer public access points free of charge, whereas in other countries people have to rely on private cyber cafés in order to gain access to the web. Costs related to networks can be partially paid by the government. There are even differences in Internet connectivity from work and schools. In order to decipher the differences, we take a look at people's Internet use according to the point of access (Table 2.2). It should be kept in mind that the question asked in the Flash Eurobarometer allowed for multiple answers.[1] Thus, one person might access the web from several places.

In the Table, countries are listed in alphabetical order. Comparisons of the shares of people who use the Internet from (a) public access points in libraries, city or town halls, schools and universities, (b) work, and (c) cyber cafés are presented. In the first comparison, Iceland, Finland, Ireland and Norway have the highest shares. In these countries roughly 20 per cent say that they use the Internet from public access points. The lowest shares are for Portugal, Austria, Italy and Greece. These countries, with the exception of Austria, were also among those least connected in the comparisons in Table 2.1. Looking at the second point of access, work, Iceland takes the lead once more, followed by the rest of Scandinavia and Austria. Even in Ireland, Netherlands and the UK, many people use the Internet from work.

Private cyber cafés are most common in Ireland, Norway, Spain, Iceland, Germany and Greece. However, the frequency of people using

Table 2.2   Where Europeans use the Internet, June 2001 (percentages)

	Public access point	Work	Cyber café
Austria	7.3	28.1	1.2
Belgium	16.3	21.6	3.3
Denmark	15.8	35.7	2.4
Finland	20.2	30.3	1.7
France	12.3	17.8	2.3
Germany (E)	13.2	16.3	5.1
Germany (W)	12.0	20.9	4.9
Greece	4.7	6.5	4.8
Iceland	22.8	41.2	5.0
Ireland	19.9	27.1	8.1
Italy	6.2	12.2	1.4
Luxembourg	10.6	18.8	1.9
Netherlands	16.5	26.3	4.2
Norway	19.3	37.5	5.6
Portugal	7.6	12.3	0.6
Spain	11.3	13.9	5.3
Sweden	14.3	36.7	3.3
United Kingdom	15.4	24.8	4.2

Source: Flash Eurobarometer 103 (2002).

cyber cafés does not match that of using the net at public access points, at work or from home (Table 2.1). It is interesting to see that in poorly connected countries, such as Spain and Greece, many people use the net via private cyber cafés. This may indicate that people are obliged to do so, since other means are not easily available. It is also worth noticing that cyber cafés do not seem to have any popularity in Finland, which in other ways is well-connected. People seem to act rationally, they are not willing to pay for a service which they get free of charge elsewhere.

The social divide in Western Europe

Let us move on to the second aspect of the digital divide, that of a social nature. We start by taking a look at access figures between different age and social groups in West European countries. Table 2.3 cross-tabulates European Internet use according to age and gender. The data are from the Flash Eurobarometer 103, which was collected by phone in June 2001. The number of respondents in each country was 2,000, with the exception of Germany, where the sample consisted of 4,000 respondents.[2]

Table 2.3 Internet users in Western Europe according to age and gender, June 2001 (percentages)

	15–29 M	15–29 F	30–44 M	30–44 F	45–59 M	45–59 F	60– M	60– F
Austria	83.1	74.3	75.2	61.8	65.7	37.1	24.7	6.3
Belgium	86.1	77.2	71.1	50.9	46.6	26.4	12.9	2.6
Denmark	88.2	82.2	83.7	80.7	68.7	70.2	29.0	24.8
Finland	94.7	92.2	78.8	74.7	65.7	63.3	16.1	10.0
France	79.5	66.2	54.9	44.3	40.6	26.8	11.3	5.8
Germany (E)	84.8	77.2	67.7	46.6	46.8	31.0	16.5	5.9
Germany (W)	88.4	81.2	76.1	65.2	59.2	44.6	25.8	11.9
Greece	60.1	38.8	28.0	13.3	13.0	3.2	2.5	0.4
Iceland	96.9	95.3	92.8	85.4	72.9	65.3	29.0	12.9
Ireland	81.8	81.1	70.7	55.2	50.0	35.1	26.9	11.2
Italy	65.8	59.9	56.2	40.3	29.0	14.3	8.4	1.1
Luxembourg	86.4	75.1	66.0	48.6	51.9	29.6	18.3	3.5
Netherlands	93.8	85.4	84.6	70.1	75.5	46.1	32.0	15.0
Norway	98.4	94.5	88.6	83.3	77.4	61.6	30.4	15.2
Portugal	65.5	53.1	46.1	23.2	24.9	9.5	3.4	1.1
Spain	76.5	67.5	53.0	27.3	31.1	13.4	6.1	1.1
Sweden	94.0	94.2	90.1	80.4	78.9	67.7	28.3	22.9
United Kingdom	81.8	76.9	70.7	62.0	57.9	47.9	30.1	12.5
EU 15 *	79.1	70.7	64.9	50.9	47.9	32.5	17.9	7.5

* EU15 stands for the 15 member countries of the European Union; thus, Iceland and Norway are excluded.
Source: Flash Eurobarometer 103 (2002).

In this particular survey the pattern of the divide between countries prevails. Actually, the smallest shares in every category can be found in Greece. Not surprisingly, age seems to determine whether people use the WWW or not. Among the youngest age cohort, the Internet is used by a large majority of respondents. The only exceptions are Greek women of whom less than 40 per cent use the Internet in this age cohort. In the Nordic countries practically everyone below the age of 30 uses the net. The share of Internet users reduces linearly as we move towards older cohorts. There is also a divide between men and women; men are in every age cohort and country more connected than women. It is also interesting that the gender gap increases with age, older women are far less connected than men. The Internet is practically unknown for the oldest age cohort in Spain, Italy, Portugal and Greece. Of the countries with generally high penetration figures, Finland seems to make an exception. Elderly Finns do not seem to use the Internet, whereas the age gap is less clear in the rest of Scandinavia and Netherlands.

A simple typology of age and gender does not cover all the possible social gaps related to the new ICTs. Therefore, an overview of access according to social strata is desirable, and in Table 2.4 a cross-tabulation of Internet access and respondents' professions is presented.

Of all the professions, the category of farmers and fishermen has the largest variation in Internet use. All Swedish farmers seem to use the Internet, and even the majority of their Austrian, German, Finnish, Icelandic, Dutch and Norwegian colleagues do so. In Spain, Italy and Portugal, on the other hand, none of the farmers claims to use the net. Of all the categories in every country, students (and people in military service, which were classified together) are the ones who make use of the web most commonly, followed closely by professionals and people in general or middle-management. The unemployed are fairly well-connected in comparison with other groups, even though variations between countries are high. The groups with the least user shares are the retired and housewives, even though there are differences between the countries even here. Almost half of the housewives in Sweden, Iceland and Finland use the Internet, compared to minuscule shares in Greece, Portugal, Spain and Italy. At the EU level (i.e. excluding Iceland and Norway), students, managers and professionals are the most wired professions. The unemployed, manual workers and farmers lag far behind.

In the above it has been established how access to the Internet varies within the West European population. The measures have been at the

Table 2.4 European Internet users according to profession, 2001 (percentages)[3]

	Farmers, fishermen	Professionals	Shopkeepers, craftsmen	General management	Middle-management	Manual workers	Retired	Housewives	Students military service	Unemployed
AT	53.3	79.3	81.0	78.3	73.9	50.9	13.7	34.7	92.2	50.0
BE	23.1	75.0	54.2	81.0	72.9	29.7	7.8	14.7	95.3	26.6
DE (E)	76.9	68.0	69.2	64.2	58.9	48.6	9.7	21.8	93.9	35.2
DE (W)	69.9	77.6	78.7	86.0	75.6	53.5	18.4	28.4	95.9	60.0
DK	25	91.7	74.1	89.1	84.1	63.5	23.5	33.3	91.5	75.8
ES	0.0	85.9	32.8	88.1	53.0	20.8	2.6	4.7	85.5	39.7
FI	55.6	56.3	68.4	89.5	85.9	60.3	8.6	46.2	98.6	60.4
FR	17.6	46.2	58.6	70.6	50.3	27.3	8.1	21.5	86.2	41.3
GB	28.6	84.1	61.0	83.3	71.4	40.4	19.7	32.4	90.8	46.9
GR	1.7	37.2	24.4	42.9	35.4	12.8	0.9	0.7	63.3	35.5
IE	18.4	80.8	56.5	86.4	69.5	46.6	20.8	24.1	87.0	53.8
IS	51.6	93.4	74.9	89.5	93.3	73.9	10.2	48.7	97.4	73.5
IT	0.0	65.6	36.5	87.5	70.8	16.1	4.7	6.7	80.6	38.2
LU	25.0	82.6	51.2	76.2	78.8	26.9	11.8	20.5	96.6	62.5
NL	59.0	83.3	82.1	93.9	80.6	61.3	20.8	29.0	96.5	47.7
NO	53.3	86.1	71.9	91.9	80.1	67.5	14.2	33.8	99.5	66.7
PT	0.0	86.1	25.6	77.8	50.2	10.5	2.7	2.5	76.0	21.4
SE	100	92.3	82.5	100.0	92.4	73.0	19.6	49.1	96.0	79.6
EU15	48.7	74.9	53.9	80.6	65.9	39.0	11.9	16.1	87.7	43.9

Source: Flash Eurobarometer 103 (2002).

individual level, and we can already see that in most countries farmers and fishermen do not use the Internet to the same extent as people in other professions. This implies that there may even be differences between different areas of a country. Table 2.5 therefore presents how well people are connected in metropolitan areas, in other towns, and in the countryside in each West European country.

In West European countries people in metropolitan areas use the Internet more than in other areas. They are followed by people in other urban areas, whereas the countryside has the lowest shares of Internet users. This pattern seems to be fairly uniform. Only Belgium, Luxembourg and the western Länder of Germany have no substantial geographical contrasts. Belgium and especially Luxembourg are geographically small, which might explain the phenomenon. Other countries with small differences between people who live in different types of environments are the Netherlands, the United Kingdom, the eastern Länder of Germany, Sweden and Denmark. The largest geographic variations are found in Italy, Iceland, Ireland, Portugal and France.

All in all, the social patterns of Internet use are rather similar across West European countries. Men use the web more than women, the young more than the old, and urban people more than people in rural

Table 2.5 Internet users according to the area of residence, 2001 (percentages)

	Metropolitan zone	*Other town*	*Rural zone*
Austria	60.4	58.2	47.5
Belgium	46.9	45.6	45.9
Denmark	72.7	69.4	63.6
Finland	67.9	62.0	54.9
France	51.6	36.0	29.8
Germany (E)	50.5	43.1	44.0
Germany (W)	54.1	54.8	51.6
Greece	27.5	24.2	13.3
Iceland	78.3	70.8	54.5
Ireland	70.1	62.9	46.6
Italy	51.7	37.8	25.3
Luxembourg	43.9	49.2	
Netherlands	66.3	63.3	60.5
Norway	78.8	68.5	67.1
Portugal	47.4	36.2	24.9
Spain	41.9	35.0	27.1
Sweden	70.7	69.1	63.1
United Kingdom	57.5	54.8	51.5

Source: Flash Eurobarometer 103 (2002).

areas. It must be kept in mind, however, that there are large differences in Internet use between countries even in Western Europe, and the levels of access vary from country to country, even though the general social pattern is similar. In conclusion it is justified to say that social divides in ICT use still exist in Western Europe.

The democratic divide

This section discusses the third aspect of the digital divide, and tries to establish if there are variations with regard to democratic uses of the ICTs in Western Europe. Suitable data are difficult to find. However, in the Eurobarometers at hand, a question was asked about how people look for information or contact public administrations through the Internet. Thus, we can ascertain the extent to which people actually use the Internet in order to contact local authorities or other public agencies in their respective countries. Table 2.6 presents the shares of people accessing public administration in European countries. Men and women are presented separately.

Using public administration services online is most common in Finland, where over 70 per cent of Internet users have been in contact with government websites. Finnish women especially seem to be frequent

Table 2.6   Internet-users who access public administration online services in EU countries, 2000 (percentages)

	Men	*Women*
Austria	63	63
Belgium	58	53
Denmark	61	51
Finland	70	76
France	28	25
Germany	56	60
Greece	46	41
Ireland	36	37
Italy	39	41
Luxembourg	43	40
Netherlands	67	66
Portugal	29	19
Spain	42	37
Sweden	48	52
United Kingdom	45	50

Source: Flash Eurobarometer 88 (2001).

visitors to the homepages of the public administration. Even in other Nordic countries and in the Netherlands, Austria, Germany and Belgium at least half of Internet users have accessed government websites. Not surprisingly, people in the least connected countries visit government websites more rarely. The exception to the general pattern is Ireland, where citizens do not seem to visit such websites, even though they are placed high in the comparisons of Internet usage.

Naturally, Table 2.6 as it stands does not measure the possible existence of a democratic divide in the European Union. In order to study the provision of public information more thoroughly, I make use of a survey conducted among local mayors in the EU, the Flash Eurobarometer no. 79. This survey was carried out in the spring of 2000, and altogether 1,774 mayors were interviewed.[4] I cover three aspects: first, I examine the number of municipalities in each member state that have their own website; second, I measure the level of transparency on municipal websites; and third, I analyse the level of interactive services of the websites. These comparisons are presented in Table 2.7. The levels of transparent information[5] and interactivity[6] have been formed through a combination of questions in the survey. The values of interactivity and transparency are national means of indices, on a scale from 0 to 100: the lowest value zero corresponding

Table 2.7 Percentages of municipalities in the EU countries with websites, and national means of transparency and interactivity, 2000

	Website (%)	Transparency (means)	Interactivity (means)
Austria	73	71	44
Belgium	38	78	19
Denmark	70	64	36
Finland	94	87	23
France	33	61	15
Germany	77	60	20
Greece	21	33	29
Ireland	52	73	19
Italy	57	63	18
Luxembourg	60	61	0
Netherlands	27	61	11
Portugal	53	34	25
Spain	41	27	7
Sweden	100	79	21
United Kingdom	92	76	34

Source: Flash Eurobarometer 79 (2001).

to no transparency or no interactivity. The highest value 100 indicates that all the corresponding features of transparency or interactivity have been implemented at the municipal website. The exact features can be read in the footnotes: there are altogether five elements in the measurement of transparency, whereas interactivity consists of nine features.

The local governments of Sweden, Finland and the United Kingdom have the most extensive online services. Practically all municipalities in these countries have a website and they have plenty of relevant information on their sites.[7] Even in Germany, Austria and Denmark a large majority of municipalities have their own homepage. The pattern of municipal websites does not fully correspond to the individual access figures given above. After Greece, the second lowest share of municipalities with homepages is in the otherwise highly ICT-intensive Netherlands. Even in France and Belgium less than 40 per cent of municipalities are online.

When it comes to transparency, Finland is, in fact, the leading country. The average Finnish municipality offers almost 80 per cent of the possible services that measure transparency. Finland is closely followed by Sweden and the United Kingdom. Belgian and Dutch municipalities, even though not many of them are online, offer high levels of information to their citizens, and even in Austria, Denmark, Germany and Ireland municipalities inform people in many ways. Spanish and Portuguese municipalities have the lowest mean scores on transparency.

Interactive services are less widely offered than transparent information. This may in part reflect the fact that the index of interactivity consists of more items than that of transparency, but it still gives an estimate of opportunities of citizens to communicate with the municipality and its decision-makers. The highest average scores on interactive services are in Austria, Greece and Denmark. The municipalities in Luxembourg, Spain, Finland, Belgium, France and the Netherlands offer the lowest levels of interactive services.

Prospects for deliberative uses of ICTs

The available empirical data do not tell us much about the extent of digital democracy in Western Europe. But if the decision-making process of a representative democracy is to be enhanced through electronic means, as Barber (1984) and Dahl (1989) among others have suggested, people must have the means of taking part in the political processes electronically. How realistic is the introduction of direct democracy via electronic channels? There are at least three prerequisites.

The first prerequisite concerns access to the technology, which has been mapped out in the preceding sections of this chapter. It has been established that people in some countries are beginning to have the required technical means, whereas some southern European countries still lag behind. Further, access to the net is still unevenly distributed even within the most advanced ICT countries. Second, people must be willing to engage in a new type of participatory democracy, which would in most of the visions include a deliberative process. Various forms of deliberation could be accomplished digitally (Stromer-Galley 2000). Instead of merely casting a vote every four years, an attentive and politically deliberative public would be needed. Third, in order to make decisions, the public needs to be informed about the relevant facts related to the political agenda. In fact, they should be able to control the agenda itself. The second and the third prerequisites are a mixture of public deeds and private needs. If we are truly interested in the quality of democracy, as outlined by Barber (1984) and Dahl (1989), the demand for a deliberative (digital) democracy must come from the people. It cannot be forced upon them.

In order to conclude the analysis, an attempt is made to establish how many Europeans are willing to commit themselves to a democracy with deliberative features. For the sake of the argument, let us consider two personal qualities that are needed for political deliberation. In order to commit themselves to political discussions, people should have an interest in public affairs on the one hand and an interest in taking part in public discussions on the other. Once again, the available data empirically restrict the theoretical interest. Luckily, however, some data are available. The first dimension, political interest, has not been asked in conjunction with the relevant Internet use in the available European data. Therefore, I am forced to make use of a somewhat vague imitation. I have simply identified people who have sent e-mail to public officials; these people have shown at least some interest in public affairs. The second dimension is the will to deliberate in public. This readiness has been measured through a question on whether the respondent takes part in discussions online (Figure 2.1).

The typology gives us four types of Internet users. First, we have the browsers. These people neither contact their public administration via e-mail nor chat on the net. Almost two-thirds of West European Internet users belong to this category. Second, we have what I call active citizens. They have sent e-mail to public agencies but they do not engage in online discussions. Thus, they might see the Internet as a service provider and themselves as customers. The share of active citizens is 16.5 per cent. Third, we have social conversationalists, who do chat on the net but have not contacted public administration via e-mail. These people may not have all that much interest in taking part in public life. The share of social conversationalists is 13.4 per cent. Fourth, we have potential deliberators. They have sent e-mail to public authorities and they take part in online discussions. As can be seen in the figure, their share is merely 5 per cent.

Figure 2.1 attempts to capture two dimensions of interactivity that could be essential in order to implement electronic democracy. Naturally, the questions are very narrow and it would be naïve to claim that only 5 per cent of people are willing to take part in political life via the net. But if we consider how many people are members of political parties, this share is not considerably lower. In the World Values Survey that was conducted in 1995–96, 3.7 per cent of respondents in the corresponding West European countries, that is Germany, Spain, Norway, Sweden and Finland claim to have been active party members, whereas the total share (active and passive) of party members was 10.6 per cent. The politically active have always been a minority, as Berelson *et al.* could demonstrate already in 1954. In their typology, voters were distributed along a continuum from social individuals via political individuals to ideological individuals. The last category consisted of the politically active, whereas even the largest group, the political individuals, normally voted in elections.

In order to establish the determinants of the digital divide I have produced two logistic regression analyses. For these purposes,

Have sent e-mail to the public administration?

		No	Yes
Take part in forums or group discussions on the Internet?	No	12,247 65.2% Browsers	3,104 16.5% Active citizens
	Yes	2,522 13.4% Social conversationalists	914 4.9% Potential deliberators

Figure 2.1   Classification of West European Internet users according to two interactive dimensions (numbers and %)
Source: Flash Eurobarometer 103 (2002).

I have chosen to treat the whole Flash Eurobarometer 103 as one sample. This can be justified through the fact that the basic social patterns within countries seem to be similar across them. The regression analyses can be found in Table 2.8.

In the first equation, the dependent variable is Internet use, whilst in the second equation the dependent variable is being a potential deliberator. Prior to the second analysis the sample was filtered leaving only Internet users for the analysis. This was done in order to avoid over-prediction: being a potential deliberator on the net does certainly require access to the net. Since the share of potential deliberators was very small, it was necessary to compare them with other Internet users, not with the whole sample.

As can be seen, predicting Internet use is easier than predicting the category of potential deliberators. In both cases, however, age is the most important independent variable. The Wald value in the first analysis is 5875. Even education and gender are powerful explanatory

Table 2.8 The determinants of Internet use and deliberative characteristics: two logistic regression analyses

Dependent variable: Internet use

	B	S.E.	Wald	Sig.
Male	0.560	0.026	451.368	.000
Age in years	−0.065	0.001	5,874.88	.000
Education in years	0.169	0.003	3,173.91	.000

Model chi square 13,483.83 (p = .000)
Cox & Snell R square = .32
Nagelkerke R square = .42

Dependent variable: potential deliberator

	B	S.E.	Wald	Sig.
Male	0.672	0.074	83.507	.000
Age in years	−0.030	0.003	105.133	.000
Education in years	0.052	0.007	62.733	.000

Model chi square 220.4 (p = .000)
Cox & Snell R square = .01
Nagelkerke R square = .04

Source: Author's calculations based on Flash Eurobarometer 103 (2002).

variables. Being an Internet user is explained by education more than by gender. Being a potential deliberator is explained more by gender than education, an interesting finding *per se*. Men are in other words more inclined to deliberate in public. The Chi square values for the two equations prove that the first model is far more valid than the second. This can be partly explained by the more equal distribution of values on the dependent variable. Also the pseudo R squares suggest a similar interpretation, even though their real significance is, as commonly known, heavily debated by statisticians. In short, the likelihood of being an Internet user decreases with age but increases with education. Even though these two variables explain most of the variation, men are also more likely to use the net than women. Being a potential deliberator is mostly explained by age, that is the young are more likely to engage themselves in the two dimensions captured by the index variable.

In this chapter I have tried to decipher access figures to the Internet in Western Europe. We have seen that there are substantial differences between the countries even in this area, which, in a global comparison, is well-covered by ICT. Further, we have been able to establish rather similar social patterns of Internet access in the countries investigated. In the light of the patterns uncovered, the prospects of digital (or electronic) democracy have also been pondered upon. It has not been possible to determine whether new deliberative forms of democracy could be introduced via the net. In some West European countries people use the Internet to a large extent and would therefore soon meet the technical requirements of becoming cyber citizens. A totally different story is the needs and wishes of the people. Some macro evidence, such as the decline of voter turnout in many established democracies, may suggest that the current representative democracies suffer from legitimacy problems. Even some soft interview data on political trust suggest this (Norris 1999: 226ff). Whether people are willing and able to deliberate electronically is a question that cannot be answered by the present data. Still, it is a fact that a certain share of people is already communicating through the net, surely even in matters of political relevance. It is likely that the new ICTs will be more mature and more evenly spread in a few years time. Then, new needs might arise among people, which is why scholars should continue debating the prospects of electronic democracy.

Notes

1 In the following, Germany has been split into two areas, former West and East Germany. This is possible thanks to separate samples in the country, and is used in order to control for differences within the nation.

2 The raw data have been weighted with the Eurobarometer weight coefficient for national analyses (WCOUNTRY).

3 The country abbreviations follow the ISO 3166-1 standard.

4 The sample size in each country varies between 30 (Luxembourg) and 362 (France).

5 Transparency was formed of the following components: 'Information on the opening hours of services', 'Information on the structure and responsibilities of the local authority', 'Indications about procedures to obtain official documents', 'A newsletter on local activities', 'Accessing legal deeds and local decisions online'.

6 Interactivity was formed of the following components: 'E-mail addresses of those responsible for each activity', 'List of frequently asked questions', 'Enabling the e-mailing of official forms through a system of electronic signatures', 'Enabling requests of official documents' (such as birth certificates, certificate of marital status etc.), 'Enabling citizens to lodge a complaint against other citizens online', 'Enabling citizens to make on-line comments on minutes of the local council meetings', 'Citizens' forums or public debates on issues of common interest online', 'Organizing public opinion polling, i.e. referenda or other voting activities on public issues', 'Contacting elected officials or the members of the local council'.

7 The amount of municipal websites is bound to have increased remarkably since the spring of 2000 when the survey was conducted. The fast pace of development is naturally a problem if we study new phenomena, and it is especially problematic with new ICTs. The problem can be turned into a positive element as well; it is important to document the paths of ICT-development.

References

Barber, B. R. (1984) *Strong Democracy. Participatory Politics for a New Age.* Berkeley, Los Angeles and London: University of Los Angeles Press.

Barber, B. R. (1999) 'En plats for kommers eller en plats för oss?' in E. Amnå(ed.), *IT i demokratins tjänst. Demokratiutredningen. Forskarvolym VII.* Statens Oftentliga Utredringar, 1999: 117, Stockholm.

Berelson, B. R., Lazarsfeld, P. F. and McPhee, W. N. (1954) *Voting.* Chicago: University of Chicago Press.

Habermas, J. (1996) *Between Facts and Norms.* Cambridge, Mass.: MIT Press.

Dahl, R. A. (1989) *Democracy and its Critics.* New Haven and London: Yale University Press.

Gallup Europe (2002) Flash Eurobarometer 112. *Internet and the General Public.* European Commission, DG Press and Communication. Survey conducted in November 2001. Report (online) 30 October 2002 <lhttp://europa.eu.int/ comm/public_opinion/ archives/flash_arch.htm>

Lewin, L. (1970) *Folket och eliterna*. Stockholm: Almqvist & Wiksell.
Norris, P. (2001) *A Digital Divide: Civic Engagement, Information Poverty and the Internet and in Democratic Societies*. New York: Cambridge University Press.
Norris, P. (1999) 'Institutional Explanations for Political Support', in P. Norris (ed.), *Critical Citizens. Global Support for Democratic Governance*. Oxford: Oxford University Press.
Nua.com 2002 'How many online?' (Online) 16 May 2003 <http://www.nua.com/surveys/how_many_online>
Stromer-Galley, J. (2000) 'Democratizing Democracy: Strong Democracy, US Political Campaigns and the Internet', in P. Ferdinand (ed.), *The Internet, Democracy and Democratization*. London and Portland: Frank Cass.

Data files

Eurobarometer 56.2. European Commission, DG Press and Communication, Unit B/1. Survey conducted in November 2001. (Computer file). Brussels: European Opinion Research Group EEIG (producer). Cologne: Zentralarchiv für Empirische Sozialforschung/Ann Arbor, MI: Inter-university Consortium for Political and Social Research (distributors).
Flash Eurobarometer 79. Mayors. European Comission, DG Press and Communication. Survey April/May 2000. (Computer file). Brussels: European Opinion Research Group EEIG (producer). Cologne: Zentralarchiv für Empirische Sozialforschung/Ann Arbor, MI: Inter-university Consortium for Political and Social Research (distributors).
Flash Eurobarometer 88. Internet and the General Public. European Commission, DG Press and Communication. Survey October 2000. (Computer file). Brussels: European Opinion Research Group EEIG (producer). Cologne: Zentralarchiv für Empirische Sozialforschung/Ann Arbor, MI: Inter-university Consortium for Political and Social Research (distributors).
Flash Eurobarometer 103. Internet and the Public at Large. European Commission, DG Press and Communication. Survey June 2001. (Computer file). Brussels: European Opinion Research Group EEIG (producer). Cologne: Zentralarchiv für Empirische Sozialforschung/Ann Arbor, MI: Inter-university Consortium for Political and Social Research (distributors).
Flash Eurobarometer 112. Internet and the Public at Large. European Commission, DG Press and Communication. Survey November 2001. (Computer file). Brussels: European Opinion Research Group EEIG (producer). Cologne: Zentralarchiv für Empirische Sozialforschung/Ann Arbor, MI: Inter-university Consortium for Political and Social Research (distributors).
World Values Surveys 1995–97. February 2000. (ICPSR 2790). Principal Investigators Ronald Inglehart *et al.* University of Michigan. Institute for Social Research. Inter-university Consortium for Political and Social Research. Ann Arbor, Michigan. (Computer file).

3
Online Democracy, Is it Viable? Is it Desirable? Internet Voting and Normative Democratic Theory

Hubertus Buchstein

Internet voting has become a challenging field of action for political scientists, computer companies and legal advisers. Its introduction is on the current reform agenda of nearly all democracies (and semi-democracies). In various projects all over the world, the technical details for 'Internet voting', 'online elections', 'cyber vote' and 'e-voting' are being worked out (I will use all these terms synonymously). The academic discussion about Internet voting is centred upon various technical, empirical, analytical and constitutional questions which arise from the new voting technique. Surprisingly, the underlying normative arguments and the implicit democratic theories which are at the core of the digital reform project and which were the driving force behind the movement for online voting have vanished from sight in the course of these debates.

The number of policy options for future reforms towards Internet voting is quite impressive. The introduction of online voting forms part of a number of measures designed to promote 'multi-channel-voting': citizens shall be free to cast their vote through the traditional paper ballot or the postal vote, the proxy vote, the vote in advance, the vote at an embassy and the Internet. The supporters of Internet voting share an implicit and rather radical vision (see Corroda and Firestone 1996; Lynthia and Pal 1998). All channels to cast votes shall still be available in the future, but the slogan of a computer business company in 2001, 'Vote in your underwear!', truly forecasts the dreams of most advocates of Internet voting. If their dreams come true, voting computers will be installed in polling stations, shopping malls or public libraries. Moreover, the regular voting procedures of the future will actually be based on the use of home PCs and cellular phones from any place in the world. According to this vision, all other channels to cast the vote will eventually become remnants from the past. Estonia is the first country to put this vision into practice; the Estonian parliament recently decided to make use of the net in their national elections scheduled for 2005.

Such plans challenge today's way of voting far beyond mere technological aspects: their implications reach to the normative self-understanding of modern democracies. The recent debate about online voting, however, is deficient in two ways: most arguments pro and con online voting are exchanged without reflecting the contextual components of elections. Thus most arguments fail to develop proper normative reasons, which are sensitive to the different contextual components of voting procedures. Accordingly, this chapter is in two parts. In the first part (the first two sections) I intend to present a systematic framework of three contextual components for e-voting by introducing three analytical distinctions, followed in the second section by the main arguments in favour of Internet voting emphasizing the high expectations originally connected with this kind of reform.

After these systematic preliminaries, I will discuss the most radical technique of Internet voting for general elections in the second part of the chapter (the remaining sections). I pay special attention to three aspects of online voting: the consequences of online voting for the legitimacy of democratic procedures; Internet voting and the principle of mandatory secret voting; and, finally, the probable effects of political decisions made spontaneously behind the scenes. These last three sections raise serious doubts:

- First, with the argument that all forms of Internet voting have the potential to undermine the legitimacy of modern democracies in those situations where election results are close. Thus reasons are given why Internet voting would lead to a serious proneness to crises of legitimacy in modern democracies.
- Second, with the argument that e-voting in the public domain is incompatible with a mandatory secret vote. Thus, Internet voting would have to be ruled as unconstitutional in most European countries.
- And third, by taking the main liberal arguments in favour of democracy as a starting point for an – admittedly partisan – speculation about the loss of democratic rationality in a future Internet democracy.

Basic distinctions: the context, form and status of Internet voting

Ongoing pilot projects are making use of different computer techno-logies, and they differ from each other with reference to their context, form and status. I will skip the technological aspects of Internet voting here, however interesting they may be. Instead, I will concentrate on those three aspects of Internet voting which become crucial when one tries to evaluate Internet voting from the point of view of democratic theory. In order to get a systematic overview of the confusing variety of current Internet voting practices, three basic analytical distinctions must be introduced (see Gibson 2001; Internet Policy Institute 2001; Lange 2002):

- The first distinction deals with the various *contexts* of Internet voting,
- the second distinction puts the emphasis on the *forms* of Internet voting, and
- the third distinction is focused on the *status* of online voting.

The contexts

On a contextual level, two dimensions appear to be of particular inter-est. First, the political definition of decisions made through the Internet (should it be considered as part of the private or of the public domain?). And second, the constituency of Internet voting and its scale or spatial distribution (ranging from the local to the international level) (Table 3.1).

The requirements which voting procedures have to meet differ accord-ing to the context. With respect to the dimension of scale, the possible difficulties which may result from Internet voting on the international level are mainly of a technical and legal character. In most cases, the obstacles are not fundamental enough to prevent joint solutions.

Table 3.1 Contexts of Internet voting

	Private domain	*Public domain*
Local and national	Clubs, firms	Local and national elections
International	Global interest groups and companies	International organizations

When we look at the distinction between the private and the public sector, things look less promising. The easiest cases are met by organizations in the private domain of civil society. The practice of elections and voting in a wide range of groups in civil society (sports clubs, civil associations, philanthropic organizations, etc.) normally meet much lower standards than in those of the public domain. Consequently, voting procedures in organizations in civil society are only marginally affected by legal arguments.

Even in cases in which voting procedures within the private domain are fixed in a detailed manner (as in private firms and stock corporations), they are more easily altered than those in the public domain. In the public domain constitutions normally prescribe particular standards which voting procedures have to meet (e.g. access, security, secrecy), and procedures are usually prescribed by constitutional law and very difficult to change (if at all). On the other hand, there is no European constitutional law which says that elections in stock corporations necessarily have to be held in secrecy.

The forms

The second matrix deals with the form of Internet voting (see also Gibson 2001: 566). The actors responsible for computer technology (public PC; home PC) and the level of mobility (fixed; mobile) add up to the four basic forms of Internet voting (Table 3.2).

A brief look at the four basic models indicates differences in concept and political practice:

- @community. In this form, the computer system simply substitutes the old Florida-like voting machines in the traditional public polling station. They may – but do not have to – be connected to a central server to allow all voters (including those who happen to be on vacation) to use any polling station they want.
- @kiosk. In the kiosk system, additional polling stations connected through the net to the central server are installed in places where

Table 3.2   Forms of Internet voting

	Fixed	Mobile
Public PC	@community	@kiosk
Private PC	@home	On-the-run

people frequently show up in their daily routines (like shopping malls and public libraries).

- @home. Voters use their own home PC to cast their vote.
- On-the-run. Cell phones and other mobile forms of communication can be used to participate in elections.

The defenders of the different forms of Internet voting claim different advantages, which it is up to empirical research to prove:

- In the @community model, the claim is that its main advantage is the provision against a repetition of the Florida disaster.
- The @kiosk system is primarily extolled for its alleged capacity to enhance voter turnout.
- Similarly, the arguments in favour of the @home system and the 'on-the-run' model say that both forms will lower the cost of political participation for voters even more and will have a positive effect on voter turnout.

The status

The third distinction is about the status of Internet voting. According to some champions of the new technology, Internet voting should be introduced – at least in the beginning – as an additional and optional form (like the postal vote today). According to others, it should become the regular form as soon as possible and substitute traditional voting practice (Table 3.3).

The status of Internet voting involves not only aspects of technology and finances; a brief look at the history of voting procedures illustrates the degree to which these procedures are part of a much more complex political culture. Voting procedures are embedded in a political culture, and they influence political culture at the same time. It is only plausible to imagine that Internet voting – as all its predecessors before – has the potential to generate and regenerate a particular dominant voting culture. There can hardly be any doubt that Internet voting as the

Table 3.3   Status of Internet voting

	Short term	Long term
Optional	A	B
Regular	C	D

official and regular form to cast the vote will influence the attitude of candidates, voters and political campaigning. However, such effects are plausible to claim, but difficult to verify empirically. I will come back to this point in the last section of this chapter.

The near future: coexistence and competition

The three analytical distinctions help us imagine the multitude of policy options reformers face when they think about introducing Internet voting. The differences between the options make a safe bet about the face of future developments in the field of Internet voting almost impossible. Most probably, the near future will be a pluralistic one: we will probably observe the coexistence and competition not only of different computer software technologies, but of different basic forms and contexts as well. The rising interregnum of Internet voting pluralism will become an era of various technological experiments and pilot projects. It will turn out to be a vein of gold for some political scientists, computer companies and legal advisers.

Part of this pluralistic picture is the large group of today's electoral reformers and leading computer companies trying to push the reform agenda on a much more radical track. They envision future elections with people voting from their home PCs or simply by using their mobile phones. Their courageous vision challenges today's mode of voting in more than just its technological aspects; the implications of their radical vision reach deep into the normative infrastructure of modern democratic theory and deserve particular attention and extensive reflection.

Promises, promises: the main arguments in favor of Internet voting

Before discussing the radical vision in more detail, one has to keep in mind the expectations originally connected with Internet voting in general. Over the last decade, advocates of Internet voting have claimed a number of positive effects for the future of democracy, and at least five different arguments have come into play (see KPMG 1998; Schweizerischer Bundesrat 2002; Local Government Association 2001):

- **Cheap democracy**. Elections and other voting procedures cost a lot of money, and the use of computer technology would make it much easier and cheaper for municipalities and communities to organize and hold elections. Internet voting would not only save paper, but also spare the communities such tasks as the appointment and training of polling officers, the preparation of suitable rooms, and the costs of the equipment required. The hope is that after a transition period of investment into new technology, future elections will be much cheaper than today and require but a small number of voluntary polling officers.

- **Fast and efficient count of votes.** The argument says that computers count votes not only faster but more accurately than human beings. The count will be much faster, which means that we do not have to wait for hours to get the final outcome. Florida is used as an example that humans are not as neutral as necessary when it comes to reading the butterfly ballot.

- **Higher voter turnout.** According to the defenders of online voting, its greatest advantage is that voting would no longer be confined to one particular location. The casting of votes from a mobile voting kiosk, the home PC or a mobile phone is less complicated and a lot more spontaneous than applying for a postal vote. The expectation is that Internet voting will raise voter turnout, in particular among the younger generation.

- **Additional election options.** A fourth advantage of e-voting is that new election procedures, which are more complicated but would be more reliable in taking into account the intentions of the electorate, will be introduced on a fair technological basis. Complicated procedures that currently exist in Ireland and in some other European countries, like the splitting of the vote, cumulative voting, the single transferable vote or the preference vote, can easily be introduced. And, in addition, new forms of splitting the vote (e.g. to give 60 per cent of my individual vote to party A and 40 per cent to party B) need no longer be confined to the imagination of those who care for the preferences of voters. Or we could think about a plebiscite, in which voters can mark intervals between just 'yes' and 'no', or list the particular percentage they would prefer for, say, the reduction or increase of certain taxes. All such visionary electoral reforms (that truly respect the authentic expressions of citizens) can easily be introduced without incurring any additional cost in time or materials while ensuring absolute accuracy of the count.

- **Strengthening direct democracy.** The fifth advantage of the cybervote is its potential to strengthen direct democracy. When elections of persons to the parliament become possible from a computer, the vote on issues no longer faces technical obstacles. Computer democracy marks a huge step in enabling voters to decide political issues directly by simply pushing a button.

Economic interests lend an additional (but still crucial) motive for the high pressure behind e-voting programmes. Politicians and managers see Internet voting as a strategic building block for the expanded use and user radius of computer technology. It is not surprising that computer and mobile telephone companies such as Cisco, Nokia and British Telecom willingly sponsor experiments of this kind. The new election technology is a big market and already highly competitive.

In the face of this variety of arguments, anyone taking a sceptical position towards e-voting could easily be suspected of suffering from technophobia, of oversleeping, of missing the boat, or of thoughtlessly thwarting the chance for the revival and modernization of democracy. However, such a reaction is not as impressive at it may look at a first glance, since the procedures of Internet voting raise at least some questions which cannot be left to wait for technological and practical answers.

Over the last three years, a second generation of arguments in favour of Internet voting has already tuned down the euphoric rhetoric of the early 1990s. The disillusion has to do with first experiences and first empirical findings (see California Online Voting Task Force 2000; Caltech/MIT 2001):

- Estimates of the financial investments necessary to start Internet voting on a larger scale seem to grow as fast as cannabis during a long hot summer.
- Opinion polls indicate that large numbers of citizens in most countries do not really trust the new technology.
- It seems that the transaction costs which voters have to cover in order to secure the vote (time, sophistication, additional technologies) are too high to be an incentive for a larger number of citizens.
- The experiences with voter turnout or the social composition of participants in pilot projects ('digital divide') are at least ambivalent.
- And the media's interest in producing quick vote totals on elections nights in the USA has switched after the Florida debacle to revile any technology that appears to produce false results.

Issues like these are at the top of the agenda of social scientists and computer technicians who deal with Internet voting. Although one can expect that some of the empirical findings about voter participation and computer security will contradict the optimistic claims made in the beginning, no reliable final conclusion can yet be drawn from the empirical findings (see the controversial results of Solop 2000; Alvarez and Nagler 2000; Lange 2002; Kriesi 2003 and Grönlund, Norris, Pratchett and Kersting in this volume). For any given empirical outcome, it could simply be the case that the first data to be obtained (this holds true for both higher and lower voter turnouts in all social groups) will find their main explanation in the pure fact that online voting is such a new practice.

Instead of relying on the weak empirical support the debate needs a normative turn. Such a turn, however, has to avoid the contradiction that usually appears when normative theory meets empirical research: normative theory starts with a demanding normative concept of democracy – only to complain in the end that the political reality is insufficient. Such a confrontation of an ideal with reality is somehow naive; life will always be insufficient to some degree, and this particularly holds true for democracy. In contrast to such an idealistic approach (at least in the first two objections), I will rely only on those normative standards for democracy which bear a broad consensus among modern democrats.

Democratic legitimacy: towards a procedural legitimization crisis

Anecdotal evidence indicates that, due to our daily experience with computers, we all have developed a healthy skepticism when it comes to trusting computer technology. Sometimes the computer works pretty well, but on some days all these crazy things happen. And on other days it looks as if the computer can be influenced by friendly words. We have developed a basic trust in computer technology and at the same time a certain kind of distrust in it. This attitude can be called our daily 'computer common sense'.

With respect to Internet voting, safety or computer security is the single most important criterion for confidence in the technology. Listening to current debates among political scientists, citizens or computer technicians, one: easily finds that one question is always stressed as the crucial one how safe is voting via the net? A majority of critics within the computer scene doubt the technical security of online elections, especially with respect to hackers and other online virtuosos (see Internet Policy Institute 2001; Grimm 2001; Mitchison 2003). Does encryption really and definitely guarantee the safe transfer of ballots from the voter to the central computer? Is it even likely that the computer will be used as a method of civilian surveillance? Is it possible to prevent and exclude manipulation of election results in the central computer?

The underlying question one has to answer is: can we (and do we) want to expose our elections to such risks? Defenders of online voting sometimes give the following reply to the question as to how high the security standards in the Internet have to be until citizens can trust the procedures: A process can be considered secure when the same people who have doubts are willing to do their financial transactions over the same system. This answer, however, is misleading. There are no comparable corrective mechanisms in e-voting and e-commerce. As opposed to an incorrect financial transaction, there is no way to reclaim a vote. In the case of fraudulent financial transactions, the victim usually realizes some time later what has happened, and he or she can normally recoup the loss to the last cent. To make possible the recoup of a vote contradicts the very principle of the equality of votes, which would be lost if someone were given the opportunity to reclaim his or her vote. Even if the voter protests that he or she will vote again exactly as on polling day, there is always the possibility that the voter will have some strategic calculation in mind, which the voters on polling day were unaware of, hence making the vote unequal.

Security is only as strong as its weakest links, and against the background of security misgivings it is hardly surprising that the question of security is foremost for all organizers of Internet voting. A recurring mantra one can hear from companies involved in the development and promotion of Internet-based voting systems is that they have conducted 'public tests' and that their systems are therefore secure. Such an argument is hardly convincing. Just because hackers have not broken into the system so far, no system can be declared definitely successful. Using such 'public tests' as a validation technique runs sharply contrary to well-established engineering verification practices and makes fun of the extensive testing processes which are required by other computer systems. In addition, it is unlikely that people with an interest in subverting electoral processes in Western democracies would contribute to the improvement of computer systems in a test phase.

But even if we were to imagine that thanks to intelligent technology all these worries about security could be dispelled, and that electronic voting systems have been officially certified to comply to high security standards – even in this highly unlikely scenario the procedural problems of Internet voting could not yet be considered as solved. And even if only a minority of voters feared security problems with online voting, this would still be sufficient to undermine the legitimacy of the entire process (For a cross national study presenting high rates of distrust in computer technology for voting procedures see Taylor Nelson Sofres (2001)). Trust in the system and its procedures are the source of any modern democratic legitimacy. In the history of political elections, traditional ballot papers have certainly been falsified, or they have mysteriously disappeared, but as votes are physically evident and because they are stored in ballot boxes and counted in the open, frauds on a massive scale are usually easy to detect. This is not the case with cyber-elections.

To emphasize my argument at this point: confidence in the procedures is crucial to modern democratic legitimacy. Therefore, democratic procedures require techniques which can be challenged and proven. Even in regular elections, there always remains an irremovable hint of distrust which will flare up every time there is a surprise or a very close call that at least seems to undermine the legitimacy of the election result – just take a look at Florida again. But at least in cases like Florida in the 2000 presidential elections, there is some 'evidence' worth inspecting, and there are witnesses who can be interviewed afterwards. This is not the case with elections via computer and the Internet. In the fall elections of 2002, voters in Florida used new and expensive touch-screen voting machines. Due to technological problems that still remain unclear, some votes obviously got lost, and there is no way to figure out which ones.

Things get even worse when intentional fraud comes into play. Take the case of spoofing: how do I know that my vote really got counted and that no smart counter-technology has yet been developed in order to overcome the official computer system? The most successful and refined cases of manipulation in the Internet stand out for the reason that nobody knows about them except the culprit. Even when there is a suspicion, it is due to the technology that manipulations are later difficult to prove with certainty

In situations in which citizens expect close election results, there will always be a suspicion that is much more difficult to counter than with the traditional mode of voting. The US presidential elections of 2000 would have triggered much harsher conflicts if the voting had been done via computers only. Would Swiss voters have believed the results of a computer count of votes in the election of 2003, which made the right-wing party the strongest group in parliament? And what about less stable democracies? To sum up my argument: the leap to electronic democracy requires having the 'courage' to risk a permanent legitimacy crisis, even in cases in which no manipulation has taken place.

Democracy not only means an equal right to vote, it also means an equal right to understand the techniques of voting procedures and an equal right to prove the results. Democracy includes full transparency in all its procedures. Thus, in a democracy, all elements of the voting process (including the software) must – at least in principle – be easy to follow and to understand for all citizens. Citizens who agree to give up that right, and to put all their confidence in technicians who will judge the security of computer software in their place, have already agreed to transfer all power to an aristocracy of a handful of people.

Constitutionality: on the road to optional secret voting

The secrecy of the vote is one of the most important principles in Western democracies. While some voters might tolerate the risk of his or her vote not being counted because of technological errors, most of them will positively not stand for a disclosure of his or her choices in public. Keeping the secrecy of the vote is a serious problem for Internet voting. If one follows the radical protagonists, Internet voting is simply a sophisticated variation of the traditional postal vote (postal vote here means – in contrast to the Scandinavian terminology of 'advance voting at the post office' – the 'absentee ballot' by mail). In both cases, citizens cast their votes in the privacy of their homes, and deliver them afterwards (by mail, computer or cellphone) to the polling station.

The analogy to the ballot by mail points to a crucial constitutional barrier to the new technique. To take the case of Germany (see Buchstein 2000a; Will 2002), postal voting (as defined above) has been practiced in West Germany since 1956, but it has been accepted only as an exception to the rule (which requires citizens to cast their vote personally at the polling station), and only under certain conditions.

The precarious 'exceptional' status of the postal ballot, is illuminated by a contrasting look at the voting practices and theories in the former German Democratic Republic (GDR). Similar to the West German Constitution, the GDR Constitution provided for a secret ballot but, notwithstanding, votes in the GDR were mainly cast in the open. And the constitutional doctrine of the GDR did not judge the electors' abandonment of the polling booth as a violation of the universal principle of secrecy. Instead, it justified it with the argument that the use of the secret ballot was not mandatory but an option. According to this doctrine, it is up to the voters to finally decide whether or not they believe they have to claim this right. Between 1949 and 1989, quite obviously more than 95 per cent of East German voters 'voluntarily' decided that there were no reasons to cast their vote in secret.

Cases of dictatorial misuse such as in the GDR have supplied reasons for a strict version of the secrecy provision in Western democracies. In this version, the *optional* claim to use secrecy is seen as insufficient. Instead, secrecy is considered a *mandatory* lawful duty. You are free to tell anybody for whom you voted; but you are not free to prove your claim. Only you will know whether what you said was true. It is easy to see how hard it is for Constitutional Courts to accept even the postal vote (absentee ballot by mail). How can the state ensure that the postal voter is not at the 'mercy' of curious glances at his vote (from family members, neighbours, or political fellows)? The difficult and highly controversial nature of the postal ballot can be observed by a brief glance at some European countries. Less than half of the current EU member states allow postal ballots (among them, Germany, the UK, Ireland, the Netherlands, Portugal) while all other countries strongly rule it out. Scandinavian countries, for example, have a tradition of stressing the secrecy of the ballot, and they enforce a rather restrictive mail-voting legislation.

On two occasions, the German Constitutional Court has ruled to accept the postal vote as constitutional (1967, 1981) – but only as long as voters convincingly claim that they have no other alternative than casting their vote by mail. The postal vote was weighed up between two basic suffrage principles – the 'universality' and the 'secrecy' of the vote. Postal votes are only accepted as an exception on important grounds (sickness, work commitments) which prevent citizens from casting their ballot at the polling station (and which have to be proved in some states). In Germany, the number of postal ballots has steadily risen from 4.9 per cent in 1957 to 14.7 per cent in 1998 and close to 16 per cent in 2002; in cities like Frankfurt, Hamburg and Berlin the ratio is already up to 30 per cent. This increase has led prominent constitutional lawyers to make demands for a stricter enforcement of the postal ballot provisions.

Speaking in the language of constitutional law: The introduction of the Internet is only constitutional in those cases in which it literally substitutes the postal ballot. But it is obvious that such a distinction of cases would be difficult, if not impossible, to implement in the real world. The only way to draw such a distinction would imply the regulation of the Internet ballot by a set of conditions for its usage (for example that voters would have to prove that they are sick or abroad for work). If one does not want to choose such a strict regulation policy, the introduction of Internet voting becomes identical with the universality of the basic framework of the postal ballot to all voters.

What is wrong with this kind of universality ? In the two models which use private computers – called '@home' and 'on-the-run' in the first section – the procedure of Internet voting has the same Achilles heel as the postal ballot. It does not provide a full guarantee that the vote really has been made in secrecy. Votes could have been cast with the help or under the influence of family members, friends, or even groups representing special interests. Just take the (empirically significant) case of the female voter who needs her husband's technical assistance. With respect to the fulfillment of the secrecy principle, one has no option but to trust the voter. Or, to put it less euphemistically: now it is up to the single voter to shield his or her vote from family members, friends, enemies or brokers.

So however it is twisted or turned, the universal introduction of voting from home PCs or cellphones puts modern democracy at a crossroad. The mandatory secret vote is slowly turning into an optional secret vote, and such a reversal of the mandatory secret ballot would be unconstitutional in most European countries.

I say 'most', because at this point the Estonian constitutional debate comes in as a possible starting point for a paradigmatic change. Wolfgang Drechsler and Uelle Madise have delivered a report on the fascinating turn in Estonian constitutional reflections about the status of 'secrecy' in the principle of secret voting. Paragraph 60 of the Estonian Constitution explicitly states that elections shall be free and that voting shall be secret. The supporters of the Estonian law which introduced online voting on a national scale for the 2005 election used a teleological approach in their argument in order to get rid of the mandatory secrecy of the vote. They argued that constitutional rules should be understood through the problems they are supposed to solve. The principle of secrecy was said to protect the individual voter from any pressure against his or her will. In this teleological reformulation, secret voting has become a means and is no longer an end in itself. So, while all voters still have the right to go to a polling station in which their privacy is guaranteed, the end of secret voting is already in sight. In this view, online voting must be seen as constitutional, since voters who choose this technique have obviously decided that they do not need this kind of shield for their privacy.

It is not yet clear whether this innovative interpretation of the principle of secrecy in Estonia will survive the integration of the country into the European Community. Recent decisions of the European High Court give no hint that they will follow the teleological line of argument given by the defenders of online voting. It is necessary, however, to come to grips with the meaning of 'secret voting' in more general terms. The mandatory secret ballot is a scheme designed to deprive the voter of any means of proving the way he voted. The perspective of the voter has been accurately described by Thomas Schelling in his classic *The Strategy of Conflict* (1960): 'Being stripped of his power to prove how he voted, he is stripped of his power to be intimidated. Powerless to prove whether or not he complied with a threat, he knows – and so do those who would threaten him – that any punishment would be unrelated to the way he actually voted' (Schelling 1960: 19). Following this logic, the conclusion is that secret voting has to be mandatory: 'It is not alone the secrecy, but the mandatory secrecy, that robs him of his power to sell his vote. He is made impotent to meet the demands of blackmailing' (*ibid.*: 148).

Mandatory secrecy is a principle which goes beyond constitutional law, its fundaments are based on the idea of auto-paternalism and it is understood as a mechanism of self-binding of autonomous citizens in order to avoid situations of external pressure or corruption. In this concept, it is not the individual him- or herself, but a warranted outside agent or authority – normally the state – that is responsible for providing the necessary means to allow for the secret ballot. I do not intend to discuss all the pros and cons of secret voting in this chapter, the circumstances for a renaissance of public voting in modern democracies are described in Buchstein (2000b: 680–721), and all I want to do at this point is call attention to the fundamental relevance of the auto-paternalistic interpretation of the principle of mandatory secrecy, which goes well-beyond all strategies designed to interpret constitutional law.

Real virtuality: junk-vote.com

My last concern deals with some of the alleged advantages of electronic elections mentioned in the second section of this chapter. To what extent does Internet voting really improve our democracy? Some observers are convinced that the new technique will lead to changes as fundamental as the introduction of female suffrage or the equal weight of the vote. But should the current technical modernization of democracy be evaluated in the same positive way? There are good reasons for less optimistic expectations, and such concerns are mainly based on a realistic self-assessment of democracy which underlies most of today's liberal concepts of democracy. Three concerns particularly deserve to be addressed:

1. First, the issue of a 'direct push-button democracy'. Supporters of direct democracy praise the innovation for the opportunity it provides to implement additional forms of direct democracy. In the eternal dispute between representative and plebiscite democracy, supporters of direct democracy now find themselves in a much improved position. Over the last 200 years, they have had little success with their criticism of representative democracy, simply because the purely technical prerequisites for a permanent and robust plebiscitary democracy did not exist in large modern countries.

   The establishment of an 'electronic agora', however, may change the direction of this discourse. One may argue about the need and use of installing more direct democratic elements into a parliamentary democratic system. The new technology, however, has the potential to create a dynamic process of its own. Technologically speaking, a direct 'push-button' democracy is on the horizon. After the introduction of Internet elections it will be only a small step to introduce plebiscitary decisions on basically every issue, and at low cost. The defenders of representative democracy will have a much more difficult stand than today; they will be accused of defending an elitist model of democracy or even an aristocracy. But the alternative does not necessary lead to more democracy. In contrast, the combination of online plebiscites with structural changes in the media system (which can currently be observed in the USA and in some European countries such as Italy and the UK) has a strong potential for giving populist politics a technological push.

2. Second, the privatization of the voting process. The places where we vote are not without symbolic meaning. Until now, the casting of votes has always occurred in a public place, the polling station. Even without harboring any illusions about the discreet charm of today's polling stations, the ritualized casting of votes in a public place symbolizes a relationship between the voter and his community. The Internet takes voting farther away from its former public habitation; e-voting hijacks the voting process and brings it into the private domain of the living room. The little cable in the living room becomes a paradigm for the place politics

may hold in computer democracy. Preferences on public issues are expressed literally from the centre of individuals' private existence; democracy is divorced from the symbolic spaces of concern for the common good.

The private context of voting will probably have consequences for the way voters experience themselves. It does not take much to imagine the extent to which the casting of votes from private homes via the net will speed up the erosion of the publicly minded spirit, change the political culture, and support the tendency of privatization in politics – with even lower voter turnouts than today.

3. Third, time and decision. There are serious doubts that the promised speed and permanent possibilities of spontaneous participation in voting procedures are really an advantage for democratic decision-making. Until now, individual citizens had to decide whether or not they could be bothered to walk to the polling station (in the US the hurdle is even higher – much too high, I believe – because voters have to do some paperwork first). Voters will only take the walk to the polling station if they take the election seriously, at least to some extent.

Until today, election procedures have almost always served as a 'census of those interested'. Only the votes of those citizens who take the trouble to go to a polling station or apply for postal votes show that they care in a minimal way for political decisions. Until now, there has also been time for citizens to consider their votes, even if it was only on the way to the polling station. These beneficial barriers disappear with computer voting. The voter can collect the most up-to-date information and be on the cutting edge, but for well-considered thought-out votes this type of information is of no importance. At the same time, Internet voting encourages non-reflective spontaneity and reduces the meaning of the act of voting to such a degree that it might actually be better for democracy if some of these 'junk votes' were not cast at all.

If the walk to the polling station is like a walk on the wild side and such a serious hurdle for uninterested voters, the cure should not consist of getting them to participate via electronic games. Real democrats would lie to themselves about the state of the political culture if voter participation increased only because of technology. If, however, one wishes to follow that road, a much cheaper and probably more successful path to pursue would be to offer a lottery-prize incentive for election participation.

The future of the debate

The intention of my arguments is to challenge the group of over-optimistic reformers who want to introduce Internet voting. The concerns and objections which I have raised are situated on different levels, and the defenders of online voting will consequently have to employ different strategies in order to counter them.

The first concern about possible future crises of legitimacy in situations of voters' distrust in the voting procedures is, admittedly, rather speculative. But I do not think that we should decide to simply wait and see whether our worries will come true or not. To begin with, these concerns are based on sound arguments, but, more importantly, what is at stake is democracy itself. Still, defenders of online voting may argue that a prognosis about the future which the author does not want to be transformed into an observable factual statement is an unfair way of immunizing the argument (in particular when the argument comes from someone who can be suspected of being influenced by a technophobe German culture). I would agree to this objection, while insisting at the same time that quite obviously we need some kind of democratic risk-assessment, and a number of joint convictions about the degree of risks we want to take for Western democracies.

The second objection – somehow hidden behind the veil of an argument in constitutional law – may be viewed by some readers as equally unfair. Why should a political community not have the right to get rid of secret voting, or at least to weaken the mandatory status of secret voting? Well, there is nothing wrong with constitutional changes. Such a counter-argument would miss the point. My argument only attempts to remind us of the fact that any additional weakening of the mandatory secret ballot will have a tremendous consequence in introducing the optional status of public voting. I would easily acknowledge that there can be good reasons to give up the mandatory secret ballot; a tradition of strong criticism of the secret vote has been transmitted from classical Athenian democracy up to the beginning of the twentieth century. My point is that the potential small-scale reintroduction of the open vote by online voting should not be admitted through a technological backdoor. As long as there is no consensus among modern democrats that modern politics are civilized enough to give up the shield the mandatory secret vote provides, the status quo has to be preferred.

The final set of arguments may be judged by some readers as the most unfair attack. Opponents may argue that the form of democracy we have today also fails in the light of normative standards. So it is worth adding that, despite all the flaws of today's democratic proced- ures, I have not yet heard of any plausible and convincing argument why Internet voting should necessarily lead to an improvement of the deliberative qualities in political communication. At any rate, empirical research on political communication via the net gives to evidence for such an optimistic claim (see Streck 1998; Bimber 1998; Wilhelm 1999).

To sum up the argument in conclusion: at least in the context of the public domain (picking up the analytical distinctions from the first part of this chapter), even weak normative concepts of democracy lead to the conclusion that the ongoing transfer of voting procedures into the Internet should be stopped. And by the way – what is wrong with the idea that a modern democracy may rely on very traditional ways to cast the vote?

References

Alvarez, M. R. and Nagler, J. (2000) 'The Likely Consequences of Internet Voting for Political Representation', <http://www. internetvoting/ivaote3c.pdf>

Bimber, B. (1998) 'The Internet and Political Transformation', in *Polity* 31(2000): 133–60.

Buchstein, H. (2000a) 'Präsenzwahl, Briefwahl, Onlinewahl und der Grundsatz der geheimen Stimmabgabe', *Zeitschrift für Parlamentsfragen* 38: 886–902.

Buchstein, H. (2000b) *Öffentliche und Geheime Wahl*. Baden-Baden: Nomos.

Buchstein, H. (2002) 'Democracy's Secret. Carl Schmitt and the Critique of Secret Voting', in *Finnish Yearbook of Political Thought* 6: 107–25.

Buchstein, H. and Neymanns, H. (eds) (2002) *Online-Wahlen*. Opladen:Leske & Budrich.

California Internet-Voting Task Force (2000) *A Report on the Feasibility of Online-Voting*. Sacramento: California Secretary of State.

Caltech/MIT (2001) *Voting. What is, What could be*. Report of the Caltech-MIT Voting Technology Project <http://www.ss.ca.gov>

Corrado, A. and Firestone, C. M. (eds) (1996) *Elections in Cyberspace. Towards a New Era in American Politics*. Washington DC: The Aspen Institute.

Gibson, R. (2001) 'Elections Online: Assessing Online-Voting in Light of the Arizona Democratic Primary'. *Political Science Quarterly* 116: 561–83.

Grimm, R. (2001) 'Technische Sicherheit bei Internetwahlen', in B. Holznagel (ed.), *Elektronische Demokratie*. München: C. H. Beck: 86–104.

Internet Policy Institute (2001) *Report of the National Workshop on Online-voting: Issues and Research Agenda*. Washington DC.

Karger, P. (2002) 'Online Voting. Not Only a Technical Challenge', in J. L. Monteiro *et al.* (eds), *Towards the Knowledge Society*. Boston: Kluwer Academic Publishers 3–13.

KPMG and Sussex Circle (1998) *Technology and the Voting Process*. Final Report. Montreal.

Kriesi, H. (2003) 'E-Voting and Political Participation', in H. Muralt-Müller *et al.* (eds), *E-Voting*. Bern: Bundes Kantlei 85–106.

Lange, N. (2002) 'Click'n'Vote. Erste Erfahrungen mit Online-Wahlen', in H. Buchstein and H. Neymanns (eds), *Online-Wahlen*. Opladen: Leske & Budrich: 127–44.

Lynthia, A. and Pal L. A. (eds) (1998) *Digital Democracy. Policy and Politics in the Wired World*. Toronto: Oxford University Press.

Local Government Association (2002) *The Implementation of Electronic Voting in the UK*. Research Summary <http/:/www.lga.gov.uk>

Mitchison, N. (2003) 'Protection against "internal" Attacks on E-Voting Systems', in H. Muralt-Müller *et al.* (eds), *E-Voting*. Bern: Bundeskanski 255–66.

Schelling, T. (1960) *The Strategy of Conflict*. Cambridge: Cambridge University Press.

Schweizerischer Bundesrat (2002) 'Bericht über den Vote électronique', <http://www.e-gov.admin.ch>

Solop, F. I. (2000) 'Digital Democracy Comes of Age in Arizona: Participation and Politics in the First Binding Internet Election', Paper, September.

Streck, J. (1998) 'Pulling the Plug on Electronic Town Meetings: Participatory Democracy and the Reality of the Usenet',. in C. Toulouse and T. Luke (eds), *The Politics of Cyberspace*. New York: Routledge: 18–47.

Taylor Nelson Sofres (2001) Government Online. *2001 Benchmarking Study*, <http://www.tnsofres.com>

Will, M. (2002) *Internetwahlen. Verfassungsrechtliche Möglichkeiten und Grenzen*. Stuttgart: Boorberg.

Wilhelm, A. G. (1999) 'Virtual Sounding Boards. How Deliberative is Online Political Discussion?' in B. Hague and B. Loader (eds), *Digital Democracy. Discourse and Decision Making in the Information Age*. London: Routledge: 154–178.

Part II
Country Studies

4
Electronic Voting in the United States: At the Leading Edge or Lagging Behind?

Frederic I. Solop

The first binding Internet election to take place anywhere in the world occurred in the United States during March 2000. Internet voting was offered as one option for casting a ballot in the Arizona Democratic Party primary election. Voters could also cast an early ballot by mail. Voters showing up at a polling location on Election Day could cast a traditional paper ballot or vote using a computer. The future of Internet voting in the United States looked quite bright at that historic moment. Turnout in the Arizona primary election doubled, the election took place without a breach in security, public opinion supported introducing Internet voting into all statewide elections, and young people (who typically vote at very low rates in the United States) expressed unprecedented enthusiasm for voting over the Internet. In the years following that election, momentum for Internet voting in the United States slowed significantly. The 2002 federal and state elections took place without a trace of consideration for Internet voting, and the United States no longer occupies the 'leading edge' in the use of Internet technology for voting. In fact, the United States has fallen behind many European nations to a position more aptly thought of as 'lagging behind.'

This chapter reviews the history of Internet voting in the United States, including an examination of several Internet voting experiments that occurred during the 2000 presidential election. An extended discussion of the binding Arizona election is included. This chapter further examines diminishing interest in Internet voting in the United States and situates declining interest against the 2000 presidential election, when a prolonged vote count left the question of who would next occupy the office of the presidency unanswered for more than a month. The peculiar structure of election laws in the United States attenuated enthusiasm for Internet voting in the wake of the 2000 election.

Internet voting is not a utopic election reform drawn from a science-fiction novel. Instead, it is a reform that extends recent trends of 'digital democracy' into the electoral arena. By now, digital democracy has become a routine part of the political landscape in the United States. As I discuss in another chapter, digital democracy involves government agencies, interest groups, candidates, and citizens moving the apparatus of politics and governance to the Internet environment. The products of digital democracy are obvious. During President Clinton's tenure in office, all major federal agencies in the United States were ordered to establish a web presence. Today, political organizations must have a sophisticated web presence or risk being viewed as irrelevant to the many people who rely upon the Internet for policy-related information.

The movement towards digital democracy was first established in the mid-1990s. What was new for the 2000 presidential election was that Internet voting was, for the first time, widely available in a variety of settings: Alaska Republicans cast a non-binding vote over the Internet, and several non-binding experiments took place in California and Arizona in the 2000 general election, Democrats introduced elements of Internet voting into their party convention, and youth participated in a national non-binding Internet election. Also new to the 2000 presidential election was that the first binding Internet election took place in the presidential primary cycle when Arizona Democrats introduced a remote-site Internet voting option into their primary election.

This binding experiment with remote-site Internet voting was a success on many fronts. In retrospect, the most successful outcome of this election may very well be that Internet voting became an ordinary part of electoral reform discourse; indeed, since that time discussions of election reform typically include the potential of introducing online voting as a future option for casting a ballot. In order to fully understand the potential of this reform, it is important to contextualize Internet voting within the broader movement towards digital democracy, outline details of the role of the Internet in the 2000 presidential election, specify the pivotal role played by the Arizona primary election, and discuss the prospects of introducing online voting into the future 'toolbox' of election reform in the United States.

A brief history of digital democracy in the United States

The World Wide Web can be thought of as the psychological Rorschach test of the twenty-first century; everyone looking at the web may see something different. A typical American looking at the web sees an 'Information Superhighway,' no doubt a reflection of the American obsession with freedom experienced 'on the road.' Another Internet user looks at the web and sees an avenue for facilitating commerce and trade. To some, the web is a social outlet. Between chat-group conversations, postings to usenet groups and e-mail, the web allows people to feel connected to others. The fact that Internet users tend to only communicate with similarly situated people (socially, economically and politically) seems unimportant. The web is simultaneously a source of serious undertakings and entertainment; it simultaneously grounds the user in reality and helps users to escape the burdens of the world. Today, United States Census Bureau statistics say that 51 per cent of households in the United States have a computer and 42 per cent have Internet access (US Census Bureau 2001). People, however, also access the Internet at work, school and in public spaces such as libraries. Capturing this broader category of Internet users, a recent UCLA report on Internet use noted that 67 per cent of Americans use the Internet (UCLA, 2000), and the projected rate of growth for access is unparalleled for the introduction of any new technology.

With this explosion of interest in the Internet and the flexibility of the technology to accommodate many different interests, it should not be surprising that the Internet has become an important location for politics and governance in the United States. The Clinton administration, with Vice-President Al Gore at the helm of technology initiatives, saw vast opportunities in Internet technology. Starting with the Telecommunications Act of 1996, President Clinton pledged the resources of the federal government to transform those opportunities into reality. During the 1990s, the government began to promote Internet technology much as it had with the railroads a century earlier or with the production of electricity in the early 1900s. Investment in the Internet was investment in infrastructure and economic growth. Many now see the expansion of all-things Internet in the 1990s lending impetus to economic growth in the United States during the Clinton era. This investment was also a major engine of globalization well into the twenty-first century.

President Clinton's involvement in the Internet took two major forms. First, Clinton facilitated widespread adoption of Internet technology throughout a variety of sectors of United States society. Second, he committed the federal government to achieving a major World Wide Web presence for the United States. Clinton spearheaded legislation making the Internet more easily available to both public and private spheres pledging, for example, that all classrooms would have Internet access by the end of the twentieth century, and then supported his pledge by increasing appropriations for educational technology from $23 million in 1993 to $769 million in 2000. He negotiated with telephone companies and Internet service providers to make low-cost Internet access readily available in rural and low-income communities. Furthermore, $2.25 billion in discounts were created to connect schools and libraries across America to the Internet. In Arizona, where some counties have as low as 40 per cent household telephone rates, Clinton negotiated Internet access for rural Native Americans, such as the Navajo, for just one dollar a month.

Clinton also eased business use of the Internet by signing the Electronic Signatures in Global and National Commerce Act, allowing online contracts signed with digital signatures to have the force of a contract signed in person. President Clinton took part in an online chat with Internet users on 9 November 1999, and took part in the first electronic bill signing on 30 June 2000. During the Clinton/Gore Administration, all major federal agencies in the United States were mandated to put essential information online. In addition, federal agencies were required to comply with the Americans with Disabilities Act (ADA) by making websites accessible by differently-abled people.

President Clinton and Vice-President Gore promoted the Internet and made sure the federal government maximized their use of the technology. This faith in the Internet spilled over to other sectors, and by the end of the 1990s candidates for major public offices (and most minor offices) had to have a website to be considered viable. Interest organizations also scrambled to have a sophisticated web presence, and the Internet became a locus of democratic conversation. Most interest groups today sport flashy websites containing position papers, voting records, research reports, news about lobbying activities, and solicitations for contributions. Left and right political groups alike communicate with and organize supporters using the Internet. World Trade Organization protests in Seattle, Washington were organized using the Internet, and the Ku Klux Klan, a racist organization with a violent history in the United States, recruits new converts using the Internet.

The first wave of cyberdemocracy in the United States used the Internet as a one-way tool for communication. Politically savvy people replicated the format of a campaign brochure or a government report in HTML format. At first, text files or database information could be downloaded through GOPHER sites or by using the File Transfer Protocol (FTP) process. The Internet quickly became information rich, but the information was not necessarily easy to access or interesting to read. The introduction of the HTML format allowed for something more than text, but something less than the flashy graphics, cute animations and interactivity characteristic of the second wave of cyber democracy. This second wave utilizes techniques of interactivity to encourage people to feel connected with websites in a personal way, and to continue returning to preferred websites. Online polls (Morris 1999), e-mail newsletters tailored to subscriber interests, topic-oriented chat groups, real-time Q&As with celebrities, and webcams providing 24-hour views into campaign headquarter sanctuaries are just some examples of how interactivity has been promoted in the second wave.

A recent study documents a shift in Internet user patterns from an early preference for surfing a wide variety of websites to a pattern today that involves returning constantly to tried and true sources of information. However, it is interesting to ask what gets identified as a tried and true source of reliable information? Successful websites today tend to have a flashy, visually attractive, graphic-laden home page where information is regularly updated (sometimes by the minute) and linked to some popular brand name. Although numerous newspapers are available on the Internet, people gravitate to the *New York Times* or the *Washington Post* websites to read the news.

Digital democracy has developed from simply making campaign literature and office hours available online, to a more sophisticated interaction taking place between users and the technology. User demands have changed over time and today's websites work hard to attract new users and to keep regular visitors. Within this ever-changing world of digital democracy, Internet voting has taken an important place in redefining how citizens can take part in the machinery of governance.

Internet voting in the 2000 United States presidential election

Some United States researchers consider 1994 to be the Year of the Internet. Others say the Internet became a mass phenomenon in 1998 as prices dropped and computers became more widely accessible. The year 2000 will undoubtedly be remembered as the Year of Online Elections in the United States. The Internet played a crucial role in the 2000 presidential election and the paradox of this development, set against problems with old technology punch ballots, has not been lost:

Ironically, it was old technology – the mechanical voting booth and the now infamous chad – that had the most enduring impact upon the 2000 presidential election. The new technology of the Internet came of age politically in 2000, with the first major election that would not have been the same without it. (Coleman 2000)

Beginning with the primary elections, each major candidate and some minor candidates for president invested resources in elaborate campaign websites. In some cases, candidate websites played a significant role in the primaries such as when John McCain, Republican candidate for president, reportedly raised $6.1 million through his website within 24 hours of winning the New Hampshire primary election. Major news organizations reported details of the election campaign over the Internet with stories updated every few minutes.

Vast reserves of information were available online throughout the election. The 'Vote Smart' website allowed users to view voting records of incumbent candidates. The 'Rock the Vote' website offered voter registration forms from the 50 states. People could download and print official registration forms and mail them in to their respective states to become registered to vote. It is only a matter of time before actual online registration is available.

What was new for 2000, however, was that Internet voting technology was available and employed in multiple ways during the election. Internet elections may be new to the public sector, but in the United States they are not so new within the private sector. For several years now, private corporations and investment companies have been holding online elections to encourage shareholder participation in management decisions. Companies such as Lucent Technologies and Xerox Corporation utilize online elections to select members of boards of directors. Online election technology has also been used by unions voting on contract negotiations. For example, after a prolonged strike, Boeing engineers voted to ratify their contract via the Internet in May 2000. Universities throughout the nation, including the three major universities of Arizona (Arizona State University, Northern Arizona University, University of Arizona), Stanford, Cornell, and many others universities, have allowed students to cast votes for student body leaders over the Internet. Election.com, the company that organized the online component of the Arizona primary election, boasts organizing more than 300 elections to date. Since 2000, election.com was purchased by the French investment firm Accenture, pushing Internet voting further into international markets.

Internet elections are big business. Election.com and Votehere.net define this sector of the economy. Phil Adler from Votehere.net has been very active speaking across the nation, promoting Internet voting technology as safe and secure. Safevote and Trueballot.com also play an active role in this business sector. Additionally, the Internet seems particularly suited to elections in that it is conceptually easy for an individual to use the mouse and move a cursor to a ballot box, click and make a selection for each particular office. This stands in contrast to the difficulty of using the Internet for other political processes that require extensive discussion and consensus-making.

Internet voting technology was employed in several ways during the 2000 presidential election in the United States. In addition to the Arizona primary election, three remote Alaska precincts allowed registered Republicans to participate in non-binding state caucuses by casting a vote over the Internet. About 35 Republicans took advantage of this option, and 3,638 primary voters in Thurston County, Washington, participated in a non-binding Internet voting pilot project during February 2000.

Following the primary elections, both the Republican and Democratic Party conventions featured exercises in integrating the Internet into political activities. In addition to elaborate websites dedicated to each event, Democratic delegates cast votes from the floor using online Internet connections, with results instantly available to the public. This Internet voting experience at the Democratic Party convention was coordinated by Election.com, and Republic Party convention efforts were coordinated by Votehere.net. The Reform Party, a third party invented by entrepreneur and sometime presidential candidate Ross Perot, conducted their presidential primary over the Internet in a system designed by Eballot.net (now Validity Systems).

Internet voting initiatives continued in the 2000 presidential general election. A select group of military personnel living abroad were encouraged to vote in the election as part of the Federal Voting Assistance Program (FVAP), but only 84 people voted in this project that cost an astounding $6.2 million to organize ($73,809 per vote). (Despite the high cost, the FVAP is planning on offering Internet voting to military personnel abroad in an expanded project designed for the 2004 presidential election; Dunbar 2001). Young people were encouraged to cast a non-binding vote in the presidential election using the Youth E-vote website organized by Election.com, and finally, five non-binding election experiments were held to demonstrate the potential of online election technology. *Votehere.net, Safevote* and *Election Systems & Software* organized nonbinding Internet voting experiments in Contra Costa, San Mateo and San Diego Counties in California. San Mateo County had the largest turnout with 1,020 voters. Additionally, 932 voters participated in an Internet voting experiment in one Phoenix, Arizona precinct organized by Election.com.

Despite the enthusiasm for Internet voting, there were forces in the United States speaking out against Internet voting during the same time period. Prior even to the first presidential primary of 2000, there was movement in California to introduce an Internet voting option into all state elections. Bill Jones, California Secretary of State, convened a panel of social scientists, election experts and computer security experts to consider the potential of this initiative (Jones, 2000). The panel wrote an influential report warning of the limitations of online elections and proposing a process of slowly phasing in the technology. Online voting could first be offered onsite at election polling locations in a secure environment; voting at kiosks would then be introduced prior to remote-site Internet voting being offered.

Responding to an executive order issued by President Clinton, the National Science Foundation, working with the Internet Policy Institute and the University of Maryland, convened a similarly constituted panel in October 2000. The main purpose of the panel was to study the feasibility of Internet voting, and to outline a future technical and social science research agenda for better understanding the potential of Internet voting. The panel concluded its work in February 2001 with a 100-page report (Internet Policy Institute 2001). Regarding the feasibility of Internet voting, panel recommendations mirrored those of the California Secretary of State study. The report determined that technical limitations prevent full implementation of remote-site Internet voting at this time. Onsite Internet voting could be implemented in a secure environment now, but much future research needs to take place before remote-site Internet voting is introduced in any significant way.

Despite the conclusions of these reports, a presidential election recount in Florida and the subsequent revelation of election improprieties raised election reform and the possibility of Internet voting to the national agenda within the United States. It became clear that antiquated election systems challenge fundamental principles of one-person-one-vote in the United States. Reliable and accurate election system technology is needed to replace old technology voting systems, And there is a great need for a ballot system that is transparent and easily auditable. Internet voting meets many of the requirements needed in a new election system, and interest in Internet voting has grown alongside increasing interest in ATM-style voting and optical scanning systems. However, a National Commission on Federal Election Reform, led by former Presidents Jimmy Carter and Gerald Ford, released a report critical of Internet voting for its technical and security limitations (Dunbar 2001; National Commission on Federal Election Reform 2001)

Although future prospects for Internet voting in the United States are now limited by technical considerations, the National Science Foundation, a federal government agency that funds academic research, has recently initiated a quarter of a billion dollar initiative to fund research on digital democracy. Internet voting research is an important part of this initiative.

International interest in Internet voting is now growing rapidly. Public officials in France, England, Germany, Switzerland and Sweden are currently considering the potential of Internet voting, and the discussion taking place in these nations makes little reference to technical limitations. Election.com has taken their concept of student voting to Europe and worked with a variety of international activists to organize a European Union – wide election for an EU student council. EU-Student Vote recently concluded its election with 82,689 students participating in the selection of a 30-member international student council.

The rich discussion of Internet voting always comes back to that moment in March 2000 when Arizona held the first binding Internet election. Arizona Democrats undertook a bold leap and captured international attention for their historic effort. We turn now to a better understanding of the Arizona Democratic primary election, the first and, until now, the only binding public-sector Internet election to have taken place.

The unique context of elections and election reform in the United States

If Internet elections had their birth in the United States, having first flourished in the private sector and then achieving success in the public sector, why has interest in Internet voting in the United States declined since 2000? Why have some European nations taken the lead in exploring Internet voting as a viable approach to election reform? The answer lies, at least partially, in the unique structure of election laws in the United States and in events specific to the 2000 presidential election in the United States. This section looks first at the structure of election laws in the United States, because it is this structure that shapes how the events of 2000 impacted discussions of election reform.

To begin, election administration in the United States is extremely decentralized. Only very broad principles establishing a standard of fairness in voting and eliminating discrimination at the ballot box are in place at the federal level. Each of the 50 states has its own election rules, administered by a chief election officer, often called a Secretary of State. The Secretary of State's office is responsible for maintaining state election records and officiating the electoral process. Furthermore, states are subdivided into counties and each county retains authority for establishing voting procedures within its boundaries. There are over 3,100 counties in the United States, each possessing autonomy to decide how votes will be cast and counted.

To further emphasize the decentralized framework for election law in the United States, there are over 5,000 legally defined election districts in the USA. I live in Flagstaff, Arizona, for example. I vote in national elections, state elections, county elections, city elections and school district elections. Each election involves a unique governing body that exercises power within overlapping territorial boundaries. Each governing entity has some autonomy over when elections will take place, how votes will be cast, and who will tally results. I may cast a vote in one location for a city-wide election and in another location for a school district bond issue. In my county, people vote using punch cards, an outdated technology developed in the 1960s involving punching holes in an 80 column computer card. The voter uses an object to punch out a hole next to the name of the candidate of their choice. Half of all Arizona counties continue to use this technology, now so old that new punch card readers can no longer be purchased. In the United States, one-third of all counties used punch card technology in the 2000 presidential election.

Unlike many democracies, The United States does not convene an independent election commission to make election law and adjudicate election disputes. The election process in the United States is firmly rooted in partisan politics. Political parties (Democrats and Republicans) make election law, administer election law and adjudicate disputes. The Secretary of State position is held by a party partisan. In the state of Florida, the site of the infamous vote-count battle of the 2000 presidential election, Katherine Harris, the Secretary of State at that time, played a defining role in the vote count struggle. Katherine Harris was a Republican working for a Republican governor – Jeb Bush, President George W. Bush's brother. Secretary Harris co-chaired the

2000 George W. Bush for President campaign in Florida. Following Election Day, Harris continued with partisan politics and promoted George W. Bush's interests in the battle over Florida's electoral votes. She subsequently ran as a Republican candidate for the United States Congress in 2002 and won.

Finally, in order to understand election reform in the United States, especially reform involving the adoption of new election equipment, it is important to point out that this process is driven by competitive, private markets. Large corporations market election equipment in the United States, travelling state by state and meeting with Secretaries of State. The Secretary of States' offices test election equipment using principles developed within each state and certify equipment that can be purchased by counties within the state. Individual counties decide which technology to adopt and are responsible for financing the purchase and maintenance of election equipment. Thus, once counties make a decision to invest in a particular technology, they typically continue to use the equipment for some time. United States studies consistently demonstrate that poorer counties and rural counties tend to use punch-card ballot technology, while wealthier counties use optical scanning equipment. Some counties continue to use lever machines.

Within the unique context of election administration in the United States, we can begin to understand how problems associated with the 2000 presidential election affected the discourse of election reform in the United States. In the 2000 presidential election, Al Gore received over 500,000 more votes, among nearly 100 million votes cast in the nation, than his opponent George W. Bush. However, because of the Electoral College structure of presidential voting, which dates back to the interests of the constitutional founders, the popular vote does not elect a president. Each state is represented within the Electoral College relative to its population size. California had 54 votes in the Electoral College in 2000, while Arizona had eight votes and North Dakota had three. State votes are allocated on a winner-take-all basis. Despite Al Gore receiving more popular votes than George W. Bush, Bush received more electoral votes, finishing with five more Electoral College votes than Gore. Florida then became a battleground because the states' 25 votes would decide the election. Because of this situation, Florida effectively put George W. Bush into the White House.

The 2000 presidential election was unresolved for 40 days. It took intervention from the United States Supreme Court to decide by one vote that presidential candidate George W. Bush would win the presidential election. The election controversy boiled down to how Florida's 25 electoral votes would be allocated because, as mentioned, whoever received Florida's votes would win the presidency. Several improprieties were alleged to have occurred in Florida on election day. One controversy involved a misdesigned ballot in one county (counties design their own ballots); this so-called 'butterfly ballot' controversy led to many liberal, traditionally Democratic, voters actually casting a vote for Patrick Buchanan, a right-wing Republican Party ideologue. Another controversy involved the removal of alleged felons from the voting roles. In Florida, as in several states, people with a felony record are denied the right to vote for their entire lives. The net for defining who was a felon was cast rather wide and many people without felony records were taken off the voting roles and denied their right to vote on election day. This situation disproportionately affected African American and Latino citizens of Florida.

The overarching issue behind the Florida election debacle, however, involved the use of antiquated election equipment and the slippage between votes cast and votes counted. Studies repeatedly show that all election equipment is associated with a known failure rate, ranging from about 1 per cent to 6 per cent. Many votes are lost each election. But in the case of the 2000 election in Florida, up to 6 per cent of votes cast in some counties were never recorded. And the older, more antiquated, problem-prone equipment resides disproportionately in low-income and minority communities. Further, when it came to hand-counting ballots cast, each county had its own rules and regulations, part of the decentralized nature of election administration in the United States. Thus it is not surprising that a vote cast with a punch card in one county might be considered a legitimate vote, while such a vote would be discarded in another county. Or, an inappropriate vote cast by military personnel abroad might be accepted in one county but not another.

The 2000 election and beyond

In the United States, the conversation about 'election reform' today is necessarily haunted by the 2000 presidential recent experience; promises made and opportunities lost are at the forefront of the public mind. As citizens, public officials, political scientists and the media discuss election reform in the post-2000 presidential election season, one requirement for reform stands above all else: how can we insure that every vote is actually counted in future elections?

The Florida recount raised concern about the quality of election equipment throughout the nation. Many states and counties began to examine equipment purchased years prior and considered replacing antiquated equipment with newer, more user-friendly equipment. For a brief moment, Internet voting was on the table as an intriguing option that guaranteed one-person-one-vote and automated recount procedures. But many agreed that Internet voting was not viable in the short run. It would be years before the technology would be tamper proof and mass public elections could be organized utilizing the technology. Election reform had to be implemented now.

The decentralized election structure in the United States and the active solicitation of customers by election equipment manufacturers turned a public policy issue worthy of debate and serious consideration into a short-term buying spree driven by market-oriented solutions. Election equipment manufacturers went on the offensive and visited Secretaries of State throughout the nation, demonstrating their equipment, seeking buyers among election officials presiding over the more than 5,000 election districts in the United States. Now, interest in Internet voting took a back seat to interest in other high-tech voting solutions, including optical-scanning machines and ATM-style electronic voting. However, even interest in these other technologies has dulled somewhat as communities realize the price tags associated with ushering in new technology. Since 2000, most states in the nation have been experiencing fiscal crises driven by exploding budget deficits. The best of intentions to usher in electoral reform have fallen short in the face of no slack resources to fund new voting technology. In the 2002 congressional and local elections in the United States, Internet voting technology was not utilized anywhere in the nation, in stark contrast to the prevalence of Internet voting in a variety of forums during the 2000 presidential election.

Arizona's situation is a case study of the broader problem. Arizona was the state to hold the first binding Internet election, and telephone surveys showed support throughout the state for having Internet voting options available in all future elections. Betsey Bayless, Arizona's Secretary of State, took the lead in promoting the need to replace old punch-card voting systems in the state with optical scanning equipment. The Arizona state legislature ultimately turned down her request for funding, although it did authorize her to seek financial support from private sources of funding. To date, new equipment has yet to materialize in Arizona. It is important to note that a new federal law allocates $3 billion to states interested in replacing old voting technology.

The viability of Internet voting in the future will depend upon improvements in Internet technology, particularly in the area of security. So, too the future of Internet voting will be influenced by the structure of election administration within a nation. Decentralized election administration (now operating in the United States as a crisis environment) leans towards short-term, market-oriented decision-making. Long-term political and economic investment in Internet voting will not emerge from within this environment. Europe's recent experiences with Internet voting demonstrate that forward movement on this issue is more likely to emerge within political systems characterized by centralized election administration and more stable sources of funding. Internet voting is a byproduct of digital democracy. But the issue, once so prominent within the United States, has lost momentum within the nation. The proverbial ball now passes to Europe and elsewhere to demonstrate the viability of Internet elections.

References

Coleman, S. (2001) 'Introduction', in S. Coleman (ed.), *Elections in the Age of the Internet: Lessons from the United States*. London: Hansard Society.

Dunbar, J. (2001) 'Internet Voting Project Cost Pentagon $73,809 Per Vote', <http://www.public-i.org/story_01_080901.htm>

Internet Policy Institute (2001) *Report of the National Workshop on Internet Voting: Issues and Research Agenda*, <http://www.Internetpolicy.org/research/ results.html>

Jones, B. (2000) *California Internet Voting Task Force Report*, <http://www.ss.ca.gov/ executive/ivote/>

Morris, D. (1999) *Vote.com*. Los Angeles: Renaissance Books.

National Commission on Federal Election Reform (2001) 'To Assure Pride and Confidence in the Electoral Process', <http://www.reformelections.org/data/ reports/99_full_report.pdf>

Solop, F. I. (2001) 'Digital Democracy Comes of Age: Internet Voting and the 2000 Arizona Democratic Primary Election', *Political Science and Politics*, 34 (2) (June): 289–93.

Solop, F. (2000a) 'The 2000 Arizona Democratic Primary Election: What We Learned From the First Binding Internet Election', e-voting workshop, National Science Foundation and the University of Maryland.

Solop, F. (2000b) 'Digital Democracy Comes of Age in Arizona: Participation and Politics in the First Binding Internet Election'. The American Political Science Association meetings, Washington, DC.

Solop, F. (2000c) 'Public Support for Internet Voting: Are We Falling Into a "Racial Ravine"?' The American Association of Public Opinion Research meetings, Portland, OR.

UCLA (2000) 'The UCLA Internet Report: Surveying the Digital Future', <http://us4.israeline.com/ucla-Internet.pdf>

United States Census Bureau (2001) *Home Computers and Internet Use in the United States* (August), <http://www.census.gov/prod/2001pubs/p23–207.pdf>

5
Electronic Voting in Switzerland
Hans Geser

In the governmental and administrative realm, Switzerland has developed a number of rather advanced Internet applications: for example by implementing electronic systems of transit traffic control or tariff payments, and by offering online options for filling out census questionnaires and tax declarations or for following parliamentary debates in real time on the Net.[1]

In the sphere of political communication, however, the use of online media has remained outstandingly peripheral. This is astonishing in the light of the extensity and intensity of grassroots-level political discussion and deliberation going along with the frequent initiatives and referenda which lead to a multitude of plebiscitarian votings (on the federal, cantonal and communal level) every few weeks. Thus, participation in online discussions and chat hours (organized by reputable politicians) is notoriously weak, and no cases are known where the Internet has been effectively used for petitions or other sorts of political campaigns.

Consistent with these trends, the 'Selects' survey conducted in 1999 has shown that only about 11 per cent of all Swiss net users are visiting any websites of political parties, and only a tiny minority of them declares to be influenced by any kind of content on these pages. And the Vox surveys (regularly conducted after each federal voting) show that only 3–4 per cent of all voters use the Internet for acquiring knowledge about the issues in question (Auer and Trechsel 2001: 27).

Thus, we face the remarkable paradox that the country most known for its traditions of direct democracy makes little use of many obvious democratic potentials opened up by online communication: its capacity for more intensive 'bottom-up politics', and for a more extensive plebiscitarian participation. Instead, the Internet has mainly given rise to rather centralized 'top-down initiatives' which tend to collide heavily with the decentralized, fragmented power structures as well as with a conservative-minded population.

We may speculate that exactly these highly established democratic traditions are the reason why the need for online channels has remained low, because they have given rise to a dense network of offline communication channels ranging from informal pub and tavern gatherings (*Stammtischrunden*) to a wide range of assemblies within the formal framework of local and supralocal party sections, citizen groups, movement activist groupings and voluntary associations. Adding the tiny geographical areas and the fine-grained settlement patterns which ensure that anybody has easy access to some of these structures (without extensive travelling), it is evident that virtual communication channels will also in the future be less needed than in countries like Australia, Canada or Russia where thousands of miles (and several time zones) have to be bridged.

Of course, the same factors have been responsible for a fine-grained allocation of ballot places, so that most citizens find a voting opportunity within walking distance.

Who then will find electronic voting attractive (or even indispensable) under such favourable conditions? And how could significant numbers of citizens be brought to use their PCs for executing the solemn act of voting, when they have never acquired the habit of using the Internet for more serious purposes of political information or communication?

The postal vote as a major step toward 'virtual voting'

Nevertheless, as voting rates have become lower and lower over the last decades, it has become folk wisdom to believe that this trend could be weakened or even broken by making voting more easily accessible through technical means. Since the late 1970s, the Swiss government has taken initiatives to implement new ballot procedures in order to increase participation levels, especially among the younger and more mobile segments of the population. Thus as early as 1979, a working group instituted by the Federal Department of Justice had come to the conclusion

> that everything possible must be done in order to reduce material or psychological hindrances to practice the right to vote. This calls for facilitating the voting process or making the trip to the

polling station unnecessary through postal voting. *(Amstutz 1999, translated by the author)*

The postal vote procedure was introduced by the federal government and most cantons in the early 1990s: a step which went along with many deep changes in voting behaviour, changes usually associated with the electronic vote.

The major modification consists particularly in the extended time span available for depositing the individual vote. In most of cantons, citizens receive voting materials about 25 to 28 days before the official polling date, and on the average, about 60 per cent of voters make use of this new procedure.[2] In urban settings like Basel or Geneva, the rate of postal voting usually exceeds 80 per cent, while in the suburban and rural towns and villages, the traditional walk to the ballot urn (open at specific hours from Friday evening to Sunday morning) is still preferred by the majority. In some cities, however, postal rates have remained low when a dense network or polling stations has been maintained.[3]

At least in the case of Geneva, empirical findings allow the conclusion that the postal vote has been effective in raising turnout rates. Since about 1997, Geneva now ranges above the Swiss average, while in the past it was notoriously far below (Amstutz 1999).

At the moment, however, we see in many places the initial phases of a vicious cycle: insofar as many polling stations are closed because usage has fallen too low, many voters are forced again to send votes by mail because walking distances have become intolerably long.

Two highly problematic dysfunctions of postal voting procedures have to be noted, which are both aggravated by peculiarities of the Swiss political system:

1 Almost half of all postal voters deposit their votes before the governmental agencies have sent out their informational material, and before the public campaigns and discussions focusing on the voting issue have gained momentum. This of course is highly inconsistent with a concept of deliberative democracy in which voting decisions should only be made after all organized groups have been able to propagate their views and information, and opinions have been shaped within widespread processes of discursive communication. In fact, such extensions of voting periods privilege larger and richer groupings and associations which have the means to start their campaigns weeks or even months before polling dates, hurting weaker groupings which have to concentrate their activities on the final days.

2   A second dysfunction concerns the exercise of two other political rights provided by the Federal constitution: the signing of initiatives and referenda. In the past, groups organizing such campaigns had an easy and cheap option of collecting signatures: by just catching citizens at the exit gates of the polling places. Today where less and less citizens still make use of physical ballots, other more costly procedures have to be used. Again, this change favours the more potent groupings and organizations, which can pay individuals to walk the streets or engage in door-to-door canvassing (Amstutz 1999).

The initiating and facilitating role of federal government

In February 1998, the Swiss government (Bundesrat) committed itself to a long-term e-government strategy aiming 'to make Switzerland one of the leading countries in this realm'.[4] Since then, this initiative has given rise to a multitude of rather loosely connected specific projects carried on by specialized agencies and offices on the one hand, and by lower-level governmental units (cantons and communities) on the other. These can be subsumed under two headings:

1   *Guichet virtuel projects*: promoting the use of online channels for administrative procedures (e.g. tax procedures, military service, renewal of passports etc.).
2   *E-voting projects*: aiming at the development of secure online methods for depositing yes–no votes in issue-related pools as well as lists of candidates in various elections. In addition, in future citizens should also be able to exercise all other political rights by online channels: for example by signing petitions, initiatives and referenda in a legally binding way.

These aims have been clearly stated by the Swiss Bundesrat in responding to a parliamentary interpellation: 'The signature to Swiss national initiatives and referenda or to National Council proposals as well as the casting of votes at Swiss plebiscites and at National Council elections are handled, transmitted, examined, counted and passed on electronically'.[5] As a major consideration, the executive hopes that electronic voting will increase voting turnout rates, particularly among the younger cohort known to be regular Internet users, but to have below-average participation rates at conventional polls. In addition, it is envisaged that population segments could be activated which were hitherto not able to vote for various physical reasons: for example tourists or businessmen absent on polling days, physically handicapped individuals (*Schweizerische Bundeskanzlei* 2002), and particularly the more then 500,000 emigrants (*Auslandschweizer*) on all continents who have retained their citizenship as well as their voting rights (even in the second and third generation).[6]

Furthermore, it is envisaged that the government should use the new online channels for making their citizens express more differentiated opinions than just 'yes' or 'no'. By inviting comments, remarks and arguments, it is hoped that government will be better able to interpret the results and to guess what kind of options citizens really prefer.

> In electronic voting systems there exists the possibility to attach facultative questions, where the voter expresses his opinions at the same time he casts his vote. This creates the opportunity to interpret voting results electronically. With this, the political opinions of voters could be taken more into account. With a strict obligation to make votes anonymous, an enhanced analyses of votes could deliver exact data. From this, an increased influence of the citizen on the political decisions making process could develop. (*Schweizerische Bundeskanzlei* 2002, translated by the author)

It is evident that the Swiss political system is especially predisposed towards the adoption of e-voting for the following reasons:

1 An extremely large number of polling activities (elections as well as issue voting) at the federal, cantonal and communal levels take place every year, so that considerable economic and organizational advantages can be gained by making use of the new technologies. In addition, the pressure for change is increased by the fact that it is becoming increasingly difficult to recruit enough volunteers to organize and supervise the polls and the counting of ballot papers.
2 Voter registration procedures are on a very high level, because registration is compulsory and registries are permanently updated (e.g. when people move from one community to another).
3 By adopting postal-vote laws in the 1990s, Switzerland has already gone a long way towards 'distant-polling' procedures no longer based on personal appearance at ballot stations, so that e-voting will not appear as a major revolution. Such far-reaching voting facilitations are themselves an indicator that polling in Switzerland is more 'desacralized' than in many younger democracies where it is a ceremonial act not easily amenable to innovative change.[7]

4 Finally, the introduction of e-voting is facilitated because norms concerning the secrecy of votes are less pronounced than in many other Western countries. This is due to a long tradition of public voting (in open assemblies like *Landgemeinden* or town-hall meetings) where this secrecy can evidently not be secured at all (*Schweizerische Bundeskanzlei* 2001).

Within Swiss society, these e-voting endeavours can currently rely on considerable support:

1 A representative survey conducted in Nov. 2000 showed that about 66 per cent of Swiss citizens were strongly in favour of electronic voting. Thus, it is certainly one of the most preferred Internet projects undertaken by government, ranging closely behind online communication with administrative offices (74 per cent) or electronic passport extensions (72 per cent).
2 On the level of organized groupings, the political parties (especially the Radical Democrats) have expressed much support for e-voting procedures, as well as the association of cantonal administrators (*Staatsschreiberkonferenz*), which will have a major role in the process of implementation (see below).

Finally, in a survey conducted in Spring 2001, all cantonal governments expressed their willingness to engage in e-voting projects – at least under the condition that the federal government provide expertise and pay the major costs.

Despite this broad support, however, the latest documents indicate that the federal government has recently become more cautious (if not pessimistic) about the whole endeavour. Thus, official agencies are eager to underline that 2010 is the earliest possible date when an official start of e-voting (on the federal level) could be envisaged, and that costs of between 400 and 600 million Swiss francs have to be expected, 50 per cent of which would have to be carried by the communities (*Schweizerischen Bundeskanzlei* 2002). In addition, some statements indicate that the government has lost enthusiasm as a result of several critical arguments brought forward by experts and organized groupings. In particular, the Bundesrat seems to share the concern that:

- the territorial basis of the Swiss voting system (organized into cantons, districts etc.) could be undermined when votes are able to be delivered from any location; and

- the use of online technologies could result in an acceleration of voting porocedures, which would have a negative impact on the time-consuming processes of political campaigning and deliberation.[8]

The ambiguous implications of decentralized federalism

Due to its historic formation (as a secondary confederation of preexisting political units) and to its multitude of locally based languages, traditions and political cultures, Switzerland has conserved a rather decentralized system of political power. First of all, the 26 cantons have maintained considerable legal, financial and organizational autonomy in many policy fields, particularly in the realm of political and administrative organization. Secondly, most of them provide rather extended autonomy rights to their communities, especially in the German-speaking regions.

From the perspective of political innovations and reform, this decentralized structure is certainly propitious insofar as it provides a rich 'variety pool' of smaller units trying out their own ways and disposed for trial-and-error experiments which involve little cost and risks because they remain bound to smaller parts of the territory and population.

In the realm of election and voting procedures, this functionality is explicitly taken into account by the federal government. Thus, while the Federal Law of Political Rights (BPR) obliges all cantons to observe traditional voting procedures (for example implying that votes have to hand-written and voting sheets have to be personally signed), Para. 84 provides space for exemptions by authorizing the federal governments to grant specific exceptions: 'The senate can *empower* the government of the cantons to create specific legal regulations for the technical instruments used in elections. Election and voting processes using technical means require the authorization of the senate'.[9] This paragraph provides a sufficient legal basis for testing out electronic voting procedures (without even specifying to what extent traditional rules may be violated), so that no additional legal (or even constitutional) rules had to be created.[10]

On the other hand, the same federalist structures hamper the implementation of political reforms insofar as:

- various cantons and communities have established their own traditional procedures and institutions over decades (or even centuries); and

• Federal agencies always remain dependent on the voluntary cooperation of subnational units, and nationwide reforms are highly dependent on reaching a consensus, which can be promoted but not authoritatively enforced.

As a result of this basic need for voluntary multi-level accordance, all federal commissions dedicated to e-government have to be recruited according to highly complex criteria, so that widespread representation of different cantons and language regions is secured.[11]

In summer 2001, the federal working group for the promotion of e-voting conducted a survey in order to assess the current state and the future plans of e-voting projects in all 26 cantons. The results indicated that while everybody is interested in implementing e-voting procedures (by collaborating with the federal government), very few cantons have started concrete projects, and even less have already created the necessary legal provisions (Table 5.1).

Most of the cantons are very far away from fulfilling one important precondition: the establishment of a central electronic voting registry. Even worse: they have no means for realizing this aim, insofar as constitutional norms don't allow them to enforce homogeneous rules and procedures on all their communities. Given the tiny population and administrative apparatus of most communities, they often lack the financial means and expertise to make the transition from physical to electronic registries on their own. And in several cases the cantonal administrations themselves lack the means to provide professional help.[13]

Table 5.1   State of e-voting initiatives in 26 Swiss cantons (survey from July 2001), number of cantons answering 'yes'[12]

	Yes
Interested in undertaking an e-voting project in collaboration with the federal government	26
E-voting project currently underway	4
Legal provisions for e-voting have already been enacted	2
Initiatives to create such provisions are underway	6
Voting registries are administrated by the Canton (not by the Communities)	4
A standardized electronic voting registry has been established	4
The communities have changed to electronic voting registries	all = 7 (some = 12)

Thus, we may conclude that the implementation of national e-voting will critically depend on major reforms:

1 on the political level: by creating the legal basis for homogeneous electronic registries; and
2 on the organizational level: by providing the personnel, expertise and technology necessary to implement such homogeneous procedures on the level of all (about 2,990) communes.

It is to be expected that centralized top-down endeavours by the federal governments to implement homogenous procedures on all subunits will never be accepted. Instead, only highly time-consuming bottom-up solutions will be viable: for example in the sense that intercommunal and intercantonal networking of voter registries occur, so that the federal government will only possess a 'virtual registry' by having access to intercantonal servers (*Schweizerische Bundeskanzlei* 2002).

Given these contingencies, the question arises whether the interest in e-voting will be sustained at a sufficiently high level to motivate such far-reaching changes. As to be expected, the few cantons actively engaged in projects have not coordinated their endeavours (despite the fact that they have invited each other to participate in the specialized commissions), and the goals they have envisaged are rather different. The most potent canton (Zürich) has currently the most modest aim of just coordinating and homogenizing the communal registries so that the transition to electronic formats will be possible in a later step. Neuchâtel is currently also still occupied by tasks of administrative standardization and centralization, but with the more ambitious aim of developing a format of electronic signatures which can be applied to e-voting as well as to initiatives and referenda. At the moment, only Geneva is seriously committed to the concrete establishment of a fully functional official e-voting procedure, confronting itself deeply with all the legal, technical, administrative, psychological and cultural implications associated with such an unprecedented step. The project strictly focusses on yes–no issue voting, so that the complications associated with electoral procedures (for example name cancelling or cumulations on lists) do not have to be dealt with.

Given the need for centralized and standardized registries and administrative procedures, it is highly significant that the more ambitious projects are exclusively found in the French-speaking region of Switzerland where traditions of direct democracy and communal autonomy are rather weak. This situation favours e-voting for two very different reasons:

1 implementation is easier because standardization has already been made, and because cantonal agencies have more authority to enforce common rules and practices; and
2 e-voting is more likely to be accepted by citizens because for many of them the community is not a relevant level of political participation, so that they have never become familiar with traditional ballot locations.

Geneva in particular stands out as a canton where the political relevance of communities is minimal, and where rather anonymous relationships between citizens (and between citizens and governmental agencies) prevail. This is at least partly due to the high demographic fluctuation, which implies that many inhabitants have just recently immigrated.

Three pilot projects currently in the stage of experimentation

Neuchâtel: a comprehensive strategy encompassing all plebiscitarian rights

Based on an unusually tight collaboration between communities and cantonal agencies, the executive of Neuchâtel has decided in favour of a comprehensive one-step concept, which should almost simultaneously establish:

1 e-voting at all plebiscitarian issue voting (on the communal, cantonal and federal levels),
2 e-voting at all elections for the legislature and the executive (on the same three levels), and
3 online subscriptions of petitions, initiatives and referenda.

In contrast to Geneva where the authorization code has only be submitted after the vote has been sent, the Neuchâtel strategy relies on an anticipatory authorization as it is used by most telebanking procedures After personal authentication, the system checks that the individual has not yet voted before. When this check has been successfully passed, the voter receives an access code as well as a password, which are necessary to gain access to the official voting site. When delivering their votes, an additional secret number has to be submitted which citizens will have received by post. Like in Geneva, online votes are stored in an encrypted 'electronic urn'. When counting begins, electronic votes are added to those delivered by postal letter or at ballot stations, and a check with the central voting registry ensures that no citizen has submitted more than one vote.

Contrary to the Geneva system, which treats individuals exclusively under the aspect whether, they are (or are not) entitled to vote, the Neuchâtel solution has the advantage of embedding e-voting processes in a larger universe of citizen–government relationships. This e-*guichet* concept implies that whenever an individual has successfully completed authentification, he or she gets access to a multidimensional universe of official relationships based on a manifold of salient relationships (e.g. taxpayer, enrolment in education, welfare receiver, public employee or member of the catholic church).

Another characteristic is that in contrast to Geneva, the cantonal administration plays a lesser role because many operative tasks (distribution of voting material, administration of voting registries, vote counting etc.) are taken care of by the communities. Instead of constituting a centralized physical registry of its own, the canton is satisfied to establish a 'virtual central registry' *ad hoc* at each polling date: by simply creating cognitive access to the 62 communal registries (which are mirroring current conditions because they are regularly updated each day or week). Thus, the Neuchâtel solution relies much more than the Geneva concept on the practices of 'cooperative federalism' between communal and cantonal agencies as autonomous actors of equal status) which are characteristic for most Swiss cantons.

Zürich: overcoming the obstacles of decentralized administrative structures

In contrast to the two aforementioned French cantons which can both rely on highly centralized cantonal administrations, the canton of Zürich displays many features typical of German-speaking regions: a highly heterogeneous set of rather autonomous communities (ranging from about 200 to 350,000 inhabitants) with highly divergent computer and software systems, as well as rather heterogeneous voter registration systems. Given these inhospitable premises, the establishment of a unified population and voter registry would already be a laudable pioneer task. As a first step the cantonal executive has chosen the only viable compromise: to establish a secondary ('virtual') voting registry based on communal registries, which have to be maintained and updated by communal administrations. Future plans are oriented towards implementing a comprehensive electronic voting system using different devices such as mobile phones, the Internet, and so on. The process of public tendering started in 2003.

For each polling procedure, a 'virtual voter registry' is created by aggregating the current communal registries. Each citizen receives an automatically generated numeric code which can be used as an identification key to gain access to the electronic polling system. On the polling paper, the same code is printed as a barcode. Whenever a citizen votes at the ballot station or by mail, this barcode is checked to verify that the same individual has not yet submitted his vote online (in which case the vote is invalid). Given that counting is administered by the communities, each commune has to have access to the central virtual registry and to be equipped with the machinery for deciphering these codes.

While Geneva and Neuchâtel tailor their systems exclusively to the personal computer, only Zürich takes into account that future citizens may rely more on mobile phones, PDAs or other lean and easily mobile devices. As a consequence, a polling system is envisaged where all problems related to reliability, security, encryption, privacy and so on are solved for a very wide range of different hardware configurations, operating platforms, software applications and transmission protocols.

Geneva: the most comprehensive and pioneering endeavour

In a comparative international perspective, the current e-voting project in the canton of Geneva stands out as one of the very few really serious attempts to implement formally binding governmental voting procedures on the WWW. This implies that all the major factors on the cultural, psychological, political, administrative and legal levels have come into play, and water-tight solutions for all preconditions necessary for legitimate democratic voting procedures (security, anonymity, reliability, controllability etc.) have to be addressed and solved on an operational level. As a consequence, the Geneva pilot project is a breeding ground for fruitful discussions, innovations and experiences which may be relevant for similar future projects within communities, governments, voluntary associations or any organized democratic systems.

Favourable preconditions

For five different reasons, Geneva is better predisposed for implementing e-voting than most other Swiss cantons:

1 A centralized electronic voting registry exists, so that no obstacles related to divergences among different communities have to be overcome.

2 Contrary to all other cantons, the voting law (instituted in 1982) authorizes the cantonal executive 'to collaborate with the communities in trying out new voting methods at variance with the present law, in order to bring voting procedures in line with new technological conditions.'[14]

3 As the rate of votes delivered by postal correspondence has recently risen to about 90 per cent, the majority of citizens have already turned away from traditional ballot urns to more anonymous voting procedures. As a consequence, the additional change to electronic voting is not likely to be felt as a dramatic change.

4 An unusually high per centage of all citizens (about 5.9 per cent) currently live abroad. Thus, there are high incentives to enlarge the effective electorate by providing a low-threshold access channel for every entitled citizen worldwide.

5 Geneva possesses a rich of supply of highly competent experts and institutions (e.g. the CERN project for expertise related to net technologies, and the Cantonal University for legal questions and issues related to political science).[15]

Goals and driving motivations

Apart from more specific goals (for example to increase turnout rates by mobilizing additional younger voters or emigrated citizens), the Geneva authorities seem to be driven by more general ideological motivations and by their ambitious endeavour to make Geneva the 'e-capital' of Europe. These broader goals are also manifest in several other electronic innovations implemented over recent years: for example the rapid transmission of voting results on WAP-enabled mobile phones. Various statements in official documents also corrobor ate the impression that the e-voting project is primarily nourished by a high-flying technological enthusiasm, not by concretely defined expectations:

> Why introduce Internet voting? Contemporary scientific advancements go beyond simple technological progress. According to the opinion of numerous observers, we live in a transitional period, the turning over of an era, like that which took place five centuries ago in the period separating the invention of the printing press (1457) from the Renaissance. Rather than suffering this technical revolution, the state must anticipate it, accompany it, and see to it that no one is excluded.[16]

On the framework of planning and implementation

In March 2000, the cantonal executive (Conseil d'État) agreed on a proposal to implement e-voting within the subsequent three years. In the first stage, it should be completely restricted to issues voting (involving only yes–no statements), while applications to the election process should be delayed to a later period.

In the course of a public subscription in fall 2000, two private enterprises (Hewlett-Packard and Wisekey SA) were selected for working out the design of the system and the adequate software requirements. At the same time, various experts from reputable local institutions (CERN, University, central hospital etc.) were chosen to study various critical issues of e-voting procedures (such as problems of voter identification, security and confidentiality of voting etc.). Following this, several smaller test runs were made in connections with federal voting in June, September and December 2001 as well as in March 2002.

The electronic voting procedures were tested inside the canton's administration and in public schools. In January 2003, in Geneva's suburb Aniere, the first online referendum took place. The introduction of postal voting in 1992, had boosted turnout by around 20 per cent, so that usually about 95 per cent of the electorate used the postal voting alternative. At the referendum in Aniere, 44 per cent took the opportunity to use online voting, 50 per cent voted by mail, and only 6 per cent cast their votes at the polling station. Although there was no tremendous increase in voter turnout, the pilot project was regarded as very much a success.

The total costs reached SFR1.25 million (of which 1 million was carried by the federal government), and were distributed as shown in Table 5.2.[17] In the longer run, it is estimated that e-voting will result

Table 5.2   Total costs of e-voting pilots (Swiss francs)

Hardware equipment	180,000
Upgrading of telephone systems	288,000
System software	40,000
Development of procedural applications	210,000
Security testing (incl. mandated hacking)	80,000
Legal and political science study	30,000
Public communication	315,000
Public hotline	50,000
Diverse costs	50,000

in increased costs of about 8 per cent for each individual voting procedure in the canton (from SFR500,000 to SFR540,000).

Voting procedure

All citizens receive official documents for voting by mail three weeks in advance. The enclosed personal voting card entitles everybody to deliver their vote online or by mail at any moment up to noon Saturday before the official election day, or by traditional ballot voting or the official day. Access to Internet voting is made very simple by using methods similar to most e-commerce applications: Without having to register in any way, individuals can point their browser to a portal site which leads them to all relevant information and form pages. They can even transmit their vote freely and experiment themselves 'whether it really works'. Formal registration is only necessary in the last phase in order to validate the submitted vote. This is also the only stage where communication with the voting server is encrypted (on the basis of SSL 3.0). The voting form is filled out by inserting (a) an individual identification number (PIN code), (b) a personal password (which can both be made visible on the voting card by scratching at specific locations), and (c) the date of birth.

By scratching the paper to read the password, the voting card is visibly invalidated so that it can no longer be used for mailed or ballot procedures. After personal authentication, voters get immediate confirmation that their vote has been accepted, and they can optionally receive an additional confirmation by e-mail (without the content of the vote) to an indicated address.

The servers dedicated to identification, registration and voting have the capacity of processing up to 2,000 voting requests per hour, while those used for presenting informational material are able to handle much larger numbers of visitors.

There procedures (used similarly for lottery tokens) have the advantage of being functional without a digital signature, but on the other hand cannot guarantee that the vote really originates from the entitled person.[18] During polling periods, the encrypted votes are accumulated in an 'electronic urn' to which nobody (especially citizens who are entitled to vote) has access. The encryption procedure is still under scrutiny. It is envisaged that two keys may be used, each of which is known to only one representative of the voting committee (which is again steered by representatives of the political parties). The two individuals are requested to define the two codes at the beginning of the polling period, so that they can be used as a basis for encryption.

During this period, the keys are kept in a closed envelope guarded by the president of the cantonal 'chamber of solicitors'. When the counting of votes begins, the chamber president opens the envelope and hands over the keys so that they can be used for decryption.

Future developments

On 28 January 2002, the committee dedicated to the study of security problems published an extensive report in which many still unsolved problems plaguing the current e-voting project are addressed.[19] The main argument is that within the sectors controlled by government and administration (for example receiving servers, counting procedures etc.), security deficiencies are rather easy to identify and can be readily and reliably solved. On the other hand, this is not true for the user-controlled sectors which are characterized by a gamut of complex, unpredictable and volatile problems related to bugs in various operation systems, to viruses and trojans as well as to intentional attempts by hackers to observe or even modify delivered votes in transit, or to redirect them to other servers.

In order to reduce such risks and dangers, the committee proposed a multitude of possible measures, many of them apt to generate considerable additional costs and organizational overheads on the one hand, and incalculable unintentional dysfunctions on the other. For instance, the establishment of a 'test urn' was suggested which would enable controllers to verify at least indirectly whether the electronic voting procedure is operational without distortions. This could be realized with the following procedures: certain segments of the electorate are selected for delivering two parallel votes (one online and the other in a conventional ballot urn), so that it may be checked whether identical results are achieved through both channels.

Secondly, it was suggested that the official voting software should be made available to all citizens on a CD-ROM, in order to create identical security standards on all peripheral computers. Evidently, this measure would engender many additional difficulties resulting from deficient hardware equipment, driving software, damaged diskettes and other problem sources, so that equal chances for online voting participation could no longer be secured.

Finally, the commission suggested opening additional gateways for e-voting (for example via mobile phones) in order to make voting procedures more independent from the PC and the WWW. Again, such measures would currently introduce additional sources of insecurity: problems even less thoroughly known than the rather well-studied deficiencies of the PC operating systems and the World Wide Web.

The authors of the report at least acknowledged the basic dilemma associated with the fact that e-voting procedures have to fulfil two equally important, but highly contradictory goals: (1) providing a low-threshold access to everybody – even users with rather simple and antiquated computer equipment, and (2) following the highest technological standards in shielding the voting process from any security loopholes and possible frauds. In fact, the first of these considerations has been predominant during these early phases of implementation (Hensler 2002).

Some longer-run concerns

The collisions with norms of transparency and lay control

Swiss political culture is highly democratic not only in the sense that most important issues are submitted to plebiscitarian voting procedures, but also in its insistence that all important governmental and even administrative processes (voting included) should be subject to lay control, which could potentially be exercised by any citizens without specialized technical, administrative or legal expertise.

In the realm of voting and elections, this implies that all ongoing procedures should be transparent such that anybody can observe them and form judgment as to whether they accord with the required rules. Evidently, the exercise of such controls is highly facilitated when low-tech offline procedures are in use, which can be understood by everybody without acquiring particular knowledge or investing costly time and labour. In such traditional systems – which certainly include voting by mail – all the documents and devices which could potentially be subject to manipulation (voter registries, voting papers, ballot urns, handwritten signatures etc.) exist in physical form, which makes them amenable to objective visibility and unimpeded examination. Such controls can easily be applied during the poll procedures as well as anytime after it has finished (for example when results are so close that a careful second or even third counting is necessary in order to eliminate all possible doubts).

A major dysfunction of e-voting is that such physical media are eliminated so that all processes of data generation, transformation and storage occur in 'black boxes' often not fully transparent even to technical experts (for example programmers who discover even sometimes on a weekly basis new surprising bugs in otherwise well-tested software applications). And to the degree that sophisticated and effective measures against frauds and errors are implemented, only tiny groups of experts know 'how they really work': groups which exclude most citizens entitled to voting on the one hand, and include unentitled specialists (for example from foreign countries) on the other.

As the Groupe des Utilisateurs Linux du Léman (Gull)[20] has articulated in an open letter directed at the Cantonal executive, such problems are aggravated in the case of Geneva because of the highly decisive role given to private corporations (HP and Wisekey). This cooperation implies that the software developed is of a proprietary nature, so that in contrast to open-source applications, only the specialists involved in creating the software (and employed by the firm owning the property rights) are able to make checks because all others have no access to the code. 'Under such conditions, the transparency essentially needed for democratic procedures can never be secured. To make an analogy: this resembles a society where only lawyers and judges have access to the text of legal statutes' (Robert and Nunes 2002).

The major consequence of all this is that the legitimacy and acceptance of democratic voting procedures becomes critically dependent on the degree of confidence accredited to the relevant experts by the general population. Given the daily news about unexpected flaws in even widely established programs developed by the most sophisticated firms (like Microsoft), this seems a rather shaky foundation for future e-democracy indeed.

The precarious role of government in the web of online information channels

A major consequence of e-voting is that acts of political decision-making are transported into the same media setting where almost all preceding political activities (campaigning, discussion and deliberation, information gathering, and so on) can take place. It is highly reasonable to assume that e-voters will have the tendency to use online sources for informing themselves about candidates or about the pros and cons of current voting issues, and that many of them will cast their votes immediately after gathering the necessary information.

Thus, there seem to be many sound reasons for governmental agencies to enhance their e-voting sites into prolific 'one-stop pages' which provide a manifold of links not only to official statements and recommendations, but also to various media, discussion fora, information sources and to the propaganda sites of candidates, committees, citizen groupings, associations and political parties (Auer and Trechsel 2002: 58ff). By reducing information costs, such sites may well be functional,

1 to increase the quality of votes by inducing more active citizens to gather more diverse and detailed opinions and information, and
2 to increase the quantity of votes by mobilizing hitherto passive voters.

On the other hand, such expansions of governmental media activities would be highly problematic for the following reasons:

(1) The 'digital divide' between e-voters and traditional offline voters would be amplified, because the latter would still need to consult newspapers and direct mail material, to watch radio and TV broadcasts (or even attend public assemblies) in order to get the same amount of relevant information.
(2) In following hyperlinks, citizens would be less able to differentiate clearly between 'official' documents and documents stemming from non-governmental sources.
(3) Governmental agencies would have to be selective in their external links: e.g. explicitly neglecting sites considered to contain false information, extremist positions or even slandering and openly racist statements. Of course, such governmental filtering would be considered as 'censorship' highly incompatible with freedom of speech, or, even worse, as an attempt by government to manipulate public opinion according to its own preferences (Niedermann 2001).
(4) By inducing citizens to cast 'just-in-time votes' immediately following accessing the e-voting sites (and some of its neighbouring first-order links), voting decisions may easily become influenced by spontaneous impressions and emotional reactions. In other words: the 'cooling-down' period between information intake and voting output is eliminated, leaving less opportunity for intellectual opera tions (taking critical distance, reflection, synthesizing operations etc.) (Linder 2001) .

Questionable potential impacts on political participation

The major driving force for spending so much money, brains and administrative efforts for electronic voting procedures stems from the hope that it will increase political participation by offering a low-threshold access to voting which should particularly appeal to rather inactive citizens who do not find it worthwhile to walk to a polling station at a predetermined time.

In March 2001, the IPSO research institute has conducted a survey of 1000 citizens from Geneva in order to gain insight into the prospective impact of e-voting on voting participation. In this survey, 35 per cent of all informants expressed the opinion that e-voting would motivate them to participate 'more regularly' in polls. Nevertheless, this effect is much more pronounced for males (43 per cent) than for women (27 per cent). This would imply that an increase in voting turnout up to about 9 per cent could realistically be expected (see IPSO 2001; Auer and Trechsel 2001: 52ff.). Such conclusions, however, are heavily contested in an expert study conducted by Prof. Wolf Linder (University of Berne) who concluded that this mobilization effect will remain below 2 per cent because most of the current Internet users are already active voters (Linner 2001).

The most significant quantitative effect of e-voting may well be a rising political participation rate among the 580,000 Swiss citizens living abroad. While this rate has risen fourfold since 1992 (from 17,000 to 70,000), it is still low because of false addresses, inefficient international mail services and other handicaps associated with postal voting procedures.[21] However, including more emigrants may well impair the rationality of democratic decisions, because voting outcomes become more influenced by individuals who are incompletely informed and who have no stake in the domestic political system.

For similar reasons, it may be questioned whether it is a good thing to introduce e-voting to increase the participation rates among rather passive citizens who have not voted so far, since this might lead to an increased weight of low-rational voters who are often undecided and poorly informed.

Notes

1 Press release of Swiss Bundesrat 5 April 2001, <http://www.admin.ch/cp/d/3acc5434_1@fwsrvg.bfi.admin.ch.html>
2 'Zwischen 97 und 2 Prozent', *Neue Zürcher Zeitung*, 15 May 2002: 17.
3 Interestingly enough, the costs of postal fees seem to be irrelevant, because rates of postal votes are similar in settings where the community pays these fees (e.g. Zürich) as in settings where they are paid by voters. See Baumann, L.: 'Gang zur Urne immer seltener / Briefliche Stimmabgabe erreicht annähernd 60 Prozent', *Neue Zürcher Zeitung*, 16 March 1999: 106.
4 Answer of the Bundesrat to the Interpellation of Ständerat Peter Briner (Freisinig, Schaffhausen) 6 September 2000, <http://www.parlament.ch/afs/data/d/gesch/2000/d_gesch_20003242.htm> translated by the author.
5 *Ibid.*

6 Presentation of M. Robert Hensler at the 2nd Forum Mondial de la Démocratie Electronique (17 May 2001), <http://www.geneve.ch/chancellerie/conseil/1997–2001/communique/2001/chan010522.html#05. Conservative parties may expect a higher voter turout in their clientele, because internet usage is higher there. It may also be that electronic voting will enhance turnout in the younger, male generation with a high level of education.

7 Thus far, only half of the EU member states have introduced postal voting procedures (Denmark, Germany, UK, Netherlands, Portugal and Sweden), and all of them practice it more restrictively than Switzerland.

8 Answer of the Bundesrat to the Interpellation of Ständerat Peter Briner (Freisinnig, Schaffhausen) 6 September 2000.

9 Para. 84 BRP translated by the author.

10 Of course, this does not mean that extralegal procedures would be allowed, because it is the responsibility of the cantons to secure the legitimacy of such innovations on the basis of democratic laws.

11 Answer of the Bundesrat to the Interpellation of Ständerat Peter Briner (Freisinnig, Schaffhausen), 6 September 2000, <http://www.parlament.ch/afs/data/d/gesch/2000/d_gesch_20003242.htm>

12 Arbeitsgruppe 'Vorprojekt E-voting: "Umfrage bei den Kantonen"', Bern 2001, <e-gov.admin.ch/dok/Erw_Auswertung_Umfrage_E-Voting.doc>

13 This is particularly true for a tiny canton like Appenzell-Innerrhoden with about 15,000 inhabitants.

14 Art. 188: Loi sur l'exercice des droits politiques du 15. octobre 1982. Nevertheless, this competence covers only non-binding trial procedures (on the communal and cantonal level) practiced during limited periods of time.

15 Particularly relevant is the 'Centre d'études et de documentation sur la démocratie directe' (C2D) which is officially engaged to follow and evaluate the whole process of testing and implementation (see <http://c2d.unige.ch/>).

16 Vote par Internet. Frequently asked questions, <http://www.geneve.ch/chancellerie/E-Government/FAQ_e-voting.html>

17 Schweizerische Bundeskanzlei 2002: 29, Beilage 10, <http://e-gov.admin.ch/vote/vote_electronique_Beilage10.pdf>

18 This deficiency also holds in the case of traditional voting procedures which also cannot rule out that voting sheets might have been filled out by unentitled individuals.

19 Rapport du Comité Sécurité sur l'application de vote par Internet État de Genève, CERN 2002, <http://www.geneve.ch/chancellerie/e-government/data/rapport_securite_Internet.pdf>

20 see <http://www.linux-gull.ch/evote/evote-gull.html>

21 Auslandschweizerorganisation http://www.aso.ch/deutsch/015_1.htm

References

Amstutz, P. (1999) 'Der Souverän entscheidet aus Distanz', in *Basler Zeitung*, 5 August 1999, <www.isps.ch/ger/stored_documents/HTML/170.html>

Auer, A. and Trechsel, A. H. (2001) *Voter par Internet?* Genève: Helbing & Lichtenhahn.

Hensler, R. (2001) 'Chances et défis du vote par Internet', <http://www.geneve.ch/chancellerie/E-Government/20011212.html>

Linder, W. (2001) 'Gutachten zum E-voting', Bern, <http://e-gov.admin.ch/ote/vote_electronique_Beilage12d_Linder.pdf>

Niedermann, D. (2001) 'Arbeitspapier E-voting. Bericht des Bundesrates an die eidgenössischen Räte', St. Gallen, 27 June 2001, <http://e-gov.admin.ch/vote/vote_electronique_eilage12e_Niedermann.pdf>

Schweizerische Bundeskanzlei (2001) 'Stimmgeheimnis, Stimmzwang und Volksrechte in den souveränen Staaten der Welt', Bern, <http://e-gov.admin.ch/vote/vote_electronique_Beilage5.pdf>

Schweizerische Bundeskanzlei (2002) 'Bericht über den Vote électronique Chancen, Risiken und Machbarkeit elektronischer Ausübung politischer Rechte vom 9. Januar 2002': 9, <http://e-gov.admin.ch/vote/e-demo-dt-09.01.02.pdf>

Schweizerische Bundeskanzlei (2002) 'Bericht über den Vote électronique Chancen, Risiken und Machbarkeit elektronischer Ausübung politischer Rechte vom 9. Januar 2002': 10. <http://e-gov.admin.ch/vote/e-demo-dt-09.01.02.pdf>

Robert, G. and Nunes, J. M. (2002) Swiss Open Systems User Group, http://www.ch-open.ch/html/oss/voting.html

6
Electronic Voting in Estonia

*Wolfgang Drechsler and Ülle Madise**

The Republic of Estonia has been, and is being, widely credited to be a pioneer in e-governance and especially e-democracy, with headlines such as 'Estonia: 10 Years from Communism to Advanced e-Democracy!'[1] It has frequently been expected, too, that Estonia will be the leading country for e-voting, having introduced it already for the national elections of 2003.[2] However, in the latest changes of the respective laws, the Estonian Parliament has voted for e-democracy, not for the immediate future, but with a delay of implementation until the year 2005. Still, to our knowledge, what follows is the first and so far only investigation into the first European case of a country that has actually passed overall e-voting laws.

Estonia is situated at the Baltic Sea and the Gulf of Finland. Tallinn, the capital, lies about 100 km south from Helsinki, 400 km east from Stockholm, 300 km north from Riga and 400 km west from St Petersburg. An independent republic between 1919 and 1940 and then a part of the Soviet Union, Estonia regained its independence in 1991 as a parliamentary democracy with a president, prime minister, and a 101-seat unicameral parliament, the *Riigikogu*. The municipal level with around 250 units has a certain degree of autonomy and also enjoys democratic elections; there is no level, other than purely administrative ones, in-between the local one and the central government.[3]

* The views expressed in this article are in no way to be construed to express the opinion of the Minister or Ministry of Justice; interpretive judgments generally, but especially those of political parties and party behaviour, are to be attributed to the first author only. We would like to thank Taavi Annus, Alo Heinsalu, Rainer Kattel, Helger Lipmaa and Vello Pettai for their very helpful comments and suggestions, but naturally we did not follow all of them. Statements, state of legislation and weblinks of this chapter are valid as of 25 May 2002.

For the political background, it is important to briefly sketch out the Estonian party structure.[4] The features that matter in our context are:

- *Keskerakond* (Center Party, www.keskerakond.ee/), the main 'transition losers' party, with a semi-charismatic leader, Edgar Savisaar, currently the Mayor of Tallinn, but without a genuine post-Socialist ideology.
- *Reformierakond* (Reform Party, www.reform.ee), the neo-liberal (indeed, market-radical) 'transition winners' party.
- *Isamaaliit* (Pro Patria, www.isamaaliit.ee/isamaa2/index_eng.html), a generally nationalist but for the most part also market-radical party that has been called 'Thatcherite' and that formed the government right after the regaining of independence.
- *Eestimaa Rahvaliit* (Estonian Peoples Union, www.erl.ee), a party similar to *Keskerakond* but with a strong and explicit rural orientation.
- *Eestimaa Ühendatud Rahvapartei* (Estonian United Peoples Party, www.eurp.ee/eng/), the most explicit post-Socialist party with a special appeal for that part of the Russian-speaking population of Estonia that may actually vote.
- *Mõõdukad* (Moderates, www.moodukad.ee/), who by their self-definition are Social Democrats but by 'Western' standards much to the right of that field.

At the beginning of our story, the governing coalition comprised *Isamaaliit* with the Prime Minister, Mart Laar; *Reformierakond*; and *Mõõdukad*. Since 28 January 2002, *Keskerakond*, together with *Reformierakond* – whose leader Siim Kallas is now the Prime Minister – forms the governing coalition; before that, *Keskerakond* was the main opposition party.[5] The governing coalition does not command a majority in the *Riigikogu* – rather, only 46 of the 101 seats.

The Republic of Estonia currently has about 1.4 million inhabitants, dispersed over 45,227 km.[6] Of these, as of 1 January 2001, 869,627 are citizens entitled to vote. In 1999, the last election year, there were 666 polling stations;[7] voting activity amounted to 57.4 per cent in parliamentary elections and 49.4 per cent in local ones.[8]

The genesis of e-voting in Estonia

Launching and first debates

The plan to introduce e-voting in Estonia was first publicly announced by the then and current Minister of Justice, Märt Rask (*Reformierakond*),[9] in the beginning of 2001.[10] At that time, the Ministry of Justice was anyway drafting several new election laws, aimed at preparing technical changes of the classic electoral process. Given the general fashion of e-related matters, which is particularly strong in Estonia, and swift developments in such fields as e-banking (see for example www.hanza.net), paperless government,[11] broadcasting of parliamentary sessions (see <www.riigikogu.ee/news.html>), SMS-parking, and so on, this was a likely step to take.[12]

Right at the beginning of the deliberation process, in early January 2001, there was some political discussion, appropriately enough, in an online debate of a business daily, *Äripäev*.[13] Küllo Arjakas, the secretary general of *Keskerakond*, voiced some doubts, but he did not exclude it as a possibility. Villu Reiljan, the chair of *Rahvaliit*, argued that Internet-voting would create inequality and that the government (*Isamaaliit, Reformierakond* and *Mõõdukad*) would merely try to dominate political life. The sociologist Juhan Kivirähk opined that e-voting would increase the success of those political parties who would have younger electorates.

The idea of e-voting was strongly supported by the then Prime Minister Laar. In the Question Time[14] of 17 January 2001, his party colleague Mart Nutt addressed to him a question regarding e-voting. The Prime Minister then proposed the idea to test e-voting in the year 2001, and to decide then whether to introduce e-voting for the 2002 local elections. Laar has continuously touted e-voting as a possibility to increase voter turnout and (partially therefore) develop democracy (see www.riigikogu.ee/ems/index.html).

Technical background

While in many states, the first step towards some form of automated vote was to use voting machines in polling stations or voting booths in order to save resources and facilitate voting or counting, in Estonia, from the beginning, there was the aim to create conditions for public remote Internet voting. ('E-voting' in Estonia has always meant public remote Internet voting.) Already, since 1999, there is an Internet- and web-based Election Information System, which enables automatic data-processing and makes the transfer of information of counted votes faster.[15] From the same year, Estonian citizens have also had no obligation to vote at a specific polling station on election day – it is possible to vote in a polling station outside of one's home station during the days of advance polling.[16] According to the *Riigikogu* Election Act and the Referendum Act (*Rahvahääletuse seadus* – RT I 2002, 30, 176), as well as the drafts of the new *Riigikogu* Election Act and the new European Parliament Election Act, citizens (respectively Estonian and European) residing permanently or temporarily outside Estonia may send their vote by mail.

Another facilitation of e-voting in Estonia was the then proposed and meanwhile realized introduction of a mandatory ID card (which had hitherto not existed; only passports were issued), which includes a digital signature possibility. Since 1 January 2002 the ID card is the primary domestic identification document and must be held by all Estonian citizens and permanent resident aliens over 15 years of age.[17] One of the ID card's features is two security certificates to supply digital signatures.[18] The digital signature is regulated by the Digital Signature Act[19] and can be used for administrative procedure.[20]

To gain an overview of the possible methods and risks of remote Internet voting, the Ministry of Justice on 1 March 2001 ordered an analysis from two scholars in the field, the cryptologist Helger Lipmaa (Helsinki) and his student Oleg Mürk, who specializes in the field from an informatics perspective (Lipmaa and Mürk 2001). A report by the Internet Policy Institute published in the USA at the same time[21] was also used as a basis of study. The commissioned analysis recommended preparation of some experiments or pilot projects first and postponing the introduction of e-voting until 2007, because an earlier date would be technically, and therefore also socially, too risky (*ibid.*). In the fall of 2001, another analysis was ordered from the mathematician Tanel Tammet (Göteborg)[22] by the Estonian Ministry of Transport and Communication (www.tsm.ee/eng/), which was to focus especially on technical questions and costs. As a result, concrete recommendations concerning the voting process were given and a provisional budget of e-elections was drawn up.[23]

The minister's drafts

Taking into account the purpose to introduce public remote Internet voting and some of the recommendations given by the experts, e-voting provisions were drafted by the Ministry and sent to the parliament. There, they were not discussed generally, but as part of four different new election laws: the Local Communities Election Act, the Referendum Act, the European Parliament Election Act, and the *Riigikogu* Election Act. The discussions in the *Riigikogu* as far as the e-voting feature was concerned were more or less seamless and not really closely connected with what Act it actually was, which is why the arguments will be presented here in a synthesized fashion. However, since local elections are scheduled for 2002, it was this Act that drew more attention than the other (followed by the Referendum Act because of its implications for European Union accession). When discussing specific features (which in the end were the same for all four Acts), we will therefore refer below to the development of the provisions of the Local Communities Election Act.[24]

(a) According to §52 of the draft law, voters who hold a certificate for giving digital signatures can vote on the website of the National Electoral Committee (www.vvk.ee/), but only on advance polling days (the sixth to fourth day before the actual election day). Every voter shall certify his or her identity by giving her or his digital signature via their ID card. After the identification of a voter, the list of candidates shall be displayed on the website. The voter shall mark the candidate in favour of whom he or she votes on the website and confirm submitting the vote. The voter shall receive a message on the website, stating that his or her vote shall be calculated.

(b) According to §55, the National Electoral Committee shall prepare lists of voters who voted using electronic means for polling divisions and forward such lists to county electoral committees not later than on the second day before election day. A county electoral committee shall forward lists of e-voters received from other county electoral committees and from the National Electoral Committee to the corresponding division committees not later than on the day before election day. After receipt of the envelopes with ballot papers and the lists of voters who voted using electronic means, the division committees shall check whether a voter is entered in the polling list of the polling division and that he or she has not voted more than once. If a voter has voted more than once, including using electronic means, the division committee shall send a corresponding notice to the National Electoral Committee immediately. On the basis of such notice, the National Electoral Committee shall not calculate the voter's vote cast using electronic means. On the parliamentary elections and referenda electronic voting is pursuant to the same procedure and conditions allowed also for Estonian citizens permanently residing in foreign states.[25]

(c) On the basis of the records of voting results of voters in the country, permanently residing in a foreign state, and who voted using electronic means received from all County Electoral Committees, the National Electoral Committee shall according to §57 verify the number of voters entered in the polling lists, the number of voters who received a ballot paper, the number of voters who participated in voting, the number of invalid ballot papers and the number of votes cast in favour of political parties and independent candidates.

According to § 60 of the Estonian Constitution,[26] 'Members of the *Riigikogu* shall be elected in free elections on the principle of proportionality. Elections shall be general, uniform and direct. Voting shall be secret.' Since the original drafting of the Constitution of 1992, these principles have not been the subject of juridical discussion.[27] As to whether e-voting would influence these principles, Minister and Ministry based themselves on two basic decisions:

1 To use a *teleological* approach to Constitutional interpretation; that is to say that Constitutional problems should be understood through the problems the given principles were meant to solve.[28] As an example in the current case of e-voting, the principle of secrecy (raised most strongly in Parliament later on) was said to protect an individual from any pressure or influence against her or his free expression of a political preference – that is, that it is a means, not an end. This includes the threat that the state or a public official can check who voted for whom. But it was said that, if privacy is guaranteed in the polling station and that all those who have voted via the Internet have the right to go to the polling station on election day and replace their electronically recorded, transferred and counted vote by a new paper-ballot (see §55 of the initial draft of the Local Communities Election law), then the aim of the principle of secrecy, the end, is actually achieved.

2 To start from the assumption that the State must 'trust the people' and not interfere if at all possible in any of their decisions. The Minister of Justice is a member of *Reformierakond*, and this party's ideology informs the current approach. As an example in our context, the problem that e-voting would facilitate some families, friends or colleagues voting together, that is practice collegiate voting, as well as the buying and selling of votes, was said to hinge on the question of whether the State would have to protect an individual only from other individuals or also from her- or himself.

In parliament

Parliamentary debate on e-voting was long and lively. The problems most discussed were equality of citizens in political life, privacy and secrecy of voting, security of electronic voting systems, and how to avoid fraud. In the plenary session, e-voting was discussed within all readings of all four drafts.[29]

Because of the above-mentioned change in government in January 2002, it had been expected by some that the strong impetus for all e-governance matters that had been a specialty of the old Prime Minister, Mart Laar, would now cease. To some extent this has been the case, although *Reformierakond* is the senior partner in the coalition; yet in fact, creating a legal basis for the introduction of e-voting is one point in the Coalition Agreement (www.riik.ee/et/valitsus/koalit-sioon.htm).

As already in the very first stages of the development of the e-voting idea, the old and new government coalition parties *Isamaaliit, Reformierakond, Mõõdukad* and *Keskerakond* were principally in favour of e-voting, with the *Rahvaliit* and *Ühendatud Rahvapartei* factions against, yet E-voting provisions were always supported in plenary session.[30]

Members of Parliament opposed to e-voting have argued that it would be unconstitutional; and have also cited technical problems and dangers. Jaanus Männik (*Rahvaliit*) and Tiit Toomsalu, the iconoclastic chairman of the tiny post-Socialist *Eesti Sotsiaaldemokraatlik Tööpartei* ('Estonian Social-Democratic Labor Party', www.esdtp.ee/)[31] mainly stressed the collision of constitutional principles of secrecy, generality and uniformity, and e-voting.[32] Rep. Toomsalu has also referred to negative or absent experiences in other countries.[33] Jüri Adams, a leading *Isamaaliit* politician active in the legal field, claimed that e-voting would not be realistic for the near future,[34] Tõnu Kauba (*Keskerakond*) referred to the weakness of technical preparations, and another *Keskerakond* member, Urmas Laht, emphasized, however, increasing voter turnout as a very important aim.[35] Jaan Pöör (*Rahvaliit*) spoke about collegiate decisions in the case of e-voting, but Kalev Kallo (*Keskerakond*) discounted that, claiming that the greatest problem would be how to avoid hackers.[36]

It may generally be noticed that a large majority of members shared the Ministry's attitude towards teleological interpretation of the Constitution, as well as the assumption that (a) e-voting increases voter turnout and that (b) this *automatically* has a positive effect on 'Democracy'.[37]

Of the anti-e-voting *Rahvaliit*, Arvo Sirendi[38] rhetorically asked whether the State would provide laptop PCs to people living in rural territories; Janno Reiljan declared that he would accept Internet voting in polling stations; Jaanus Männik said that going to the polling station would be a valuable action by itself.[39] Rep. Toomsalu said on different occasions that e-voting would just be another opportunity for the more successful people in society to have an impact and therefore not fair;[40] Jaanus Männik, a member of *Rahvaliit*, asked in his speech, 'Are we totally going to the liberal swamp?'[41]

As a result of the parliamentary debate, the initial e-voting provisions were adopted according to the principles and provisions of the draft as described above. However, to all laws or drafts,[42] the principle was added that the voter shall vote himself or herself (e.g., §50(1) in the Local Communities Election Act). Most importantly, apparently in deference to the *Rahvaliit* faction, it was explicitly stated that e-voting should not be applied before the year 2005 (e.g., §74(5) in the Local Communities Election Act). As was mentioned, the government commands at best a minority of 46 out of 101 seats; the *Rahvaliit* votes are therefore important.

Conclusion

Whatever the long-term effects of e-voting on democratic decision-making and, indeed, democracy might be – and this seems to be entirely unclear as of yet – it can hardly be doubted that this is the 'train into the future'. Estonia is noticeable for its strong proclivities of anything e-related among its politico-economic elite, as well as for an extremely low level of resistance against, and indeed discourse about, any 'progressive' developments that might have unwanted side-effects (biotechnology is another example) (see Weber 2001). There was hardly any accompanying discussion of e-voting in media or society (with the exception of a few newspaper articles and simple and emotional anonymous comments to them in online newspapers and info-portals);[43] likewise, neither were there any significant public comments by social scientists or lawyers – one of the reasons why this chapter has focused on the formal political process and on parliamentary and ministerial actors only. One can safely conclude that the e-voting initiative came from a political elite, and that it was and is largely detached from 'the people' whose participation it is supposed to increase.

Still, while Estonia could easily have been the world leader in e-voting by introducing this as a regular feature for the local elections of 2002, probably genuine worries that technical problems would not be solved by the Fall of that year, as well as the scepticism of individual members of parties generally in favour of e-voting, were among the reasons that prevented such an outcome. But in the end it was mainly the resistance of the rural opposition party (whose votes may be important to create a majority for the governing coalition) which – probably reasonably – feared that such a feature would increase the vote of its competitor parties, and which therefore would have very rightly and properly fought against it in Parliament, that led to the postponement of e-voting in Estonia until 2005.

Notes

1   <http://www.e-smartransaction.com/asp/application.asp?cle=80&cat= Government>
2   See, e.g., <http://www.time.com/time/interactive/stories/society/e_politics.html; http://www. newsbytes. com/ news/01/160092.html>; <http:// www.imaginemedia.co.uk/newsletter/apr2001.htm>: 'You can't stop progress though and it looks as though Estonia will be the world's first nation to provide e-voting at its next General Election in 2003.'
3   On local government in Estonia, see Drechsler (1999). On recent attempts by the Tallinn political party power cartel to forbid candidates outside of party lists to participate in local elections, see Annus (2002).
4   One could argue that Estonia does not really have an established party system; most parties are functionally vague associations of friends that represent certain interests (and funding sources) but hardly any ideological direction. This statement, as well as the characterizations of parties given below, are intended to give readers wholly unfamiliar with Estonian politics a rough first orientation; it is certain that all of them can and must be taken with a grain of salt. Although a bit dated already, the best analysis and description of the Estonian party system and the matrix it sets is still Pettai and Kreutzer (1999). The members of all parties are listed on the Ministry of Justice's 'Centre of Registers' website, <https://info.eer.ee/ari/ariweb_package9. erakonnad? keel=1.>
5   According to the descriptions given above, this means that the coalition consists of 'transition winners' and 'transition losers'. However, as explained in note 4, in Estonia this is not necessarily a contradiction, because *Reformierakond* indeed does promulgate a libertarian ideology appropriate for its clientele, but *Keskerakond* does not; rather, it is perhaps most fair to argue that it has hardly any ideology at all – it is, therefore, a classic populist party. Given both parties' particularly strong interest in power and government positions, they are therefore not unlikely coalition partners at all.
6   General information about the Republic of Estonia (in English) <www.riik.ee/en/; www.gov.ee/en/eestiriik.html>; <www.undp.ee/nhdr00/ en/general.html>
7   For information about the election committees for all levels of elections, including location and opening times of polling stations, < www.vvk.ee/ r99/kom_start.stm>
8   See the turnout among eligible voters, 1989–99, <www.undp.ee/nhdr00/ en/1.2.html>

9   See <www.riik.ee/valitsus/kabinet/mart_rask.html>
10 On 8 January 2001, the editorial of the business daily *Äripäev* was devoted to the idea of the Minister of Justice to introduce e-voting in Estonia. The editor asked why Estonia should wait until 2003; rather, Internet voting should be introduced for the local elections of 2002, <www.aripaev.ee/1836/arv_juhtkiri.html>. Concrete legal solutions were first presented at the press conference of the Ministry of Justice on 4 April 2001; see, e.g., *Eesti Päevaleht Online*, <www.epl.ee/artikkel.php?ID=154564>
11 Since August 2000, the Estonian government can work on the basis of web-based electronic documents without using paper versions for its sessions. See <www.cnn.com/SPECIALS/2001/ukvote/stories/epolitics/ estonia.html>
12 See overall, e.g., the Estonian Agenda 21, <www.agenda21.ee/english/EA21/3_4.html>
13 *Äripäev* Online, 5 January 2001, <www.aripaev.ee/1836/arv_kysitlus_183601.html>
14 According to the *Riigikogu* Internal Rules Act (www.riigikogu.ee/legislation.html), the Question Time, during which the Prime Minister and ministers reply to questions from Members of Parliament, shall be held from 13:00 to 14:00 h on the Wednesdays of the plenary working weeks of the *Riigikogu*.
15 Votes are counted by hand in local precincts, and the resulting local protocols then have to be transferred to the National Electoral Committee.
16 Advanced polling is possible between the sixth and fourth day before the actual election day. Every person entitled to vote can cast the ballot in the polling station of his or her permanent residence or any other polling station. *Riigikogu valimise seadus* (from §§34[1] on) – RT I 1994, 47, 784; 1998, 105, 1743; 107, 1765; 1999, 1, 1; 18, 298; 2001, 95, 588. – Estonian laws are published in, and always cited according to, the *Riigi Teataja* (RT), which also publishes international agreements, decisions of the Supreme Court, etc. English translations of Estonian Laws can be generally found on the website of Estonian Legal Translation Centre, www.legaltext.ee/. The *Riigikogu valimise seadus* can be found there as *Riigikogu Election Act*.
17 Concerning the ID card, see <www.pass.ee/2.html>
18 *Isikut tõendavate dokumentide seadus* – RT I 1999, 25, 365; 2000, 25, 148; 26, 150; 40, 254; 86, 550; 2001, 16, 68; 31, 173; 56, 338.
19 *Digitaalallkirja seadus* – RT I 2000, 26, 150; 92, 597; 2001, 56, 338. *Digital Signature Act* (in English): <www.riik.ee/riso/digiallkiri/digsignact.rtf>
20 There is e.g. the e-Tax Board: www.ma.ee/ema/; general provisions for digital administrative procedure can be found in *Haldusmenetluse seadus* – RT I 2001, 58, 354; *Administrative Procedure Act* (in English): <www.legaltext.ee/et/andmebaas/ava.asp?tyyp=SITE_ALL&ptyyp=I&m=000&query=Administrative+Procedure+Act>
21 See <www.riik.ee/evalimised/yldanalyysid/e_voting_report.pdf>
22 About Tanel Tammet, see www.cs.chalmers.se/pub/users/tammet/ home.html; see also, about OÜ IT Meedia, www.itmeedia.ee/eng/ index.html
23 IT Meedia (Tanel Tammet and Hannu Krosing) (2001),'E-valimised Eesti Vabariigis: võimaluste analüüs' ['E-voting in Estonia: An analysis of the opportunities']: H33–8,. <ats.riik.ee/amphora/home/projektid/e-valimised/materjalid/evalimisteanalyys24okt.doc>

24 The initial draft of the Local Communities Election Act can be found at www.riigikogu.ee/ems/index.html: *Täiskogul menetletud eelnõu nr 747. Menetlusetapid. Algtekst.*

25 §46 *Rahvahääletuse seadus* – RT I 2002, 30, 176.

26 *Eesti Vabariigi põhiseadus* (RT 1992, 26, 349). *Rahvahääletusel vastu võetud 28.06.1992 seadus nr 1. Jõustumiskuupäev 03.07.1992,* <lex.andmevara.ee/estlex/kehtivad/AktDisplay.jsp?id=7020&akt_id=7020>; English translation <www.gov.ee/en/eestiriik.html#const>

27 See Annus 2001: 64–70, and *Põhiseaduse juriidilise ekspertiisikomisjoni lõparu-anne [Final Report of the Juridical Expert Commission for the analysis of the Constitution of the Republic of Estonia]*, www.just.ee/index.php3?cath=1581

28 It is interesting to note that Supreme Court decisions in Estonia hardly ever use teleological interpretation; see Drechsler and Annus (2001); Annus (2001): 42.

29 See the minutes at www.riigikogu.ee/ems/index.html. The draft of the Local Communities Election Act was discussed on 14 June 2001, 23 January, 27 February, and 27 March 2002; the draft of the *Riigikogu* Election Act on 14 June 2001, 30 January 2002, 27 March, 15 and 22 May 2002; the draft of the Referendum Act on 19 September 2001, 30 January and 13 March 2002; the draft of the European Parliament Election Act on 23 January 2002.

30 See the debate and voting results according to the minutes as cited above (note 29). About the voting process, see the Riigikogu Internal Rules Act, <www.riigikogu.ee/legislation.html>

31 This party does not have a parliamentary faction of its own; Toomsalu is a member of the faction of the *Eestimaa Ühendatud Rahvapartei.*

32 See the minutes referred to above at note 29.

33 Minutes of 13 March 2002.

34 Minutes of 23 January 2002.

35 Minutes of 30 January 2002.

36 Minutes of 30 January 2002.

37 See the minutes referred to note 29. It is interesting to see how the results on e-voting provisions were changing: while in January 2002, the result was about 24:8 per vote, in March, it was about 51:13 ('about' meaning average vote of all amendments voted on, hostile meaning against). The *Riigikogu*, one will recall, has 101 members.

38 Minutes of 30 January 2002 – It may be mentioned here that Rep. Sirendi and his colleague Elmar Truu are members of the *Rahvaliit*, but they form in the *Riigikogu* the faction of the (expired, but former senior government) party *Koonderakond*, which – almost – always votes with the *Rahvaliit*. (The situation is even more complex than this, but does not really interest us in our context.)

39 Minutes of 30 January 2002.

40 Minutes of 23 and 30 January 2002.

41 Minutes of 30 January 2002.

42 The Local Communities Election Act was adopted by Parliament on 27 March 2002 and entered into force on 6 May 2002. RT I 2002, 36, 220. The Referendum Act was adopted on 13 March 2002 and entered into force on 6 April 2002. RT I 2002, 30, 176. The drafts of the European Parliament Election Act and of the *Riigikogu* Election Act are pending in Parliament; see

the *Riigikogu* proceedings nos 906 and 748 <www.riigikogu.ee/ems/index.html>

43 See, e.g., <www.postimees.ee>; <www.delfi.ee>. As all comments are anonymous, their level is indeed exceedingly low, and they often do not connect with the subject at hand. Certainly, here, the Dreyfus/Kierkegaard criticism of anonymous and ignorant discourse in the public sphere strongly applies; see Dreyfus (2001): 73–89, Drechsler (2002).

References

Annus, T. (2001) Riigiõigus, Tallinn: AS Õigusteabe Juura.

Annus, T. (2002) 'Valimisliitudele kriips peale!? Sunderakonnastamise põhiseaduslikkuses võib kahelda', in Postimees, 25 March 2002 <www.postimees.ee/index.html>

Drechsler, W. (1999) 'Kommunale Selbstverwaltung und Gemeindegebietsreform: Deutsche Erfahrungen, generelle Erwägungen, estnische Perspektiven', in W.Drechsler (ed.), *Die selbstverwaltete Gemeinde: Beiträge zu ihrer Vergangenheit, Gegenwart und Zukunft in Estland, Deutschland und Europa, Schriften zum Öffentlichen Recht*. Berlin: Duncker & Humblot: 119–35.

Drechsler, W. (2002) 'Review: Dreyfus, Hubert L. 2001: On the Internet. London', in *Philosophy in Review / Comptes Rendus Philosophiques*, 22(2) (April) 87–90.

Drechsler, W. and Annus, T. (2001) 'Die Verfassungsentwicklung in Estland von 1992 bis 2001', in *Jahrbuch des öffentlichen Rechts der Gegenwart*, 50: 473–92.

Dreyfus, H. L. (2001) On the Internet. London: Routledge.

Lipmaa, H. and Mürk, O. (2001) 'E-valimiste realiseerimisvõimaluste analüüs' ['An analysis of the possibility to organise e-voting']. Analysis ordered by the Estonian Ministry of Justice, < www.just.ee/oldjust/JM/lipmaamyrk.pdf>

Pettai, V. and Kreutzer, M. (1999) 'Party Politics in the Baltic States: Social Bases and Institutional Context', in *East European Politics and Society*, 13(1).

Weber, A. (2001) 'Baltikummer. Das verkaufte Volk', in *SZ Magazin*, 23 September, <www.zbi.ee/~uexkull/german/aweber.htm>

7
Electronic Voting in Austria: Current State of Public Internet Elections

Alexander Prosser, Robert Krimmer and Robert Kofler *

The Austrian constitution states in article 1 that, 'Austria is a democratic republic'. Public elections are the key element of a democratic country, as the right of a republic is derived from the right of its inhabitants. These mandatory elections are also a human right as stated in article 3 of the protocol to the convention of human rights to guarantee free and secret elections.[1]

Although these high standards for elections had already been discussed during the time of the Hapsburg monarchy in the nineteenth century, they had only been partly installed. It took until 1918 with the foundation of the first republic of Austria for the standards of common, equal, free and secret elections with proportional representation to become a reality for the Austrian population (Welan 1991).

Although the election procedures and laws were the subjects of considerable discussions, still very little changed, and Parliament has passed only two notable election reforms since then. In 1970 the number of members of the parliament was increased to 183 and the constituencies were reduced to nine. The reform of 1992 resulted in the possibility for Austrians abroad to take part in elections through postal votes, and the lowering of the age of voters and candidates to 18 and 19 years respectively.

The participation rate in the first-order elections to the Austrian parliament is, in an international comparison, remarkably high, well above 90 per cent. It has decreased only at the end of the twentieth century, reaching an all-time low of 80.4 per cent (Table 7.1). Still,

* The work of Kofler and Krimmer was supported by the City of Vienna Jubiläumsfonds.

109

Table 7.1 Voter turnout in elections to the Austrian national parliament from 1945–99 (percentages)[2]

Year	Voter turnout	Year	Voter turnout
1945	94.3	1975	92.9
1949	96.8	1979	92.9
1953	95.9	1983	92.6
1956	96.0	1986	90.5
1959	94.2	1990	90.5
1962	93.8	1994	91.9
1966	93.8	1995	85.9
1970	91.8	1999	80.4
1971	92.4		

discussions on the current reform have not concentrated on how to reach the former mark of 90 per cent turnout but, as in the past, on how certain political parties could increase their shares by either generally lowering the voting age to 16, or introducing postal voting also for domestic Austrians.

The Second Republic also experiences a large number of second-order (and less important) elections. The reason for this is the Austrian concept of the social partnership (*Sozialpartnerschaft*) as a network of chambers, where each citizen is represented according to her social or work status.[3] All those chambers are characterized by a compulsory membership, elected representatives and a law with their rights and duties. How often elections are conducted varies from organization to organization, and ranges from every two to five years. The stable political and social life in the Second Republic in contrast to the First Republic is attributed to this concept (Karlhofer and Tálos 2000).

Whereas voter turnout for first-order elections is by international standards high, the organizations of the social partnership do have to consider their turnout much more seriously. Turnout here ranges between 30 to 60 per cent (Table 7.2). Due to this fact, two chambers – the National Student Union and the Federal Chamber of Commerce – started in 1999 to look into electronic voting with the expectation that this new method would raise voter participation.

In this chapter we are going to present the current state of electronic voting in Austria in two steps. First, we seek to assess factors that influence the introduction of e-voting in Austria; we then continue with an analysis of two pilot projects and experiences so far.

Table 7.2 Voter turnout in second-order elections (percentages)

Austrian Student Union elections, 1983–2001		National Chamber of Commerce elections, 1985–2000	
Year	Voter turnout	Year	Voter turnout
1983	36.25	1985	70.0
1985	29.79	1990	61.9
1987	34.68	1995	54.74
1989	30.1	2000	59.27
1991	30.56		
1993	30.42		
1995	29.31		
1997	27.6		
1999	27.53		
2001	28.52		

Paper-based voting

The current method of elections as we know it has evolved over time. Every country has its special variations based on political tradition, current legal jurisdiction and social conditions. Hence, all forms can be grouped into two categories where the basic criterion is whether or not the vote is cast in a polling station: voting at the polling station and distance (remote) voting.

Voting at the polling station

Article 26 of the Austrian Constitution[4] sets the basic rules for elections to the national parliament. The principles of voting (*wahlrechtsgrund-sätze*) in Austria are thereby (Walter and Meyer 2000):

- *Universal*: all citizens are entitled to vote and be elected with a few exceptions explicitly named.
- *Equal*: the vote of every voter has the same impact on the election result.
- *Immediate*: voters elect members of parliament directly; no electoral college as intermediate elector.
- *Personal*: the voter him/herself has to vote (no representatives are allowed).
- *Secret*: the public and the election administration may not receive notice of the content of anyone's vote.

Further regulations are the use of proportional representation in contrast to the Anglo-American democracies (that is, US, UK or New Zealand) and the requirements of Austrian citizenship and age over 18 years to be eligible to vote. Another difference to the USA is that Austrian citizens residing within the country are automatically registered to vote whereas Americans have to sign up to vote at their elections.

Distance (remote) voting

Germany and Austria both have very similar principles of voting (Jarras and Pieroth 2000), but the Austrian legislative prohibited any form of remote voting until 1989. Germany had already introduced postal voting in the 1960s, but the Austrian constitutional court (*Verfassungsgerichtshof,* VfGH) declared in 1985 that this form of remote election is in contradiction of the principles of personal and secret election (Marschitz 2002).[5] The main issues revolved around the possibility of proxy voting and the protection of secrecy and privacy of the individual vote. In comparison to Germany, it can be said that the Austrian constitution requires a higher protection for the voter from any undue influences that could weaken the status of voting principles.

The court apparently changed its opinion a couple of years later, when an Austrian citizen living abroad sued the Austrian state because he was not included in the voter register of his former home town. He was therefore not allowed to vote. At that time the right to vote was linked to two facts – to Austrian citizenship and to residence in Austria. In its ruling in 1989, the VfGH said that the entitlement to vote may not be bound to residence in Austria and so the Austrian parliament had to change §2 of the voter registration law (*Wählerevidenzgesetz,* WevG) and §38 of the national election regulations of 1992 (*Nationalratswahlordnung,* NRWO) to include Austrians living abroad in the national election register.[6] Austrians remain listed in the elections register of their former residence for 10 years after having left the country, after which they may reapply to be included in the register by stating their interest in taking part in Austrian elections. For the voting procedure itself, the legislative used the two-phase concept which already existed for the use of voting cards.

Phase one: some time before the election the voter (in Austria or abroad) can apply for a voting card, which exists in two versions: (i) enabling the citizen to vote in Austria but not in his/her city of residence, or (ii) a voting card which can be used abroad. In both cases the voting card consists of three parts: the ballot sheet, a neutral envelope and another envelope with the voter's name and constituency on it, so the vote can be correctly addressed. For the 2002 elections many cities and embassies accepted applications for voting cards over the Web.

Phase two: As Austria does not allow distance voting within the country, there is now a distinction between Austrians living in and outside Austria. Austrians in Austria are required to cast their vote in any polling station, while Austrians abroad are not required to vote in the presence of an election officer. They can vote anywhere as long a person of equal status of an Austrian notary confirms by her signature and timestamp on the constituency envelope that the vote was filled out in privacy and independently. Following §60 NRWO, the notary can also be replaced by two Austrian citizens. Then the vote has to be mailed to the regional election administration and is only valid if it is received at the latest eight days after election day.

Although there have been many initiatives to allow distance voting for regional and local elections, and not only from abroad for national elections, none of them has managed to get support from enough parties (a two-thirds majority is required to change the constitution), as was the case recently for Federal Councillor Weiss (2002).

Electronic voting

The concept of electronic voting can be implemented with both presence and distance voting concepts as it is basically the use of computers for the election processes of (i) voter identification, (ii) vote casting and (iii) ballot counting. Nevertheless e-voting as it is understood in this chapter is considered as a means of remote voting through the Internet. Any remote e-voting system that is to be used for public elections following common principles of elections (as outlined below) implies that it fulfills all of the following considerations:

- *identification*: it must be known WHO voted;
- *anonymity*: but it must not be known WHAT the voter has voted; and
- *administrative fraud*: nor must the election administration have the capacity to manipulate the results

Legal issues
The Austrian jurisdiction has been very strict about remote voting for national, regional or local public elections as will become clear. But the

VfGH imposed its view on the requirements for elections of social partners and made it possible for the national parliament in 2001 to change the Student Union law (*Hochschülerschaftsgesetz*, HSG) and the Federal Chamber of Commerce law (*Wirtschaftskammergesetz*, WKG) to allow electronic voting.[7]

Besides the common voting principles that require an election of ÖH and the Chamber of Commerce to be equal, personal and secret, paragraph §34 of the HSG and §73 of the WKG address the problem areas described above more in detail by requiring:

- the voter to use a qualified digital signature on a smart card in accordance with the Digital Signature Law (*Signaturgesetz*, Sig-G) in order to establish unambiguously the identity of the voter;
- the e-voting system to keep the vote secret in accordance to the Data Protection Law (*Datenschutzgesetz*, DSG 2000) in §4 to secure anonymity; and finally
- to check the system against the possibility of fraudulent manipulations by the election administration by requiring an appraisal of non-fraud ability by A-SIT[8] and a permission by the commission for data security following §19 DSG2000.

Infrastructure issues

Parliament passed the Digital Signature Law in 1999 (Austria was the first country of the European Union to do so), but it took till December 2001 for the first trust centre to be accredited by the national regulator (RTR 2002). Furthermore, the smart cards are rather expensive with a price of around €50 and it thereby remains doubtful whether these cards will become popular without useful ('killer') applications like e-voting.

The strategy is now to combine smart card functionality with already existing ID cards like the social security card. The first significantly large number of smart cards being rolled out are the student ID cards of the Vienna University of Economics and Business Administration (WU). This institution issued for each of its 20,000 students a photo-ID card with the digital signature feature in fall 2002.[9] Other institutions are still at the planning stage, like the Department of Social Security that wanted to roll out its social security card for all members residing in Vienna, but had to postpone the plan for another year due to technical reasons (Palme 2002).

Even if smart cards are used to identify the user, it is still not guaranteed that the user's credentials also comply with the citizen in the election register even though the name and date of birth match. This problem can be solved either by (i) the smart card issuing organization being the same as the election conducting body, or by (ii) using a unique identifier like a citizen ID number that is stored on the smart card. Austria chose to realize the second variant with the registration law in 1995, and thereby Austria is one of the few countries in Europe where such a central register (ZMR) for all citizens exists. It started public service on 1 March 2001 and every Austrian citizen was appointed one unique 'ZMR identification number. However, in spite of its usefulness for e-voting, it should be noted that critics such as the data security specialists from ARGEdaten warned of possible misuse and called the system the first step to a surveillance state.[10]

With a smart card a digital document can be signed and everyone who gets this document can access a public server to verify your identity and that you signed the document. The standard certificates[11] on the smart card include only given and surnames, and the numbers of the certificate and the card itself (the latter is unique worldwide). Even by looking it up in the public certificate server of the certification authority (in Austria a-trust, http://www.a-trust.at) the only further information one can get is the status of validity of the certificate and if it has been revoked.

Through storing the national citizen ID on the citizen's smart card it becomes a national ID card (Bürgerkarte), which can then be used to anonymously cast a vote. Currently this card still imposes a security problem for e-voting as it is not an anonymous data-store medium (Kofler, Krimmer and Prosser 2003).

Current e-voting initiatives

Currently, there is no national e-voting project articulated or planned, which is probably due to high voter turnout. In contrast, the social partners all suffer from low voter turnout and two of them have been considering e-voting for some years now. In the following, we outline the current status of their work and their experiences.

The Austrian student union

As described above, the Austrian Student Union (ÖH) is a member of the social partnership and has undergone a major crisis in the 1990s. Turnout in student elections was very low and hovered around 30 per cent despite the compulsory membership of every student. In a strike ballot in 1991, 80 per cent of the students were in favour of keeping the system of a Student Union with mandatory membership for every student. This ballot finished an Austria-wide discussion and confirmed the Student Union as the only representation of students. This led to a Student Union legal reform in 1998 in which this system was introduced for all higher academic study programmes in Austria, and the ÖH is now a union for all Austrian students.

Every two years elections take place and students can participate on up to four levels related to their field of studies, faculty, university, and finally for all students the national body of representatives. To do so, the system allows two ways of electing officials – the study programme representatives are elected personally by name, and for the other three levels (faculty, university and national) one votes for political parties. This makes the system quite complicated and error-prone. For the other side – the election officials – it is also hard to organize the election, as more than 100 polling stations are required and more than 500 voluntary workers have to be found who do not belong to a political party.

These challenges led to two developments, on the one hand to automate the election processes and on the other hand to introduce remote e-voting. The remote e-voting initiative started in 2000, where a cooperation agreement was settled between the ÖH, the Ministry for Education, Science and Culture and the research group Internetwahlen of the University of Osnabrück (Germany). The aim of this was to hold the ÖH elections in 2001 over the Internet using the digital signature of the WU student ID card. As an outcome of this agreement, the HSG was changed to accommodate remote e-voting but finally the project failed in March 2001 because the mandatory certification process of the digital signature card couldn't be finished early enough to run tests.

Even though remote e-voting could not be implemented, the ÖH at WU and the university IT department developed a voter identification system to accelerate the complicated check of identity and voter eligibility. The card was placed in the card reader and on the monitor a picture of the student was shown (to check the identity of the voter) and the relevant ballot sheets were handed to the student to be filled out by hand. Positive experiences with the voter identification system then led to an agreement with the WU institute for information processing and information economics, department of production management to further pursue remote e-voting. A first work agreement has been a study of whether or not students are into e-voting or not.

The study showed that 84 per cent of the students would prefer the use of electronic voting, with only 5 per cent rejecting this technology.

The findings also showed that two groups of students exist: first a group that frequently uses the facilities of the university and because of that does not have a real preference for or against e-voting; and a second group that is strongly in favour of e-voting as they only come to the university campus for exams and mandatory seminars and don't have a strong attachment to the university. However, they still find it an obligation to participate in elections but the lack of time prevents them from voting at the polling station. This group will grow at the WU, as space is limited and the number of students is still growing. With new services such as the e-learning platform http://learn.wu-wien.ac.at the necessity to attend the main facilities will diminish and with that comes the danger of a further voter-turnout drop if the election process is not available online as well.

In a further step, an e-voting prototype has been developed with the support of the City of Vienna and was first used during the test election in May 2003 in parallel with the Austrian Student Union elections at WU Vienna. This has been the first Austrian Internet election and the first Internet election worldwide that could guarantee General Voting Principles. As at this test election the national ID card was not available in large enough numbers, the project team had to replace the two national ID card roles by using the identification facilities at the WU computer centre. The electronic voting token was saved on a non-specific medium. 978 students that major in IT relevant studies were eligible to participate in the test election. The application for the voting/validation token could be signed from 1–19 May 2003, the vote casting itself took place during the regular student union voting days, from 20–22 May. On 22 May at 3 pm the ballot box was opened by the election committee and votes were decoded and entered the tally. The voter turnout for the test election was 36 per cent, compared to the real-paper-based student union election that attracted 26 per cent. Hence the turn-out in the electronic election was 40 per cent higher than in the conventional paper-based system. The allocation of votes in the test election corresponded to the result in the real election.

Federal chamber of commerce

The Federal Chamber of Commerce is in a similar situation to the student union although their voter turnout has never been comparably low, but still critical with just above 50 per cent turnout in 1995. And, like ÖH, their analysis led to a similar two-way strategy; first accelerating the election processes, and at the same time developing a remote e-voting strategy for deployment later.

For the elections in 2000 the Chamber of Commerce of Vienna developed a system to connect all 64 polling stations. This enabled the election administration to automate voter identification by offering one central electronic database of voter registrations in replacement for the thousands of paper pages previously needed. Voters were able to use any one of the different stations to cast votes in the regular way on the paper ballot sheet. For the counting process the administration again used a central scanner unit with OCR to automate the vote count and the publication of results; they do not want to use e-voting machines for the vote casting process due to the high development cost. In the opinion of the Chamber of Commerce this money is better invested in the remote e-voting project as described by Schinagl and Kilches (2000) who presented a three-step plan for the introduction of remote e-voting:

1 develop a technical and organizational concept for an election with remote e-voting capabilities as the basis for,
2 a change of the chamber of commerce law WKG, and then allow
3 pilot projects to gain experience for the use of remote e-voting in the 2005 elections.

So far steps 1 and 2 have been realized with Parliament passing the bill in June 2001 (four months after the student-union law HSG). Currently pilot projects have been discussed internally but no deployment date has been fixed or decision taken as to whether or not e-voting will be used in 2005. More likely they will pursue a broader deployment of networked polling stations in the City of Vienna.

Assessment

Remote voting as such (and e-voting in particular) is a very controversial topic at the Austrian national level. This is not only demonstrated by the legal point of view depicted above, but also finds its (non-) representation in the national strategy papers.

The report *Austrian Information Society* published by the working group installed by the federal chancellry in 1997 was the most recent document containing an opinion on e-voting (Knoll and Grossendorfer 2000). This ambitious programme concentrated on how to lead Austria in the next century and has been the first Information Communication Technology (ICT) strategy to be centrally organized and coordinated. A broad range of relevant topics including e-business, e-government and even e-democracy were discussed. The working group was very skeptical towards e-democracy. On one hand it was seen as positive that using ICT could raise the level of transparency, but on the other hand the so called digital divide could result in unequal conditions in the ability to access public services for citizens. As far as e-voting was concerned, it was not seen as an alternative to regular elections until 100 per cent security could be guaranteed and manipulation of votes or violation of voters' secrecy can be ruled out.

Currently the Austrian ICT strategy is dominated by the EC e-Europe initiative [eEur99] where 'e-Austria in e-Europe' is the Austrian (Östereichisches Bundeskanzleramt 2002). This initiative is led by the e-Austria taskforce with Prof. Posch as the National Chief Information Officer in charge (Posch 2001). But not one of these documents contains any judgment or strategy pointing towards electronic voting. This is in contrast to the high level of attention e-voting was given by the passing of laws that enabled remote e-voting as an alternative way of voting. To our knowledge, no other country in the European Union has passed a national law so far that allows e-voting in more than pilot projects. More interestingly, so far, no such pilots or public tests have taken place in Austria. This makes it necessary to develop a national strategy for the use of e-voting. At present, only the Austrian Computer Society (OCG) has established a working group for e-democracy and e-voting.[12]

Notes

1 That is, Switzerland hasn't ratified it so far as in one canton it is still casting the *Ständerat* publicly at the commencement of the *Landsgemeinde*; see Glossar zur Wahl 1999, <http://www.parlament.ch/dL/D/Wahlen/Wahlen99/Glossar_A_Z_d.htm>
2 'Die österreichischen Nationalratswahlen von einst bis heute', <http://www.modernpolitics.at/publikationen/ jahrbuch/wahlergebinsse/wahlen_index.htm>
3 Examples would be the National Student Union representing all students in Austria, the Federal Chamber of Commerce representing employers, or the Federal Chamber of Labour representing employees.
4 The Austrian Constitution and any other Austrian law or finding of the Austrian constitutional court can be found in the online Law Information system of the Federal Chancellery at http://www.ris.bka.gv.at
5 See Erkenntnis G18/85. Verfassungsgerichtshof on 1985-03-16.
6 See Erkenntnis G218/88. Verfassungsgerichtshof on 1989-06-13, For more on the voting of Austrians living abroad see Dujmovits (2000).
7 See Erkenntnis WI-2/95. Verfassungsgerichtshof on 1995-02-29.
8 A-SIT is the organization appointed by the Chancellor to check the security of trust centres and their services required by the Digital Signature Law.

9   See, Wirtschaftsuniversität Wien', <http://www.wu-wien.ac.at>
10   See Überflüssiges Meldegesetz, <http://www.ad.or.at/news/20010108.html>
11   For a more detailed view on smart card standards see Hass (1995).
12   More information about the work group 'e-Democracy/e-Voting' of the OCG can be found at http://egov.ocg.at

References

Dujmovits, W. (2000) Auslandsösterreicherwahlrecht und Briefwahl, Wien: Verlag Österreich.

Jarass, H. and Pieroth, B. (2000) *Grundgesetz für die Bundesrepublik Deutschland*. Vol. 5. München: Beck.

Hassler, V. (2002) 'IT Security and Smart Card Standards', <http://www.infosys. tuwien.ac.at/Staff/vh/papers/std.ps.gz>

Karlhofer, F. (2001) 'Interessensverbände im Umbruch', in Forum Politische Bildung (ed.), *Materialpaket Politische Bildung*. Wien.

Karlhofer, F. and Tálos, E. (2000) 'Sozialpartnerschaft unter Druck', in A. Pelinka, F. Plasser and W. Meixner (eds), *Die Zukunft der österreichischen Demokratie. Trends, Prognosen und Szenarien*. Vol. 22. Wien: Signum-Verlag, 381–402.

Knoll, N. and Grossendorfer, E. (2002) *Informationsgesellschaft*. Wien: Bundes-kanzleramt.

Marschitz, W. (2002) 'Internet-Voting', http://www.plattform.or.at/down-load/POP_Art_ Internetvoting.pdf>

Östereichisches Bundeskanzleramt (2002) *Aktionsplan eEurope, Umsetzung in Österreich"*, <http://www.bka.gv.at/bka/service/publikationen/infogesellschaft/ apmaerz02.pdf>

Posch, R. (2001) 'IKT-Strategie des Bundes', <http://www.iaik.at/news/2001-06-25.IT-Strategie.pdf>

Kofler, R., Krimmer, R. and Prosser, A. (2003) *Electronic Voting – Algorithmic and Implementation Issues*. HICSS-36. Hawaii.

Palme, L. (2002) *Chip-Card-Chaos*, <http://www.profil.at/export/profil/>

RTR (2002) 'RTR akkreditiert Datakom Austria', <http://www.rtr.at/web.nsf/>

Schinagl, W. and Kilches, R. (2000) *Online-Wahlen und E-Voting: Entwicklungstendenzen zu elektronischen Wirtschaftskammer-Wahlen im Jahr 2005*. Vol. 3. Graz: Fakultätstag der Rechtswissenschaftlichen Fakultät, 291–339.

Walter, R. and Mayer, H. (2000) 'Bundesverfassungsrecht', Vol. 9. Wien: Manz.

Weiss, J. (2002) Gesetzesantrag 'Einführung der Briefwahl auf Landes- und Gemeindeebene', <http:// www.parlinkom.at/pd/pm/XXI/I/his/000/I00005 _. html>

Welan, M. (1991) *Verhältniswahlrecht – Mehrheitswahlrecht*. Wien: Institut für Wirtschaft, Politik und Recht, Universität für Bodenkultur Wien.

8

Electronic Voting in Finland: The Internet and its Political Applications

Maija Setälä and Kimmo Grönlund

Being a rich Western European country, Finland certainly belongs to the wired world. Based on a comparison of different aspects related to the information and communication technology (ICT) sector, such as research, development and employment, the OECD (2000) classifies Finland as a high ICT-intensive country. According to survey results, most Finnish households seem to be wired to the web. This is a relatively high proportion in the European context, although other Nordic countries and the Netherlands are ahead of Finland in this respect. According to other survey results, 61 per cent of Finns claim that they use the Internet personally. The usage is not evenly spread, however. Among young Finns, practically everyone uses the Internet. Moreover, students and professionals use the Internet much more extensively than other professional groups. Yet, unlike in many other countries, one cannot trace a substantial gender gap in the use of the Internet in Finland (Flash EB 88, 2001; Flash EB 112, 2002; see also Grönlund's contribution in this volume).

This chapter deals with three aspects of the political uses of the Internet in Finland, and Internet voting in particular. First, an overview is provided on Internet services provided by the Finnish state and municipal authorities. Second, an account is given on the current Finnish electoral system, and the political initiatives and discussions concerning electronic voting are dealt with. Special attention is given to the autonomous province of the Åland islands. Third, the chapter is concluded with some arguments for and against the adoption of electronic voting in Finland.

Public services on the Internet

This section deals with services provided by the public authorities on the Internet. Finnish public officials, both at the municipal and at the national levels, have been eager to provide information and services through the Internet. The Finnish parliament (*Eduskunta*), all ministries and major governmental agencies have websites that describe their tasks and the ongoing activities in their fields. Practically all municipalities have their own websites with plenty of politically relevant information. The willingness of Finnish officials to provide information and services on the Internet is reflected in what people actually do on the Internet. Using public administration services online is common in Finland, and over 70 per cent of Finns have reportedly visited governmental websites. Finnish women especially seem to be frequent visitors of public www pages (Flash EB 88, 2001).

A good example of the use of information and services on the Internet is the recently opened portal for all public authorities (www.suomi.fi). The portal is maintained by the Government Information Management Unit in the Ministry of Finance, and covers both governmental and municipal public information and services. The site is structured by different subject areas, for example taxation, education, housing and employment. This is expected to help people to find the particular information or services they need. The portal also has an extensive search facility. There is also another service (see www.lomake.fi) through which one may access a large number of public administration forms mostly free of charge.

A specific law regulating electronic communication and the provision of services in public administration was passed in 1999.[1] The law obliges Finnish public officials to develop their electronic services in user-friendly ways. The law defines the key concepts of electronic communication, such as electronic messages, electronic documents and terms related to electronic identification. Moreover, it sets the legal framework of their use in public administration and services. The law also provides the legal basis of the use of the electronic identity card. This looks like a normal identity card, and they are both issued by police officials. The electronic identity card, however, is a smart card that includes a microchip with an 'electronic service code' that can be used together with a personal identification number (PIN). The Population Registration Centre maintains the identification system and thus provides the microchip and the PIN for each user. The identification of the user requires, in addition to the card and the PIN, a special device for reading the card.[2]

The electronic identity card allows the transfer of personal and confidential information on the Internet, and at the moment the system may be used in transactions with a variety of public officials.

The card may be used, for example, for registering removal or for application for study allowances. Some private companies, such as banks and insurance companies, also allow the use of the electronic identity card for their online services. Furthermore, in some munici-palities the card may be used for lodging individual citizens' initia-tives for the municipal government, and for following the progress of the initiative.

Yet, the electronic identity card has not become as popular as first expected. In fact, by the beginning of the year 2002, only about 13,000 individuals had acquired the card.[3] One of the reasons for its low popularity might be that it still does not qualify for all public ser-vices. The investment for the card and the card reader seems to be too much for those with an Internet access at home, and there is still a very limited access to readers in public places. In order to make the card more popular, more services should be available and there should be easier access to card readers in frequently visited public places, such as libraries.

In addition to the information and public services, there have been some attempts to increase interactivity between decision-makers and citizens through the Internet. A discussion forum, Take-a-Stand (*Otakantaa*), has been opened in order to enhance exchange of opinions between citizens and ministries in charge of topical issues. Various ministries host the discussions in turn, and the min-isters responsible participate in the debates at certain points. So far, there have been quite lively discussions, for example on renewable energy, climate change policy, security policy and immigrant policy (http://www. otakantaa.fi/). Moreover, there is a register of ongoing projects of various ministries on the Internet, and by using a subject-wise search it is possible to find a short description of the projects and to give feedback (http://www.hare.vn.fi/).

In 2001, discussion forums were been implemented on 15 per cent of the municipal websites. (Flash EuroBarometer 79, 2001). One of the most innovative forms of public participation through the Internet is the Idea Generator (Ideahautomo),[4] first adopted by the Youth Council of the city of Espoo (http://www.nettiparlamentti.fi/ideahautomo/). The Idea Generator develops citizens' initiatives through the following stages. First, a registered participant may make a proposal for an improvement in local government. Second, this proposal is com-mented on in online discussion and modified on the basis of those comments. Third, the proposal is submitted to a vote among the regis-tered participants who may vote for or against it. Finally, a number of signatures are collected in support for the proposal accepted by a majority of voters, and the proposal is put forward as a citizens' initiative to decision-makers of the local government. The Idea Generator may be considered as an example of a well-designed Internet discussion forum, and it provides deliberative and transparent procedures of making local initiatives via the Internet.

Elections in Finland

This section introduces the central features of the Finnish electoral system. Moreover, the initiatives and discussions concerning Internet voting are analysed in this setting. Finnish municipal elections and the national parliamentary elections are held every four years. In the municipal and parliamentary elections, as well as in the elections of the Finnish Members of the European Parliament (MEP), a system of proportional representation with preferential voting is followed. This means that each voter votes for an individual candidate on an open list rather than a party list. The D'Hondt formula of allocating seats is applied, and the seats are awarded to the candidate with the highest average.[5] In the parliamentary elections, 200 MPs are elected from 15 constituencies. The Finish MEPs are elected in a single constituency (*Electoral Law* 2, October 1998).

The Finnish president is elected every six years by the two-stage majority-runoff method in the constituency of the whole country. This method has been used since 1994. In addition to local and national elections, there is a possibility of holding consultative national and municipal referendums. The parliamentary majority may pass a law required for the organization of the referendum, and the municipal councils may make a decision on holding a municipal referendum. There have been only two national referendums during the history of independent Finland since 1917: in 1931 a referendum was held on the repeal of the Prohibition Act, and in 1994 Finns voted in a referendum on EU-membership (Suksi 1996).

Voter turnout in Finland has varied over time, and since the beginning of the 1980s it has been declining. Table 8.1 presents the development of voter turnout in municipal and parliamentary elections. The decline has been especially strong in municipal elections, and in the latest municipal election in 2000 the turnout was as low as 55.8 per cent. In the West European comparison of turnouts at parliamentary elections in the 1990s, Finland is among the countries with lowest turnout, together with France, Ireland and Portugal (Idea 2002).

Table 8.1   Voter turnout in Finnish elections, 1945–2000 (percentages)

Parliamentary election		Municipal election	
1945	74.9	1945	54.9
1948	78.2	1947	66.3
1951	74.6	1950	63.0
1954	79.9	1953	71.3
1958	75.0	1956	66.2
1962	85.1	1960	74.8
1966	84.9	1964	79.3
1970	82.2	1968	76.7
1972	81.4	1972	75.6
1975	79.7	1976	78.5
1979	81.2	1980	78.1
1983	81.0	1984	74.0
1987	76.4	1988	70.5
1991	72.1	1992	70.9
1995	71.9	1996	61.3
1999	68.3	2000	55.9
2003	69.7		

Source: Statistics Finland.

Finnish citizens do not normally need a separate registration for voting because the Population Registration Centre maintains a register of those eligible to vote. Finnish electoral law allows three possible ways of casting a vote in elections and referenda as follows: (1) people may vote at polling stations on the electoral day, (2) people may vote in advance at certain public offices, and (3) those with handicaps and illnesses may vote at their homes, and people in various institutes (e.g. hospitals, prisons) may vote at those institutes. Mail-in voting is not possible, apart from the autonomous province of the Åland Islands (see below).

Polling day in Finland is nowadays a Sunday, and polling stations are open between 9 a.m. and 8 p.m. Advance voting is possible during one week beginning from the eleventh day before the polling day. Until recently, advance voting has taken place at postal offices. Finnish citizens living abroad may vote at Finnish embassies and consulates during four days beginning from the eleventh day before polling day. Advance voting at private homes takes place in the presence of an official appointed by the local electoral committee. The person who is by his or her physical condition entitled to vote at home needs to notify the local electoral committee by mail or by phone at latest by the twelfth day before polling day.[6]

The opportunity to vote in advance at postal offices was introduced in 1978, and the proportion of ballots cast in advance has risen significantly from 7.2 per cent at the election of 1978. The rise was especially sharp in the parliamentary election of 1991 which was the first election taking place on only one day instead of two. Since that election, the average proportion of advance votes has been more than 40 per cent of all cast ballots. The proportion of advance votes varies between urban and rural areas: in the 1999 parliamentary election, the proportion of advance votes was 36.4 per cent in cities, 43.8 per cent in towns, and 47.9 per cent in rural municipalities (Statistics Finland 1999: 40–1). This might be explained by longer distances to the polling stations in the countryside; rural voters may simply vote in advance when they run errands at the centre of the municipality during the week of advance voting.

Since the commercialization of the state-owned mail services, the number of postal offices has been reduced drastically. At the moment there is no postal office in a number of small municipalities, where postal services are provided in shops and kiosks. These are not, however, considered capable of organizing advance voting. Because of this, the responsibility for organizing advance voting has recently been given to the municipalities. According to the amendment of the electoral law passed in April 2002, each municipality is obliged to provide at least one place for advance voting in their areas. The municipalities are, however, allowed to choose the particular public offices or institutes for advance voting, such as the municipal halls, schools or libraries. The municipalities may also make a deal with the Finland Post Corporation on organizing advance voting.[7]

After closing the polls, votes are counted at polling stations by voting areas. The vote count is relatively efficient and the result is normally known with great accuracy within a couple of hours after closing the polling stations. The recount is conducted either by the electoral committees of the 15 constituencies used in parliamentary elections or, in the case of municipal elections, the municipal electoral committee. The recount is started on the Monday after polling day, and normally the recount is finished during that day. Because of the high numbers of advance votes, in some voting areas the number of ballots handed in on the actual polling day has been so low that it has created problems of voting secrecy. Normally, advance votes are counted in the whole municipality separately from the votes cast on the actual polling date. This may create some incentives to vote in advance in order to guarantee voting secrecy. In the amended electoral law, it is required that if the number of ballots cast at an individual polling station is smaller than 50, the ballots will be counted together with advance votes given by people living in that area. If even these two together are less than 50, the ballots are counted together with ballots from some other polling station (Finnish Ministry of Justice 2001a).

The cost of the election is divided between the municipalities and the state, and the current cost of elections varies between €11 and 20 million depending on the type of election, the (typically) two-stage presidential election being the most expensive. In the European elections as well as the referendum on EU membership in 1994, the state has taken responsibility for all costs. The state has also expressed willingness to take a larger responsibility for the costs of parliamentary and presidential elections in order to guarantee the equality of citizens in their use of the right to vote. Yet, in municipal elections, a greater economic responsibility will be given to the municipalities (Finnish Ministry of Justice 2001a).

All in all, the Finnish electoral law gives very detailed instructions on how votes are cast and counted. These instructions leave very little room for maneuvering in the actual organizing of the elections. One of the fundamental principles of the electoral law is that the act of voting is always monitored by a public official, and the amendment of the electoral law passed in April 2002 upheld this principle. When commenting on the proposal for the amendment given by the Ministry of Justice, certain organizations, that is the Social Democratic Party and the city of Espoo, suggested that the possibilities of electronic voting should be explored, especially electronic voting at polling stations on polling day (Finnish Ministry of Justice 2001b). Yet, no such steps were taken in the actual law.

In general, it appears that there is little interest in electronic voting in the relevant ministries in Finland, especially the Ministry of Justice. For example, in November 2000 the Minister of Justice Johannes Koskinen replied to an individual MP's written question on the issue of the use of the electronic identity card in voting (Finnish Ministry of Justice 2000). Johannes Koskinen emphasized that there are two ways to guarantee that a voter's authentic will is registered during the event of voting: monitoring the act of voting and voting secrecy. Monitoring requires that voting takes place under the surveillance of a public official, even in the case of home voting. In his reply, Koskinen appeared to be somewhat open-minded to the idea of electronic voting at polling stations, but argued that existing electronic ballot systems do not guarantee voting secrecy and are not completely reliable.

Therefore, he concluded that electronic voting and the use of the electronic identity card for this purpose is not necessary.

Although there are no immediate prospects for the adoption of Internet voting in Finnish elections, Finnish officials, especially the Ministry of Justice, have been interested in developing other electronic services related to elections. The forms required for the nomination of candidates are available on the Internet as well as information about all relevant deadlines related to the preparation of elections. For voters, essential information on all candidates is provided before the elections on the Internet. Moreover, there is a voters' checklist and a list of locations of advance voting in Finland and abroad. Electoral results are released on the Internet already during election day.

In addition to official information, there is a large amount of unofficial information on elections on the Internet. For example, in the past parliamentary and presidential elections, the commercial television channel MTV, the public broadcasting service Yle, as well as several newspapers provided a service called Candidate Selection Machine (*Vaalikone*). The user fills in a questionnaire on the Internet, and the computer program compares the answers to those given by the candidates and finds the candidate who has the views closest to the voter on these questions. This service has proved to be very popular. Moreover, there have been some Internet polls before elections, the most notable of which was organized by a company (Hi-log Oy) at the time of the parliamentary elections of 1999 in the constituency of Central Finland. The poll had a sloppy design without any proper solutions to the identification problem and, hence, large-scale spamming occurred. The result of the poll also reflected the inherent bias among those who have access to the Internet and interest in participating in such polls (Karhulahti and Laine 1999).

A more open-minded attitude towards internet voting: the case of the Åland Islands

Compared to the prevailing reluctant attitude to Internet voting in Finland, there has been a much more open-minded attitude in the province of the Åland Islands. The Åland Islands is a Swedish-speaking autonomous and demilitarized province of Finland with about 25,000 inhabitants. It has its own legislative body, the *Lagting,* which has budgetary powers and legislative competencies in the areas defined in the Autonomy Act 1921, revised in 1993.

In May 2000, the provincial government appointed a committee to study the possibility of electronic advance voting in the *Lagting* and municipal elections of 2003. The committee gave two reports, a more extensive Intermediate Report in February 2001, and a shorter Final Report in September 2001. In its Intermediate Report, the committee stated the particular benefits of the adoption of Internet voting in Åland. It was pointed out that a relatively large number of those eligible to vote lived outside the islands, and there have been very low turnouts among these people. In the latest Finnish presidential election in 2000, for example, only 2.5 per cent of those eligible to vote and absent from Åland voted at the first round, and 4.8 per cent at the second round of the election. The overall turnout in Åland in that election was 59.1 per cent at the first round and 61.5 per cent at the second round (Statfin Online 25, May 2002).

Yet, in the *Lagting* and municipal elections there are even fewer opportunities for advance voting outside the islands than in the national elections. In these provincial elections, it is not possible to vote at Finnish embassies abroad or at the locations of advance voting on the Finnish mainland. For this reason, mail-in voting has been introduced as a form of advance voting in municipal and *Lagting* elections. Mail-in voting has not been particularly popular, attracting only about 1–2 per cent of all votes in municipal and *Lagting* elections.

In its Intermediate Report, the committee studied the introduction of Internet voting as an alternative method of advance voting in the provincial elections. The main advantage of Internet voting was considered to be its global accessibility, which in turn was thought to be helpful in increasing or at least stopping the decrease of the electoral turnout. The improvement of the IT profile of the Åland Islands was also mentioned as a reason for exploring the possibility of Internet voting. Yet, the report stated that sufficient expertise required for the cryptographic solutions does not exist in Åland. Therefore, the committee suggested that the voting system should be bought from elsewhere.

For the identification of voters in electronic voting, systems based on PINs distributed before the election and systems based on the electronic identity card were compared. The former method was used in the presidential primary of the Democratic Party in Arizona in March 2000. Because of many security risks involved in this method, the committee recommended the use of the electronic identity card. It stated, however, that if the electronic identity card does not attract much wider popularity, the identification problem calls for another solution.

It was also argued that from the voters' point of view, home Internet voting could actually decrease certain kinds of difficulties involved in voting, such as stress during voting, and the possibility of voting for a wrong candidate by mistake. The report admits, however, that there are also significant problems involved in Internet voting. The main problems are due to the fact that Internet voting is unmonitored, which causes two kinds of risks of abuse: outside pressurizing of a voter, and selling votes. In this respect Internet voting does not, however, crucially differ from mail-in voting that is already in use in the provincial elections in the Åland Islands. The committee stated that in mail-in voting, the main method for eliminating risks of abuse is to maximize the number of contacts between voters and officials. Compared to mail-in voting, there are even fewer risks of abuse in Internet voting. Using the electronic identity card especially in Internet voting would decrease the risk of selling votes, because voters' identities would be checked immediately at the act of voting. Moreover, when electronic identity cards are used, selling votes would involve selling the person's whole electronic identity. Yet, the risk of pressurizing cannot be totally eliminated in Internet voting.

The Intermediate Report also included considerations on other issues, such as the transparency of the system. At a more practical level it was pointed out that in the currently existing forms of advance voting, the voter's eligibility to vote is not checked before voting but only when the vote is counted. The committee suggested that in Internet voting the eligibility to vote should be checked in advance. Moreover, the committee recommended that electronic votes should be transformed into paper format for control recounts and archiving. Finally, more general problems of voting secrecy due to the small size of many municipalities in the Åland Islands were considered.

The Intermediate Report was published on the Internet, and an Internet forum was opened for the public discussion.[8] The report was also sent out for expert comments. On the basis of feedback, the problems involved in Internet voting proved to be more serious than stated in the Intermediate Report. As a result, in its Final Report released in September 2001 the committee did not end up recommending voting on the Internet in the forthcoming *Lagting* and municipal elections in 2003. Yet, it suggested that developments in other countries, such as the United States and Sweden, should be followed. Moreover, the committee suggested many other ways of making use of the Internet in the electoral process. For example, personal information in the register of those eligible to vote should be accessible and notification on the eligibility to vote should be available on the Internet with electronic identity cards. This was considered to be particularly helpful for those living outside the Islands.

Concluding remarks

In terms of access and use of the Internet, Finland belongs to the most advanced societies in Western Europe. As for the use of public services on the Internet, Finland is, in fact, one of the leading countries. Finnish public officials are obliged to develop their services and communication on the Internet. It also appears that Finns are already used to searching for public information and using public services via the Internet, yet it seems that people are not particularly willing to pay anything for these services, as the experience of the electronic identity card shows.

Considering the decline of electoral turnouts during the past few decades, Internet voting could be regarded as a possible means to encourage especially young citizens to the polls. Also the large size of the country and the relatively sparse population could be considered as grounds for allowing remote Internet voting. In view of this background, the Finnish government has been surprisingly reluctant to explore the possibilities of electronic voting. The committee set to investigate the possibility of Internet voting in the Åland Islands may be considered as the most far-fetching step in this respect.

In the current Finnish political system there may, however, be rather good reasons for not taking steps towards electronic voting and to rely on the rather old-fashioned techniques based on paper and pencil. Remote Internet voting especially would require fundamental changes in the Finnish electoral laws. Most notably, all current forms of advance voting, including home voting, take place in the presence of an official nominated by the local electoral committees. Remote Internet voting would entail the introduction of unmonitored voting, and hence it would be a major change in the Finnish electoral system.

The current electoral system is reliable, guarantees a high degree of secrecy and minimizes abuse. And some flexibility is guaranteed by advance voting at postal and municipal offices. It is likely that the introduction of remote Internet voting would somewhat reduce the integrity of the voting system. Since remote Internet voting is not monitored, the method may – more than current systems – expose the voter to undue pressures and temptations of vote-selling. Moreover, the electoral systems used in Finland are relatively simple and the vote count is quite efficient. Furthermore, polling days are fairly few in numbers in Finland and election costs are therefore relatively modest. Hence, there is no strong systemic pressure towards the introduction of computerized systems.

The Finnish political system and political culture rely strongly on the principles of representative democracy and citizens' roles in the system are mostly limited to taking part in elections. Therefore, a likely explanation of the lack of interest in implementing electronic voting is the tradition of indirect, representative democracy. Of course, the adoption of Internet voting in national and local elections would not, as such, include any major changes in the political system. The adoption of such Internet applications that would actually increase citizens' direct influence in political decision-making would require fundamental changes of attitudes especially among the political elites.

Notes

1 See Law on Electronic Services in Public Administration 1318/1999, 30 December 1999.
2 In summer 2002, the electronic identity card costs 29 euros and is valid for three years. For comparison, a normal identity card costs 26 euros. The price of the card reader and the programmes needed was about 60 euros or more.
3 The number of cards is based on the estimate made by the Minister Martti Korhonen in his speech in a seminar on the Finnish information society in Helsinki in 29 January 2002 (see <http://www.yle.fi/teema/ tiedeuutiset/ arkisto/sahkoinenhenkilokortti.shtml>). The number of cards may soon increase significantly as the eTampere projects of the city of Tampere has a project for acquiring and distributing 5,000 smart cards for students living in the city.
4 The idea generator has been developed by the company Nettiparlamentti Oy.
5 This is obtained by dividing the total number of votes for all candidates on the list by the ranking of the candidate on a list determined by the number of personal votes.
6 See Electoral law, 714/1998, 2 October 1998.
7 See Amendments of the Electoral Law 247/2002, 5 April 2002.
8 See <www.ls.aland.fi/itval>

References

Ålands landskapsstyrelse (2001) 'Informations- och kommunikationsteknik (IKT) i valprocessen. Slutrapport frÅn Arbetsgruppen för Internetröstning', *The Final Report of the Committee on Internet Voting*, Mariehamn, September 2001, <http://www.ls.aland.fi/itval/>
Ålands landskapsstyrelse (2001) 'Rösta per Internet? En mellanrapport fr ån Arbetsgruppen för Internetröstning', *The Intermediate Report of the Committee on Internet Voting*, Mariehamn, February 2001, <http://www.ls.aland.fi/itval/>
Flash Eurobarometer 112 (2002) *Internet and the Public at Large*. European Commission, DG Press and Communication. Survey, November 2001. Analytical Report 21 January 2002.

Flash Eurobarometer 79 (2000) *Mayors*. European Commission, DG Press and Communication. Survey, April/May 2000 [computer file].

Flash Eurobarometer 88 (2000) *Internet and the General Public*. European Commission, DG Press and Communication. Survey, October 2000 [computer file].

Karhulahti, M. and Laine, J. (1999) 'Vaalit vai karnevaalit?' A Research Report Elections of Carnivals? Kunnallisalan kehittämissäätiö, <www.kaks.fi>

Finnish Ministry of Justice (2000) 'The Minister's Reply to the Speaker of the Parliament, 6 November 2000, <http://www.om.fi/8168.htm>

Finnish Ministry of Justice (2001a) 'A Proposal of the Finnish Government to the Parliament (*Eduskunta*) on the Amendment of the Electoral Law', 18 June 2001, <http://www.om.fi/11003.htm>

Finnish Ministry of Justice (2001b) 'The Technical Development of the Electoral System. A Summary of the Comments on the Committee Report. A Memorandum', 26 October 2001.

OECD (2000) 'Measuring the ICT Sector, <http://www.oecd.org/pdf/M00002000/M00002651.pdf>

Statistics Finland (1999) 'Parliamentary Elections 1999', Official Statistics of Finland. Elections 1999: 1. Helsinki.

Statistics Finland Online Services, 25 May 2002, <www.statfin.fi>

Suksi, M. (1996) 'Finland: The Referendum as a Dormant Feature', in M. Gallagher and P. Uleri (eds), *The Referendum Experience in Europe*. Basingstoke Macmillan–: Palgrave 52–65.

The International Institute for Democracy and Electoral Assistance (Idea) (2002) 'Voter Turnout – Global Data on Voter Turnout', continuously updated, 10 June 2002, <http://www.idea.int/vt/index.cfm>

9

Electronic Voting in Germany: Political Elections Online, Utopia or the Future?

Pia Karger[*]

During the boom of the New Economy, it was impossible to sufficiently applaud the possibilities offered by the Internet: particularly euphoric were the hopes and expectations that it could shape a more democratic society and activate a democracy initiated by its citizens. This also includes ideas about electronic marketplaces where everyone would be able to vote, as in the times of the Ancient Greek agora. However, do these ideas show a realistic picture of the future, or will online political elections remain utopia for quite some time to come?

In the year 2000, most German experts agreed on the answers to this question: in 2010 all elections will be able to be carried out via the Internet, but postal votes and polling stations will, however, still exist, as Geschka (2001: 125) predicted on the basis of two scenario studies drafted in 2000 using methods of scenario technique. Accordingly, online plebiscites will also take place more frequently in 2010 (*ibid.*). In addition, the trend analysis based on a survey of experts carried out by the Federal Office for Security in Information Technology (Bundesamt für Sicherheit in der Informationstechnik) stated that in 2010 direct electronic voting in elections would be conceivable if a sufficiently large number of citizens have Internet access (BSI 2000: 141).

However, in 2002 the experts' response to this question was less consistent and less optimistic (see BSI 2003). The initial euphoria seems to have dissipated.

---

[*] Until June 2003 the author was project manager of the Internet and Democracy project, and head of a working group dealing with online voting, both of which were set up by the Federal Ministry of the Interior in Berlin.

Objectives of online elections

So far, political elections in Germany have taken the form of voting at polling stations or by postal voting. The discussion of online elections is not intended to replace these forms of vote-casting; the intention is, rather, to supplement them with a newer, modern form, which is considered to be appropriate in a mobile, aging society.[1] This is supported with the rising number of postal voters (nation-wide average of 16 per cent,[2] in cities up to 30 per cent[3] at the election of the German Parliament 1998).

It is becoming increasingly difficult to find the voluntary election board members needed to implement elections. The introduction of electronic voting would enable votes to be counted much more quickly, and hours of counting at polling stations would no longer be necessary. This could encourage more citizens to volunteer as election board members. Technical support can also help to avoid invalid votes being cast inadvertently. This has already become evident in the use of electronic electoral equipment in some German cities (cf. Stadt Köln 2001).

A further problem, which can also be solved by adequate technical design, is accessibility: technical support should be designed to enable disabled persons to cast their votes without having to rely on help from others. In addition, online voting is sometimes expected to lead to substantial increases in turnout in elections.[4] However, a lack of political interest or low turnout may also have other causes than citizens' alleged idleness.

Some basic conditions

The large number of elections for various political and social levels[5] alone makes it desirable to reduce the efforts required of those taking part in elections, as well as implementing them. Information technology and the Internet appear to be suitable aids for these purposes. In order to master the challenges of information technology, more than technological aspects must be considered. It is not the characteristics of a technology itself, but rather its socio-cultural embedding which determines the manner and degree of its use. Therefore social and cultural aspects must also come into focus.

Internet access and media competence

Technology alone does not create social renewal. People are needed who are able to use the technologies, and who can use them to help shape society. For this, the following precondition must apply: citizens must have access to the Internet, and they must have media competence. Media competence[6] includes much more than the ability to simply use information technology; it must also encompass the ability to use the new media in a responsible manner.[7]

Achieving this and actively preventing a digital divide in society is the goal pursued by Federal Chancellor Gerhard Schröder's 'Internet for All' initiative. Federal Minister of the Interior Otto Schily (2002) named, amongst others, the following indicators of success in his speech held on the annual congress of the D21 Initiative:

- The number of Internet users has more than doubled since 1998; 50 per cent of the German population will be online at the end of 2002. This development has been made possible by the federal government's active telecommunication deregulation policy, which led to a reduction in Internet access costs.
- Internet corners have been established in all public libraries with the support of the federal government.
- All German schools were equipped with Internet connections at the end of 2001.
- In order to support the integration of information technology into the curricula, the federal government established the 'New Media in Education' programme. A total of more than €300 million is available in order to develop high-quality teaching and learning software.

This political initiative was supported by campaigns from the business community, in particular the D21 Initiative[8] which initiated its own 'Internet for all' sub-working group. Its most important activities are to equip social facilities with Internet cafés and to train the staff in cooperation with the German Red Cross, the 'mission Internet' and the 'Kids to the mouse' roadshow. The telephone hotlines activated for these campaigns are now being continued by the Digital Opportunities Foundation (Söhlke 2002).

The Digital Opportunities Foundation (www.digitale-chancen.de) was founded in January 2002 under the patronage of the Federal Ministry of Economics and Technology. Its aim is to support people in gaining access to the Internet, and in particular to support those groups of the population who as yet are still underrepresented in using this new medium. The Foundation focuses on publicly-accessible computers in social and educational environments. People can learn about their closest public Internet access by using the telephone hotline (Söhlke 2002).

These and similar initiatives create the framework for political commitment and elections on the Internet.

Security requirements on information technology

Well-tried and approved democratic principles should not be placed at risk by using the web. Therefore the preconditions for online voting are technical systems and organizational processes

- which render fraud impossible,
- which are reliably protected against attacks and failures, and
- which fulfil high requirements under constitutional law in terms of general, direct, free, equal and secret ballots.

These principles must not be changed at all when we put an 'e-' in front of voting and use electronic media for this purpose. At first sight, online balloting seems to be as easy as postal voting. However, political elections are not merely expressions of one's opinion which can be sent over the Internet without security measures. For the democratic legitimacy of anyone who is elected, strict compliance with electoral principles under constitutional law[9] is absolutely necessary; therefore, online election procedures must fulfil demanding requirements in terms of both reliability and efficiency. Election systems must be especially designed to ensure:

- that only voters who are clearly identified and authenticated as 'entitled to vote' can cast their votes,
- that every voter can cast her/his vote once only and that this vote can only be counted once,
- that the vote cast is kept secret permanently – and that this really means 'for ever',[10]
- that manipulations throughout the election process including the counting of votes are impossible both during data transmission and storage, and
- that the system is available on election day.

In particular, the combination of 'unambiguous authentication of the voter' and 'secrecy of the ballot' – ensured at the same time – is not a task to be taken lightly.

Intensive discussions and research are being conducted to discover how these requirements can be met (for example Grimm 2001a, 2001b; Ullmann, Koob and Kelter 2001). If such security is not guaranteed, voters will not trust the new technical opportunities, and consequently will not use them.

In 1999, the White House directed the National Science Foundation (NSF) to undertake a study on Internet voting. With the report – published in March 2001 – Internet voting systems fall into three categories: poll-site voting, kiosk voting and remote voting (Internet Policy Institute 2001; see also California Internet Voting Task Force 2000, Caltech/MIT Voting Technology Project 2001). For poll-site voting or kiosk voting, security problems are mainly solvable using the available technology. But remote voting (in which citizens could vote from any terminal, for example at home or work) poses substantial security issues[11] in addition to other risks. Therefore it should not be used in public elections until the substantial technical and social science issues have been addressed. In contrast, poll-site voting could be responsibly deployed within the next several election cycles.

Political culture

Until recently, the technical modelling of vote-casting was at the core of research in Germany. However, information technologies are primarily technologies for change. They change how we do business, how we communicate and how we learn (see Kircher, 2002: 70). Will they thus also change the way we vote? In order to be able to *actively* shape technology, questions of political and social science regarding our understanding of voting and democracy must be in focus.[12] Neymanns (2002a) stresses the symbolic function of elections. To date, elections have been organized in polling stations (or in well-founded exceptional cases by postal voting). Public access and speed are important political factors in this case, which would be changed were online elections from home to be introduced (Neymanns 2002b). Ballots are cast secretly, but are carried out in a public place; the act of voting is thus publicly visible. By going to a polling station, the process of voting is decelerated, so that there is time to reflect on the coming vote. Both factors would be eliminated were voting to be carried out online from home, and this would change the basic nature of elections (*ibid.*).

Further on, Buchstein (2001) mentions the possibility of online voting as a gateway for direct-democratic forms of politics, and discusses a possible trend towards 'push-button democracy'.

Were ballots to be carried out from private PCs, the casting of votes would be transferred from the public to the private sphere. Buchstein (2001 and 2002) therefore points to the lack of legitimacy in constitutional law terms, and to the threat of eliminating obligatory secret balloting by online voting from private PCs.

The public nature of the ballot means that election processes, including calculating the results of the ballot, can be verified by the public. Today's voting procedures are visible and transparent; each citizen is able to observe them at polling stations, or can contribute to their proper implementation as a voluntary election-board member. This verification of ballots by voters leads to a high degree of legitimacy and confidence. Online voting – be it at a polling station or from home – would move many of the previously visible election procedures into the field of technology; they would no longer be visible to all, and hence no longer verifiable by everybody. Verification of these election procedures would have to be delegated to experts able to assess the reliability of the technology and the proper organization of the technically-operated election processes. But do citizens (wish to) rely on the judgment of experts?

As Buchstein (2001: 153) has stated, a security problem (falsely) feared by a sufficient number of voters is sufficient to undermine the legitimacy of an online election. Therefore, online elections can only be justified if it can be ensured that citizens have confidence in the correctness of elections and their results and the procedure is accepted. But how does acceptance of online voting and confidence in voting procedures become possible?[13]

The discussion of these and further aspects must lead to active design of technology. Eventually those issues, but not the technological possibilities alone, must determine the political decision concerning political online voting.

Experiences from the future (learning from pilot projects)

Online ballots have been and are still being tried in Germany in a large number of pilot projects in a variety of areas of application (see Kersting 2002). With the 'elections on the Internet' project launched by the Federal Ministry of Economics and Technology in the spring of 1999, the technical framework was created for an Internet election for the first time. The 'i-vote' online election system[14] developed in this process was tested in two realistic simulations – 'social elections' of the Techniker Krankenkasse (health insurance fund) in 1999, and elections to the Staff Council of the Statistical Land Office of Brandenburg in June 2000[15] – as well as in the legally valid elections to the students' parliament of Osnabrück University in February 2000 (Bundesregierung 2002: 25).

These test runs have shown that all necessary technical elements are available for elections on the Internet.

Since then, further pilot projects have been carried out by a variety of players using different election systems. For instance, in December 2000 the elections of student representatives at Hanover Technical College[16] were organized as a simulation of a postal vote; the security requirements made were those of postal voting. In the second half of 2001, local Youth Councils in the two German cities Esslingen[17] and Fellbach[18] and the Academic Senate and the Faculties' Councils at Bremerhaven University[19] were elected online, the City of Cologne tested an election system for the election of the senior citizens' representation,[20] and interested postal voters in the county of Marburg-Biedenkopf were able to participate in an online test election for the chief executive officials of the county.[21] The common denominator of these projects is the small number (mostly a few hundred) of voters covered.

With 7,000 persons entitled to vote, the legally valid elections to the Staff Council of T-Systems CSM GmbH,[22] which took place on 6–8 May 2002, assumed another dimension. On 24–31 May 2002, a further legally valid election to the Staff Council was carried out in the Statistical Land Office of Brandenburg. An experimentation clause here paved the way for a legally-valid ballot. Both elections are connected in the 'WIEN' project (voting in electronic networks), which started in June 2002, funded by the Federal Ministry of Economics and Technology. This project aims to further develop and test technologies for Internet elections in networked polling stations, to try online elections in the non-parliamentary field and to conduct a social science assessment of electronic ballots. Cultural and sociological aspects such as confidence, acceptance and election culture are to be examined. Another focus is the test of mobile electronic signatures.

In September 2002, so-called junior elections[23] were being organized nationally at selected schools. This project focused on political education and the practice and experience of democracy: in lessons, the content of the election is prepared in its overall context. The project is finished by a symbolic election implemented as an online ballot. The fact of it being held at the same time as the campaign and election for the federal parliament in 2002 created a particular topicality, so that considerable interest on the part of students and parents *was to be expected.*

The exchange of experience between these approaches has been and is coordinated by the federal government, together with the business community in the D21 Initiative. In order to discuss the approaches and the results of pilot projects conducted so far, the second workshop on 'online voting' was held in December 2001, organized by the Federal Ministry of the Interior in cooperation with the D21 initiative, and prepared by the 'Telecommunications' study group of Bremen University.[24]

While the first of these events in September 2000 served to develop the exchange of information and views between election organizers, suppliers of technical equipment and legal experts, the goal of the second workshop was to discuss and learn from the approaches and results of pilot projects that had been conducted in the meantime. The discussion showed that there are not only legal and organizational hurdles, but that considerable technical development is still needed (Kubicek, Karger and Wind 2002). Let me refer to some examples:

- Protection against attacks by third parties continues to be a weakness, and in particular (distributed) denial-of-service attacks pose a great risk.
- Effective security measures against manipulations from within – i.e. by the administrators of an online election system – are also necessary.
- Various technical solutions are available to substantiate 'the citizen's right to vote'; they are based either on transmitted keys (e.g. PIN/TAN combinations like those used for e-banking) or on the use of electronic signatures. Identification by means of entered key combinations has the advantage of ease of handling, but might facilitate the purchase or sale of votes. By contrast, a voter would not be very likely to hand out his/her personal signature card.
- Greater attention must be paid to operability and user-friendliness both for voters and for election board members.

It became apparent during the discussions how important it will be to ensure the same degree of transparency and verifiability of election results as exists with our traditional election process, and how difficult it will be to achieve. This links directly with the question of how acceptance of online voting and confidence in voting procedures can be supported.

Step-by-step towards online political voting

Online elections have gained considerable attention in the political environment in Germany.[25] To analyse the requirements and conditions of online elections, the Federal Ministry of the Interior has set up a working group (Karger 2002a). In a dialogue with computer special-ists, legal experts and the organizers of elections, the working group is examining:

- the requirements in terms of functionality and security of technical election systems, and
- the legal frameworks for their approval, as well as
- the criteria for the organization of online elections resulting from the use of technology.

A strong interaction between these task areas is needed (see Figure 9.1). The federal states (Länder) and the German Association of Cities and Towns also participate actively in this working group. Election projects at Federal state (Land) and municipal levels do not fall under the responsibility of the federal government, but there is close cooperation in this area. The pilot projects form part of this joint venture.

The design of election processes continues to be a political task, which must not be driven only by technological opportunities. In our reflections on online voting for political elections, we have to consider that no risks – of any kind – are acceptable. When using new technologies, the prin-ciples of election law prescribed by the Constitution must be adhered to without exception, and electoral errors must be securely ruled out, according to Federal Minister of the Interior Otto Schily (2002).

Apart from the fact that repeated elections caused by a system failure would entail immense costs, the citizen's trust in the correct-

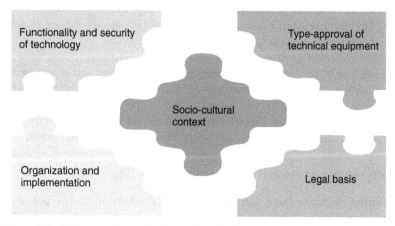

Figure 9.1   Task areas for analysing political online voting

ness of elections and in their results, and hence in the democratic legitimacy of the elected persons, would be severely affected. This would have disastrous consequences for our democratic system. The opportunities and risks, costs and benefits, must therefore be carefully weighed. In order to meet the high requirements, online political elections may only be implemented step by step (Bundesregierung 2002: 34): The German Federal Ministry of the Interior follows a gradual approach,[26] guided by experience, which initially would submit electronic voting in a networked polling station. A second step could consist of elections from special public Internet terminals before electronic voting could, in a third step, be possible from any point of Internet access, for instance from home (see Karger 2002a).

With a system of networked polling stations, it would be possible to vote at any arbitrary polling station of choice. Then, voters would have the opportunity to cast their votes not only in the constituency in which they reside, but also at any other polling station. Voters who are on holiday on polling day (and are still within the voting area) would then also be able to cast their votes in a polling station instead of having to use postal voting.

Some issues still require clarification for this first stage of networked polling stations (see Kubicek, Karger and Wind 2002):

- Access to all electoral registers from any polling station might become necessary. For this purpose, substantial technical and organizational integration efforts will be necessary because the electoral registers are maintained differently in the various cities.
- Polling stations must be equipped with the type-approved technology for electronic voting. In some polling stations, it would first of all be necessary to establish access to the Internet or another network.
- And finally there is the question of the necessary funding for implementation and for current costs.[27]

It is not until we have gathered sufficient experience that we will be in a position to decide responsibly whether online voting in political elections can be implemented in accordance with our Constitution and in a technically secure and economically reasonable manner, stated Federal Minister of the Interior Otto Schily (2002). We should work to achieve this, although not full steam ahead and at any price, but at a cautious and secure pace.

Outlook for e-democracy

Online balloting appears to be particularly attractive, as it suggests a high degree of security and confidence. The great expectations of its proponents suggest that online balloting would lift online political communication from the level of discussion which allegedly has no impact, to the more demanding level of collective decision-making. However, this is countered by critical voices which express reservations not only concerning security or constitutional matters, but which also criticize the considerable effort required to secure and legitimate these procedures (see Leggewie 2002: 159 ff).

The current discussion on online elections primarily aims at a technical mapping of the existing procedures in the Internet. However, the potential of the Internet may lie more in quality gains than in quatitative increases of voter turnout. The democratic potential of the Internet may primarily be the improvement and extension of public debate (Leggewie 2002: 160).

The Internet's potential for overcoming citizens' disenchantment with politics seems to be its capacity to enhance the transparency of political processes. This can be achieved, for instance, by political information and discussion forums on the Internet; and these may at

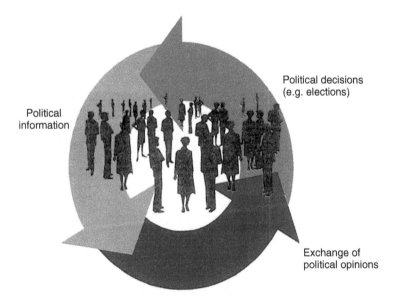

Figure 9.2 The 'informing, discussing and voting' electronic triad

the same time help voters making their voting decisions. The added value of online elections can be highlighted through the electronic triad of 'informing, discussing and voting' (Karger 2002b; Figure 9.2).

It would be basically irresponsible not to use the Internet for our democracy; we would be excluding a medium which is being used by an ever-increasing number of citizens. The Internet offers considerable opportunities to strengthen our commitment for the benefit of fellow citizens and of democracy, and we are determined not to disregard this opportunity.

Notes

1 According to the information to the Federal German Parliament by the Federal Government (cf. Bundesregierung, 2002: 25).
2 cf. Federal Statistical Office (Statistisches Bundesamt, 1998: 28).
3 cf. Federal Statistical Office (Statistisches Bundesamt, 1998: 31).
4 At present there are insufficient reliable empirical results to answer the question of whether online elections will increase electoral turnout.
5 In addition to political elections, for instance social, works council and shareholders' ballots are also promising areas of deployment.
6 In order to be able to participate in and help shape societal processes, media competence must include the individual ability to handle media and to gain new skills independently, to orient in the media world in a self-determined and responsible manner, to take on, process, understand and appropriately assess media contents, and finally to involve themselves creatively in the media process (see Forum info 2000, 1998: 10).
7 For Karger (1999), media competence must include the competence to use information technology (IT) in a self-determined and secure way. Thus, IT security competence is required, including awareness and knowledge. Besides traditional ways of learning, IT security competence can be learned in a self-organized, informal way (see Hartmann and Karger 2000).
8 The Deutschland 21 initiative is an association of well-known companies which has the aim of speeding up the transition from an industrial to an information society in Germany. This is done in cooperation with the political sphere. The Advisory Board for this initiative is headed by Federal Chancellor Gerhard Schröder. The work is carried out in working groups, each headed by one representative from politics and one from the business community. Their aims include:
    • policy-makers, the business community, scientists and society collaborating to develop optimum frameworks for the transition to the information age;
    • the state and its institutions setting good examples in the use of modern technologies;
    • the state and the business community promoting the acceptance of new information technologies.
9 The electoral principles based on constitutional law are explained e.g. by Rüß (2000; 2001), Holznagel and Hanßmann (2001).

10 This corresponds to the requirement to keep secret the voting which takes place at polling stations or by postal vote. According to Ullmann, Koob and Kelter (2001), to date no process is known which can assure a high degree of anonymity of votes for an unlimited period of time when it comes to remote online voting.

11 Grimm (2001b) points out that it is very difficult to reliably avoid individual cases of home PCs being manipulated. The only way to achieve non-manipulated voting terminals securely is to use public voting terminals in polling stations.

12 Kubicek and Wind (2001) describe four options of connecting online elections in a broader context, which are named as 'content-motivational', 'socio-cultural', 'legal-institutional' and 'technical-organizational'.

13 As yet there are virtually no surveys in Germany considering the degree to which online ballots fit the political culture of Germany. This would ultimately be the vital factor for acceptance of and confidence in online elections.

14 See http://www.Internetwahlen.de/projekt/index.html

15 See http://www.brandenburg.de/evoting

16 See http://www.fh-hannover.de/hochschulwahlen/Internet/

17 See http://www.jgrwahl.esslingen.de/

18 See http://www.fellbach.de/wahlen/

19 See. http://www.hs-bremerhaven.de/

20 See http://www.koeln.de/news/bereich1/artikel.php3/1614/ uebersicht.html /900/30/uebersicht.html

21 See http://www.marburg.de/esi/index.html

22 See http://www.heise.de/newsticker/data/tol-11.07.02-006/

23 See http://www.juniorwahl.de

24 The talks held at the workshop can be downloaded at http://www.fgtk.informatik.uni-bremen.de/ wahlworkshop2001/

25 For instance, the topic of online ballots was dealt with in two proposals in the 14th legislative term of the German Federal Parliament (see Deutscher Bundestag 2001, 2002).

26 In accordance for instance with recommendations of US experts (see Internet Policy Institute 2001; California Internet Voting Task Force 2000; Caltech/MIT Voting Technology Project 2001).

27 In comparison to political online ballots, for instance in-company online ballots have a better cost–benefit ratio since the required technology is generally already available.

References

Buchstein, H. (2001) 'Modernisierung der Demokratie durch e-voting?', in *Leviathan (Zeitschrift für Sozialwissenschaft) Sonderdruck Westdeutscher Verlag*, 2: 147–55.

Buchstein, H. (2002) 'Online-Wahlen und das Wahlgeheimnis', in H. Buchstein and H. Neymanns (eds), *Online-Wahlen*. Opladen: Leske und Budrich: 51–70.

BSI (Bundesamt für Sicherheit in der Informationstechnik) (2000) *Kommunikations-und Informationstechnik 2010 – Trends in Technologie und Markt*, SecuMedia Verlag Ingelheim.

BSI (Bundesamt für Sicherheit in der Informationstechnik) (2003) *Kommunikations- und Informationstechnik – Trends in Technologie und Markt (Arbeitstitel)*, SecuMedia Verlag Ingelheim, im Erscheinen.

California Internet Voting Task Force (2000) 'A Report on the Feasibility of Internet Voting', Sacramento CA < www.ss.ca.gov/executive/ivote/>

Caltech/MIT Voting Technology Project (2001) *Residual Votes Attributable to Technology. An Assessment of the Reliability of Existing Voting Equipment*. Cambridge, Mass: MIT Press.

Deutsche Bundesregierung (2002) 'Fortschrittsbericht zum Aktionsprogramm "Innovation und Arbeitsplätze in der Informationsgesellschaft des 21. Jahrhunderts"', Unterrichtung des Deutschen Bundestages, BT-Drs. 14/8456, 7 March 2002.

Deutscher Bundestag (2001) 'Voraussetzungen für die Durchführung von Online-Wahlen', Antrag der CDU/CSU-Fraktion, BT-Drs. 14/6318.

Deutscher Bundestag (2002) 'e-Demokratie: Online-Wahlen und weitere Partizipationspotenziale der Neuen Medien nutzen', Antrag der Fraktionen SPD und BÜNDNIS 90/DIE GRÜNEN, BT-Drs. 14/8098.

Forum info 2000 (1998) *Bildung und Medienkompetenz im Informationszeitalter*, Arbeitsgruppenbericht der AG 4, Bonn, Stand: February 1998.

Geschka, H. (2001) 'Der vernetzte Bürger. Ein Szenario über unser Privatleben im Jahr 2010', in W. Gora and H. Bauer (eds); *Virtuelle Organisationen im Zeitalter von E-business und E-Government*. Berlin: Springer-Verlag: 115–36.

Grimm, R. (2001a) *Security Requirements for Internet Voting*, ACM Multimedia Security Workshop, October, Ottawa: 1–4.

Grimm, R. (2001b) 'Technische Sicherheit bei Internetwahlen – Anmerkungen aus Sicht der Informationstechnik', in B. Holznagel, A. Grünwald and A. Hanßmann (eds), *Elektronische Demokratie – Bürgerbeteiligung per Internet zwischen Wissenschaft und Praxis*, Schriftenreihe Information und Recht, Band 24, München, 86–104.

Hartmann, A. and Karger, P. (2000) 'Modern Learning for a Secure Information Society', in E. Riedling and G. Davies (eds), *Proceedings of the International Conference on Information and Communication Technologies for Education*, EDICT 2000; December, Vienna. Österreichische Computer Gesellschaft: 193–200.

Holznagel, B. and Hanßmann, A. (2001) 'Möglichkeiten von Wahlen und Bürgerbeteiligung per Internet', in B. Holznagel, A. Grünwald and A. Hanßmann (eds), *Elektronische Demokratie – Bürgerbeteiligung per Internet zwischen Wissenschaft und Praxis*, Schriftenreihe Information und Recht, Band 24, München: 55–72.

Internet Policy Institute (2001) *Report of the National Workshop on Internet Voting: Issues and Research Agenda*, sponsored by the National Science Foundation. Washington, DC, <http://www.Internetpolicy.org/research/results.html>

Karger, P. (1999) 'IT-Sicherheitskompetenz – Qualifizierung für IT-Sicherheit', in Bundesamt für Sicherheit in der Informationstechnik (ed.), *IT-Sicherheit ohne Grenzen?*, Tagungsband 6. Deutscher IT-Sicherheitskongreß des BSI 1999, Ingelheim: 327–41.

Karger, P. (2002a) 'Online-Wahlen im Dreiklang der e-Demokratie', in M. Fluhr (ed.), *Neue und bewährte Applikationsfelder der Chipkarte*, Dokumentation des Kongresses OMNICARD 2002, Berlin: 156–8.

Karger, P. (2002b) 'Informieren, diskutieren, votieren im elektronischen Dreiklang', in Initiative D21 (ed.), *Mit Internet Staat machen. E-Government und die Zukunft der Demokratie*, Tagungsband des Jahreskongresses der Initiative D21 am 28 June 2002 in Leipzig, 79f.

Kersting, N. (2003) 'Internet-Wahlen im Vergleich. Deutschland, USA und Schweiz', in A. Siedschlag *et al.* (eds), *Kursbuch Internet und Politik 2/2002*. Opladen: Leske.

Kircher, H. (2002) 'Die technologische Revolution – Alte und neue Innovationsfelder der digitalen und vernetzten IT-Welt', in E. Staudt (ed.), *Deutschland online – Standortwettbewerb im Informationszeitalter – Projekte und Strategien für den Sprung an die Spitze*: Berlin and Heidelberg: Springer-Verlag: 61–70.

Kubicek, H., Karger, P. and Wind, M. (2002) 'Online Wahlen – Stilles Wettrennen', *Kommune*, 21 (4): 12–13.

Kubicek, H. and Wind, M. (2001) 'Elektronisch Wählen. Unterschiede und Gemeinsamkeiten von Online-Wahlen zum Studierendenparlament und zum Bundestag', in *Verwaltung und Management, Zeitschrift für allgemeine Verwaltung*, 3: 132–41.

Leggewie, C. (2002) 'Internet und Politik – wo stehen wir heute?', in Gesamtverband der Deutschen Versicherungswirtschaft e.V. (ed.), *World Wide Web – Gesellschaft im digitalen Aufbruch*, Verlag Versicherungswirtschaft, Karlsruhe, Berlin: 152–63.

Neymanns, H. (2002a) 'Die Wahl der Symbole: Politische und demokratietheoretische Fragen zu Online-Wahlen', in H. Buchstein and H. Neymanns (eds), *Online-Wahlen*, Opladen: 23–37.

Neymanns, H. (2002b) 'Be creative! Online-Wahlen und der Verlust der Wahlsymbole', in politik-digital, 25 July 2002, <www.politik-digital.de/ e-demokratie/evoting/creativ. shtml>

Rüß, O. R. (2002) 'Wahlen im Internet – Wahlrechtsgrundsätze und Einsatz von digitalen Signaturen', *MMR*, 2: 73–6.

Rüß, O. R. (2001) 'E-democracy – Demokratie und Wahlen im Internet', *Zeitschrift für Rechtspolitik*, 11: 518–21.

Schily, O. (2002) 'Der Staat im Internet – Standortvorteil Deutschlands', Rede anlässlich des Jahreskongresses der Initiative D21 am 28.06.2002 in Leipzig, <www.bmi.bund.de/ dokumente/Rede/ix_87164.htm>

Söhlke, N. (2002) 'Internet für alle – Digitale Chancen versus digitale Spaltung', in E. Staudt (ed.), *Deutschland Online – Standortwettbewerb im Informationszeitalter*, Berlin Heidelberg, 179–88.

Stadt K. (2001) *Elektronisch wählen in Köln!* <http://www.koeln-wahlen.de/_fs/fs_ elekw.htm>

Statistisches Bundesamt (1998) 'Wahl zum 14. Deutschen Bundestag am 27.09.1998', Fachserie 1, Heft 5: Textliche Auswertung der Wahlergebnisse.

Ullmann, M., Koob, F. and Kelter, H. (2001) 'Anonyme Online-Wahlen – Lösungsansätze für die Realisierung von Online-Wahlen', *Datenschutz und Datensicherheit*, 11: 643–7.

10
Electonic Voting in Sweden: Hare or Tortoise?

Jan Olsson and Joachim Åström

Democracy as well as modern information and communication technologies (ICTs) are two issue-areas that have each been high on the Swedish political agenda for quite some time. Sweden is often described as a good democratic example in terms of having well-informed and interested citizens and a high degree of public participation in elections. In modern times, about 80 per cent of the electorate has participated, which also holds for elections for local self-government institutions (local authorities and county councils). In the latest elections of the 1990s we have witnessed in Sweden a decrease in the number of votes, but not a dramatic change. There is still nearly 80 per cent participation in voting. Despite this there is a great debate going on concerning the state of Swedish democracy, and how to improve it. As in many other countries it has commonly been suggested that the public has become increasingly disenchanted with the traditional institutions of representative government, detached from political parties, and disillusioned with older forms of participatory activity.

The political ambitions concerning new information and communication technologies are as high as for democratic development. Sweden, the government says, is to become world-leading in the field of ICT, and the information society in Sweden will become an information society for everyone. Sweden is already a forerunner when it comes to ICT, especially the fast expansion of the use of the Internet and broadband expansion. In the year 2000, 76 per cent of the Swedish population between 16 and 79 years of age had access to a computer at home, and 65 per cent had access to the Internet at home (SCB 2001).

As the use of the Internet and the World Wide Web has increased, many have touted the web as a means to increase citizens' political involvement. But when the two issue-areas of information and communication technologies and democracy meet there is no obvious stand the Swedish government will take. On the one hand, there are some good reasons for believing that Sweden would take a lead in developing strategies and reforms towards an electronic democracy, such as Internet voting experiments, discussion forums, online polls and so on. The democratic tradition and technological development taken together point towards such a development.

On the other hand, in light of the Swedish policy-making tradition, we could expect a rather different strategy from the Swedish government, more like the strategy of the tortoise in the fable of the Hare and Tortoise. The Swedish political scientist Lennart J. Lundqvist (1980) uses this fable as a fruitful metaphor in his comparative analysis of American and Swedish environmental policies in the 1970s. Thus, the Swedish policy style was that of the tortoise, which could be described in more academic language with the aid of the following three concepts: proactive, consensus-seeking and based on professional expertise. Such a policy style means that Sweden would not be expected to be a forerunner, but rather someone coming from behind at a slow but steady tempo.

The purpose of this chapter is to describe the state of the art of Internet voting in Sweden, focusing on the debate, state investigations and policy of the Swedish government as well as relevant experiments. After this introduction, we describe the background of Swedish electoral traditions in order to have a historical point of reference. In the following parts of the chapter we try to understand the Swedish way by relating it to institutional factors, especially Swedish electoral traditions and what they mean when it comes to balancing competing democratic values. Is Sweden a European forerunner in Internet voting? Is Sweden best in class in combining old and new forms of democratic institutions, or is there rather a Swedish cautiousness about changing democratic institutions which seems to work quite well? Is Sweden a hare or tortoise when it comes to I-voting?

Swedish electoral traditions

Given that experimentation and innovation will take place within the existing frameworks, we would argue that understanding the existing and preexisting institutions and incentives provides the best guide to predicting the implications of the Internet for different cultural settings. Irrespective of cultural setting, the voting procedure must fulfil different types of demands. Of decisive importance are high demands on security and reliability. For instance, elections have to guarantee voting secrecy and to be organized in a way that makes it impossible to manipulate the results. Elections need also to function in a smooth and easy way in order to produce widespread participation. Both these demands must be satisfied in one way or the other in order to give legitimacy to the electoral system and the basic idea of rule of the people. The two demands may, however, conflict with one another in different situations and have to be balanced. In these situations, we would argue, the cultural setting is of utmost importance.

In the following section we will examine the Swedish tradition when it comes to remote voting and technical support in elections. For Internet voting, these aspects of the voting system concern the conflicting demands of security and reliability versus participation. Thus, the historical background is important (i) in order to understand the Swedish I-voting policy, and (ii) to assess to what extent the Swedish government is seeking to change the balance in any way, that is in a more participatory direction thanks to the new possibilities offered by the Net.

Opportunities for remote voting

The main rule in the Swedish Election Law is that voting shall take place on election day in the polling station of the district where the voter is registered. Voters that are prevented from voting in accordance with this rule can vote before the election day and/or in another place. The Swedish tradition is that quite a lot of voters use the option of voting in permanent or temporary post-offices. The share of postal voting in Sweden has been steady at over 30 per cent during the last 25 years. Postal voting started in 1942 local elections, which was a service for soldiers on military duty. The postal voting option was extended in the 1970 elections, after which its popularity increased and it has since the beginning of the 1980s become an important aspect of the voting behaviour of Swedes. The highest postal-voting figure was 37 per cent in 1988. This transformation of voting behaviour has also meant that more and more voters voted in advance. Some temporary post-offices are tailor-made for specific groups of voters (for instance voters in hospitals, in prisons and so on), which is only about 1 per cent of the total number of voters. Swedish voters abroad have, in almost all foreign countries, the opportunity to vote at Swedish foreign authorities (such as consulates and embassies), and voting is also possible on Swedish ships in traffic abroad, both for crew and passengers. Thus, foreign authorities and ships may also be temporary polling stations (or ballot reception stations) (SOU 1992: 108, 194–9; SOU 2000: 125).

A considerable reduction in the number of post-offices in recent years has meant that the Swedish government has given local authorities more responsibility in organizing polling stations. There are some worries that there will be a reduction in the number of polling stations, which would lead to larger distances for voters and perhaps a decreased turnout. This is of central importance for the Swedish voting system because the local polling station is the true soul of the Swedish electoral tradition (SOU 2000: 125, ch. 11).

The Swedish tradition of stressing secrecy of the ballot has for a long time motivated a restrictive overseas mail-voting legislation; it has only been accepted as an exception for Swedish citizens staying in Germany and Switzerland. Since the election of 1956 no ballot reception at Swedish consular representations had been possible in Switzerland. The same type of rules had been implemented in Germany since the election of 1979. When Germany accepted that foreign citizens could participate in elections in their home countries by sending voting papers by overseas mail, the Swedish government decided to test mail voting from Germany for the election of 1982 (Government bill 1981/82: 224). For the 1985 election, the same type of rules were also tested in Switzerland (Government bill 1984/85: 119). Since then, the Swedish Parliament has taken new decisions to reassert the rules at the time of elections. Thus, Swedish overseas mail voting has really been an exception on a short-term basis (SOU 1992: 108, ch. 10; SOU 1994:30, ch 6; SOU 2000: 125, ch. 12).

In the 1990s both Germany and Switzerland accepted ballot reception at Swedish consulates and therefore the need for overseas mail voting no longer exists. However, overseas mail voting was retained as an alternative to temporary polling stations at foreign representations. In the government proposal of 1996/97, the first step was taken towards a more overseas mail-voting-friendly policy. The government stated, with reference to the German experiences, that overseas mail voting in combination with voting at foreign authorities had been implemented without practical problems in the 1994 elections as well as the election for the European Parliament in 1995 (Government bill 1996/97: 70 p. 148).

The next step, which was a major one, was taken by the Election Technical Investigation in the year of 2000. It proposed that overseas mail voting should be extended to cover all Swedish voting from abroad and that a general rule about this should be included in the Swedish

Election Law. It was also suggested that the possibility of voting at foreign authorities should be retained. The enquiry motivated its proposals with arguments about making participation easier rather than strengthening security and reliability. According to the view of the enquiry the preconditions are in many places of such a kind that it is impossible to vote or that the distance is so huge that it is impossible to participate in the election without really big sacrifices by the individual voter. In addition to this, the investigation argues, increasing internationalization means that more and more Swedes are abroad for shorter or longer periods of time. At the same time, the number of embassies and consulates that can function as ballot reception places has, according to the investigation, decreased a little. Even though it would be possible to open up more voting stations, a large number of Swedes will be abroad at places where there are no ballot receptions. The government and Parliament incorporated the enquiry proposal into Swedish law in the year 2001 (SOU 2000: 125, ch. 12; Government bill 2001/02: 53).

Apart from the general internationalization argument above, there are other important forces behind this rather quick policy change. One driving force is probably European integration, which has meant a more adaptive Swedish policy style. Decreasing voting turnout in Sweden, and in particular the extremely low level of voting for the European Parliament among Swedish citizens, are important background factors. Finally, there is also lobbying in this policy area. Swedes in the World (SVIV – Svenskar i Världen) is an association for Swedes living abroad. It has existed for more than 60 years and specializes in issues related to moving abroad or moving home. SVIV argues that the new general overseas mail-voting legislation is a victory for Swedes abroad and for the association itself, because it has managed to convince the national parliament (<hhtp://www.sviv.se>).

The history of voting technology

Thus, the possibility of widely distributed locations where votes can be cast via technical means challenges many aspects of the carefully controlled Swedish elections, as we know them. Furthermore, the Swedish voting tradition is characterized by scepticism and cautiousness when it comes to technical support in elections. Technical equipment is used in a limited sense in the Swedish voting system, mainly to register voting results in computers in order to report results and allocate seats in decision-making bodies. Thus, it is still basically a traditional paper-based, manual system (SOU 2000: 125, chs 6 and 13).

Questions about technical support in the voting procedure were already taken up in a technical investigation on voting in 1965 (SOU 1969: 19; SOU 1971: 72). A new election system was proposed which would use technical equipment both in voting and ballot counting. The proposal was intended to modernize voting procedures and the most important aim was to make the procedures simpler and cheaper, and to speed up the presentation of results. That is, to make the system more efficient. During the process of consideration, relatively strong criticism was directed against the proposal. Most importantly, the procedure was thought to be too complicated to guarantee reasonable demands in terms of reliability and simplicity. The minister responsible asserted finally that technical equipment certainly could contribute to the smooth and easy running of elections, but that it also implied security risks which could undermine voters' confidence in the system. On this background, the minister found it unsuitable to start a process of transformation towards the use of technical equipment in elections (Government bill 1972: 105, s. 91).

The question was brought up again by the 1978 Election Law Committee (SOU 1980: 45). It was believed that among large groups of voters there is a marked distrust about the use of technical equipment, that voters might be worried that ballot counting equipment could be misused to register how individuals vote. The Committee also saw a risk that public control of the counting procedure and checking the election result would be severely limited. The Committee came to the conclusion that the existing routine of double manual control of the election result, with a preliminary ballot count done by an election committee and the presiding officer at the election, and a final counting at the county administrative board, is of great importance for trust in the voting procedure among voters. Interestingly, the Committee added that the extensive distrust of technical equipment among voters is, from a merely technical point of view, groundless. However, this distrust, groundless or not, has to be taken into account when new technical equipment is considered. According to the Committee, new technical equipment should not be implemented if that would undermine the confidence in the voting procedure among a significant number of voters (SOU 1980: 45).

Another example of this cautiousness concerning use of technical equipment was brought up in the 1990s in relation to the introduction of personal political mandates in Swedish elections. At that time, Swedish voters were given the possibility of voting for individual politicians on party lists; that is, voters could for the first time vote on individuals as well as parties. The reform made it more difficult for political parties to foresee the voting result in terms of who would be elected. The planning work of parties after elections became more problematic due to time delays, and initiatives have been taken to address this problem. In the governmental directives of the Election Technical Investigation it was said that the investigation should consider if it is possible to perform the vote counting and distribution of seats in a shorter time than before (SOU 2000: 125, 223).

The Election Technical Investigation came to the conclusion that it would be possible to execute the vote counting faster within the framework of the existing system, by simplifying the rules and introducing technical equipment, but also by using more staff in the vote-counting section of the county administrative boards. It also said that a faster vote count could be achieved by changing the distribution of tasks and responsibilities among the existing public authorities, but this could not be done with the same level of security, according to the enquiry experts. Thus, the ambition to design a faster counting process could, in the light of the traditional stress on security, only be attained by higher costs. The investigation therefore concluded that it could not recommend any of the above-mentioned alternatives (SOU 2000: 125, ch. 13).

Internet voting: debate and policy

Like earlier proposals for using technical means in elections, the argument in favour of Internet voting includes efficiency gains. It should be clear that the term 'Internet voting' encompasses a variety of concepts. Principally, it can be distinguished both by the voting site (poll site, kiosk, or remote) and the nature of the election (public or private) (Internet Policy Institute 2001; Gibson 2001). By using modern information and communication technologies, elections can be conducted easier, faster and cheaper. The most interesting aspect of Internet voting is, however, the increase in access to the democratic process that it would offer. The biggest arguments in favour of I-voting include higher voter turnout, and the possibility of conducting referenda more frequently. In this section we will describe the main arguments in the debate, the most important conclusions in the latest state investigations, and the I-voting policy of the Swedish government.

Main arguments for and against Internet voting

The fact that Sweden is one of the most wired countries in the world has contributed to current interest in using the Internet in elections.

As the number of Internet users increases, the problem of equality of access becomes smaller. At the same time, the explosion of the Internet culture in Sweden has caused many to question why we should not be able to cast our ballots in the same manner as we do other things on the web – from home or from work. A recent survey from the National Statistical Office of Sweden (SCB 2001) shows that 55 per cent of Swedes between 16 and 64 years of age would prefer to vote via the Internet in national, regional and local elections and referenda if there was a choice. About 40 per cent say that they would not prefer the Internet and the rest say that they do not know. In relation to this, the proponents of Internet voting argue that the adoption of such systems would increase voter participation, especially among youths, overseas personnel, business and holiday travellers, and institutionalized or housebound voters (SOU 2000: 1). As Table 10.1 shows, there are, however, great differences in attitudes between different age groups. Most positive are citizens between 20 and 34 years of age, where no less than 64 per cent say that they would prefer to point and click rather than use the traditional ballot paper. Among the oldest age group, 55 to 64 years of age, the corresponding number is no more than 35 per cent. In spite of these differences, there has not been that much talk about the so-called digital divide in relation to Internet voting, and the possibility that online elections could be seen as an infringement of voting rights (Solop 2000). The important thing is, many tend to think, that the electronic vote becomes a complement to the traditional ballot paper and that voting is not restricted for those who do not wish to use the Internet (Lindholm 2001).

Sweden is not exactly known for its direct democracy ambitions. According to a report from the Council of Europe, Sweden is among those countries in Europe where instruments of direct democracy are used least frequently (Olsson 2001). Despite this, the possibility of conducting more frequent referenda by means of the Internet has been one of the main arguments for the use of Internet voting

Table 10.1 Would you prefer to vote via the Internet in national, regional and local elections and referenda if there was a choice? (percentage of 'yes' by age group)

Age group	16–19	20–24	25–34	35–44	45–54	55–64
	56	64	64	60	51	35

Source: National Statistical Office of Sweden (2001).

(Lindholm 2001; Olsson 2001). The ideal of direct contact between all those eligible to vote has long seemed outdated, if only because of the much greater size of the modern state. But if technology could enable citizens to come together in some 'virtual' form, then it might be possible to restore a more genuine, and more profound form of deliberative democracy. For example, it might be possible to organize deliberations and regular referenda on important issues. It is often recommended that experiments like this, aiming to increase public integration in democracy, should start at the local level rather than the national level. The important question is, then, how leading local politicians relate to these ideas. Do they believe in the use of the Internet in the political process, for polls and for voting in local issues?

Table 10.2 summarizes the results of a survey from the year 2000 showing the views of Swedish chairmen of municipal executive boards on different proposals for changing democracy by using ICTs. The proposals are placed in order of preference; the most favoured proposals are found at the top of the table, and the least favoured at the bottom. The results reveal that there is a majority of positive attitudes towards four out of five proposals. Thus, the majority of the proposals seem to appeal to most politicians. However, the number of positive opinions decreases when moving from proposals that concern dissemination of information to proposals that concern two-way communication and direct participation. The most attractive proposal when it comes to communication concerns the possibility of creating a discussion forum on the Internet, which indicates that politicians are more positive towards proposals that lean towards a more 'interactive' democracy, rather than 'direct' democracy (Åström 2001). However, with 32 per cent of politicians positive to conducting online referenda, the Internet could be a valuable instrument for local governments trying to get in contact with their citizens. Of course, the questions put in this survey, as in the survey from the National Statistical Office of Sweden, are unconditional. They are not related to any specific properties within the Internt-voting system. Probably the politicians who support online elections take for granted that the Internet-voting system must be secure and reliable before it is used.

An inspection of the opponents' critique shows that security and trust are important issues. Ensuring the privacy of the voter is one concern; it must be provable that each ballot has been unexamined and is accurate. Another concern is verifying the accuracy of the voting system in collecting and counting votes. There is also the issue of

Table 10.2   Attitudes towards a number of proposals for using ICTs in the democratic process among local politicians (percentage and balance)

	Positive	Neutral	Negative	Total per cent	Balance
Publish political records online	91	8	1	100	+90
Publish documents before meetings online	85	11	4	101	+81
Use online discussion forums	76	16	8	100	+68
Conduct online polls	65	17	19	101	+46
Conduct online referenda	29	20	50	100	–21

Source: Åström (2001).

authentication and verification of the voter. Is the voter the person that sent this ballot? Is this the only ballot that the voter has sent? There are obviously a number of concerns voiced about the security of Internet voting. Even if these concerns can be satisfactorily met from a technical point of view, there might still be problems of trust and legitimacy for the system. The argument, used for example by some leading political scientists in Sweden, resembles that in earlier debates concerning the use of technical means in elections. One should be very careful when introducing new methods, which all citizens do not or might not trust in full (Olsson 2001).

Next to security and trust, the debasement of the vote is one of the most common arguments used by critics of Internet voting (Lindholm 2001; Olsson 2001). This argument is centred on the understanding that voting is an important act that cements civic life and requires a public ritual to instil and perpetuate it. The basic problem with Internet voting is, according to these critics, the fact that Internet voting will transform voting, an inherently public activity, into a private one. Even with the secret ballot, the mechanics of voting are still explicitly designed to remind us that, in principle, we are all equal members of a community. On Election Day, we leave our homes and offices, travel to a polling place, and physically mingle with the people who are plainly our equals that day, no matter what other differences we have. By eliminating this ritual, Internet voting stands to diminish the meaning attached to voting. As a consequence, Internet voting might lead us to voter apathy and a lower turnout in the long run.

State investigations and government policy

The Swedish government's Internet voting policy is formulated in the governmental bill titled *Democracy for the New Century* (Government bill 2001/02: 80). The policy position in this bill is mainly based on two state investigations; one about democracy in general (the Democracy Investigation), and one with specific focus on election technical matters (the Election Technical Investigation) (SOU 2000: 1; SOU 2000: 125).

The democracy investigation

This has been very optimistic in its general formulations about modern information and communication technology in relation to democracy. For rule by the people of tomorrow, the investigation states, it is important to raise the question of what democracy we want ICT to support. It goes on to declare that it wants to increase the opportunities for citizens to influence society much more than before. So far, ICT has mainly been used to increase the information flow from political institutions, and, the investigation continues, technology has been an instrument for what is called service democracy, or as some critics of this traditional form of democracy would rather like to express it, a 'democracy of audience'. The Democracy Investigation seems to stress participation at the expense of security (SOU 2000:1, 98–9). However, in the part of the investigation where more concrete I-voting suggestions are formulated, a slightly more cautious position can be registered (SOU 2000: 1, 188).

The Democracy Investigation says that increased use of ICT would probably increase accessibility, particularly among young people where participation really ought to be strengthened. As long as ICT is not accessible for all citizens, the Democracy Investigation finds no reasons to believe that voters with a weak socio-economic status would increase their participation in elections. Furthermore, it says, there is a risk that I-voting would only have the character of an opinion poll and not the weight, dignity and symbolic importance that a legal act of voting has. The Democracy Investigation is well-aware of the problems related to ICT. It argues for instance that voters must be able to identify themselves in an effective way in order to preclude electoral rigging and to secure the secrecy of the ballot, and so on. The Investigation goes on to say that even though there are a number of well-known difficulties, there are also good reasons for testing in practice if and to what extent the new information technology can stimulate interest in politics and increase participation. Moreover, it stresses a need for experiments with Internet-based voting, for instance in some local government elections and in school elections. Experience from these experiments as well as those made in other countries ought to be evaluated by researchers, according to the Investigation (SOU 2000: 1, 188).

The election technical investigation

According to the Election Technical Investigation, three points of departure are important in constructing a voting system. These are that the election system must fulfil high demands on reliability; that the system must be able to guarantee that the election is implemented in such a way that the secrecy of the ballot can be secured; and finally that the voting procedure must function in a smooth and easy way. This means that an electronic voting system through the Internet must fulfil the following five basic demands (SOU 2000: 125, 83–5):

- Only those persons that have a right to vote shall be able to vote.
- It shall only be possible to use the right to vote on one occasion.
- Secrecy of the ballot must be absolute.
- A vote cast can not be changed by anyone other than the voter.
- The system shall secure a correct counting of ballots on all levels.

The Election Technical Investigation cooperated with a research group at the Swedish Institute of Computer Science in order to try to develop an electronic voting system that fulfils the basic demands described above. In the traditional paper-based, manual system these demands are satisfied with the aid of physical barriers. It is, for instance, almost impossible for a person to vote more than once in the same polling-station without being recognized. Furthermore, the geographical spread of polling-stations implies that large-scale rigging is impossible in practise. An electronic voting system must replace these types of physical barriers with electronic locking devices. The investigation's proposal of an electronic voting system is of a rather technical nature, and consists of four procedural stages (SOU 2000: 125, 87–91):

- Voters, i.e. persons with the right to vote.
- An electronic ballot box, which collects the ballots.
- Two or more electronic mixers that can give anonymity to the voters.
- An electronic ballot computer that counts all the votes and presents the result.

The investigation stresses that its position is that before electronic voting via the Internet is tested in an election, there must be extensive experimentation, for instance in school elections. Only after this can a final decision be taken whether to test the electronic procedure in a real election or not. The investigation relates to the argument of the Democracy Investigation about the risk that I-voting would only have the character of an opinion poll and could undermine the traditional Swedish Election Day. It goes on to say that questions of security and integrity are also important, but these questions, it continues, can be handled without extensive experiments, in contrast to the one about the traditional election day. Thus, the most difficult problems would then be of a social-institutional character, rather than security-technical. The Election Technical Investigation also formulated a strategy in four stages of how to proceed with the experiments. These stages are (SOU 2000: 125, 91–3):

1 Internet voting in the voter's polling-station.
2 Internet voting in any polling-station.
3 Internet voting from public computers.
4 Internet voting from any computer.

The Swedish government's position

The point of departure of *the* Swedish governmental position is that the use of information technology in general elections should maintain public confidence by securing a safe election system, including voting secrecy among other things. The government is more cautious than the Democracy Investigation and the Election Technical Investigation, focussing on those parts of the investigations where the problems are discussed, rather than those where the possibilities are developed. The Secretary of the Democracy Investigation commented in a television news interview that the government had slammed the door on the idea of I-voting.

The government focuses on the Election Technical Investigation's basic demands that have to be fulfilled if Internet voting is to be used, stating that a majority of the organizations that had the proposal under consideration agreed to this, which of course is a quite obvious judgement. Among them were some really important institutions; specifically mentioned by the government are the IT-commission and the Federation of Local Authorities (Government bill 2001/02: 80: 43).

Thus, the government concludes that for the time being Internet voting in public elections away from polling-stations is not suitable. This formulation undermines that it is decisive for the government to uphold voting secrecy and to manage voter identification. The process of voting must be organized in such a way that the voter can cast the ballot alone without influence from others. Even if voter identification can be defined with a high degree of certainty it is not possible, according to the government, to guarantee that individual voters are not exposed to undue influence at the moment of voting. The government also makes clear that it sees an obvious risk that an electronic voting procedure will weaken the weight, dignity and symbolic importance of the traditional election day (Government bill 2001/02: 80: 44).

The pessimistic outlook of the governmental policy becomes even clearer when it states that ICT ought to have an important role as a complement to facilitate traditional voting in polling-stations and for the counting of votes. This would obviously mean no radical change of the voting procedure. The government has given the Election Authority a mission to follow the Swedish and international development of electronic voting, but no other activities of a more constructive policy-oriented kind. The Election Authority shall even keep a low profile in promoting participation in elections. Furthermore, the government is positive to and wants to support the use of the Internet for citizens to express their *opinions* on different issues. This can be organized in different ways, such as citizens' panels, citizen juries and so forth. The new technology has, according to the government, a potential to extend the participation and influence of citizens. A working group has been formed within the Governmental Office, which has the mission to follow the research and development of new techniques and methods in the area of ICT. This is important, according to the government, to support a representative democracy with extensive citizen participation (Government bill 2001/02: 80: 44).

As a concluding remark on the Swedish governmental policy, we can say that it is quite cautious in terms of testing Internet technology in 'real' elections for traditional political institutions. Some of the policy formulations also indicate a rather pessimistic view on the future possibility of Internet voting. The government does not even take an active role in implementing experiments, in line with proposals of the Democracy Investigation and the Election Technical Investigation. At best, the government seems to believe that ICT can work as a complement to the traditional electoral institutions, more like a modern form of opinion poll. Perhaps we can interpret this as a strategy of protecting established democratic institutions from ideas of renewal that could undermine them and change their structures. Thus, it may be about conservatism in terms of democratic institutions, rather than distrust in technology.

Internet voting in practice

As stated earlier, the most important objection to Internet voting by the Swedish government has been the secrecy of the ballot. In democratic elections, the link between the ballot and the voter must be irreversibly severed to ensure that votes are cast freely. An important factor affecting the degree of secrecy in any election is whether the balloting – either conventional or electronic – is conducted remotely or at a poll site. In a controlled environment, such as a poll site, election officials and observers can ensure that people cast their ballots unimpeded by any outside influence. Conversely, remote voting – over the Internet or by conventional absentee ballots – can be observed, opening the door to the possibilities of vote selling and coercion. This is why the cautious Swedish government has recommended that experiments with Internet voting should start with poll-site voting. Despite this, the first pilot projects in Sweden have been on remote Internet voting. The reason for this is surely that remote Internet voting probably has the greatest potential for increased participation and thus has the greatest power of attraction. Poll-site and kiosk voting offer voters some potential benefits in increased convenience, such as the ability to cast their ballot from many more places. One would expect, however, that this more modest increase in convenience would have a smaller effect on turnout compared to remote Internet voting.

Analysing I-voting experiences it is important to distinguish between public and private elections. Public elections are conducted under the jurisdiction of state election officials and are subject to state election laws. Public elections meet standards and legal tests that are generally more rigid and rigorous than for private elections. The legitimacy of democratic institutions depends upon the extent to which the will of the people is represented. Because public elections are the vehicles by which that will is determined, the integrity of the election process is a matter of the highest national interest. As such, public elections tend to attract greater attention and face a higher likelihood of fraud and attack. Also, voter privacy and ballot secrecy are fundamental requirements for public elections since the adoption of the Swedish ballot at the turn of the twentieth century. This has, as we have seen, brought about great caution when it comes to using the Internet in general public elections. As a consequence, most online elections conducted in Sweden are hybrids between public and private elections, that is within political parties, and among youths. There are, however, examples where local governments have conducted consultative online elections, at least in part in conflict with the jurisdiction at hand. Although not subject to the rigorous tests of public elections, these elections are all important as they provide experiences in Internet voting that can be useful for future public elections. In this section we shall account for some of the experiences from I-voting among young people, in local governments, and within political parties, early Swedish experiments that are all examples of remote Internet voting.

Youth elections

A number of possibilities associated with the Internet's impact on voting have been advanced. One is that the convenience, attraction and familiarity of the Internet, especially among young voters, would lead to a sustained increase in turnout. It is often suggested that younger voters would be more likely to participate in elections than they do now if they were given the opportunity over the Internet. The survey from the National Statistical Office of Sweden (SCB 2001) showed that younger voters are more likely to support Internet voting than older voters. This, and the fact that experiments with Internet voting among young people would be good from a learning perspective, promoted the Democracy Investigation (SOU 2000: 1) as well as the Election Technical Investigation (SOU 2001: 125) to suggest that Internet voting should be tested among young people, in for example school elections. Since these investigations, there have been two Internet elections among young people in Sweden: the college election in the city of Umea 2001 and the Young Election among senior high-school pupils in 2002.

One important aspect of assessing the college election in Umea is, thus, whether the possibility to vote via the Internet enhanced voter turnout. Conditions for increased participation in the election were in this case particularly good, not just because the group of voters consisted of youths used to computers and the Internet, but also because turnout has often been very low. In the last election it was only about 11 per cent. The ambition in 2001 was at least to reach a figure of 17 per cent. However, when the election was completed, it appeared instead that the turnout had decreased to 9 per cent. This must be interpreted as a failure, especially since the students were probably better informed about this election than ever before. There are, however, circumstances indicating that the turnout could have been even lower if the Internet alternative had not existed. Firstly, it was clear that the Internet was used in preference to the other alternatives, the traditional ballot paper and mail voting. A majority of those who voted, 62 per cent, used the Internet. Also, 90 per cent using the

Internet thought that it was good not to have to go to a polling station. The fact that the turnout decreased may be due to the fact that the number of polling stations was fewer in 2001 compared to 2000, and perhaps more importantly that the motivational measures did not succeed. The main reason mentioned by those who refrained from voting was a low interest in the activities of the Student Union of Umea (Statskontoret 2001; Grönlund and Hällgren 2002). This could be held as an argument for the reinforcement thesis concerning the Internet's effects on political participation, that suggests that the use of new information and communication technologies will mainly perpetuate, albeit not radically transform, already existing patterns of communication and participation. People who use the Internet are drawn from the population that is already among the most motivated and informed in the electorate (Norris 2001: 218).

A second important aspect that the college election in Umea can illuminate is whether the constitutional standards of a secret ballot are respected. The evaluation shows that about 90 per cent of the voters who used the Internet were alone at the moment of voting. It can really be seen as a positive result that a large majority of students had upheld some sort of personal sanctity of voting, even though the physical conditions in the home do not guarantee anonymity. To this we can also add that the risk of voters being exposed to undue influence by somebody else was minimized, because there was a possibility of changing the vote. The advantage of being able to change one's vote is that it can restrain problems like vote-selling and threats, since it is possible to change the vote after being threatened without any possibility of the perpetrator tracing the vote. 45 per cent of voters thought that the possibility of changing the vote was good. Despite this, it is, arguably, problematic that about 10 per cent of the voters made the choice not to be anonymous and allowed a friend or a member of the family to be present during voting. Also, 16 per cent of the online voters thought that the secrecy of the polls could not be satisfactorily protected (Statskontoret 2001).

Security was otherwise acceptable for the college election, even if some technical problems arose during voting. The most common problem was that the program crashed, which could be solved by restarting the computer, but other problems occurred to some extent too. The technical problems were much more severe in the second election among youths in Sweden, Young Election. In Young Election 2002, 91,744 pupils at the senior high school voted via the Internet. The administrators said that it was the biggest pure Internet election in the world so far, as well as the greatest expression of opinion from senior high-school pupils in Swedish history. The Young Election was, however, troubled by a severe bottleneck problem, caused by an over-whelming number of contacts occurring simultaneously. The result from this was that after the election, 47 per cent of the pupils said that their attitude towards Internet voting had changed for the worse. The problems in Young Election illustrate (i) that research must be done to determine if web capacity is adequate for the volumes that will be experienced, and to determine what an adequate capacity would be for web-voting servers and equipment; and (ii) that experiments may be really difficult to implement.

Also, the result was almost twice as high as the corresponding con-ventional election in 1998. The massive publicity drive undertaken by Young Election and the intense media focus on the event meant that it had a much higher profile than ordinary elections. Such increased attention combined with the novelty factor of voting online arguably made it a unique event.

Consultations in local governments

There has been a great interest in digital democracy issues in Swedish local governments. As the use of the Internet has increased, many have touted the web as a means to increase citizens' political involvement and to revitalize local democracy. The municipal referendum could be a good testing area for Internet voting, because it only has an advisory status and does not have the same type of insistence on precision of allocating seats in decision-making bodies (Statskontoret 2001: 58). However, the existing laws, that is the Election Law and the Law on Municipal Referenda, do not tolerate a net-based municipal refer-endum if it is to be a referendum in the true meaning of the law. In practice, however, there have been three experiments with Internet voting in Swedish local governments. These votings are called citizen advisory polls and not referenda in the formal meaning, even though the result is treated as a true referendum result.

The first two experiments with I-voting took place in the Kalix municip-ality (www.kalix.se), a city of 20,000+ inhabitants in the very far north of Sweden. The 'Kalix Deliberation' concerned the remodelling of the city centre and took place in September 2000. It received a lot of attention in the press, not only in Sweden but also internationally. Since then, there has been a second deliberation in Kalix dealing with tax levels, in October 2001. The background of these exercises has been a series of efforts to renew city politics. In 1998, a 73-year Social Democrat rule was ended by a coalition of all the other seven parties, led by the Greens. A democracy programme was formulated, including open committee meetings, a citizen proposal right, and an effort to make better use of ICTs. The third experiment, also dealing with tax levels, took place in the Nyköping municipality in November 2001 (<www.nykoping, se>).

To administer these pilot projects, both the Kalix and Nyköping municipalities employed the services of Votia Empowerment, one of several companies in Sweden specializing in e-democracy (<www.votia.com>). The general design in all three experiments included information for citizens, opportunities for debate on the Internet by means of chat and discussion forums, and voting. In the first Kalix Deliberation, the municipality preferred to keep an open dialogue about comprehensive solutions for the town centre instead of presenting citizens with fixed proposals; there were no ready-made drafts or plans. In order to find out how people in Kalix visualized their downtown area, all citizens over the age of 11 were asked to participate in the process by answering questions over the Internet, the phone or in a questionnaire during two weeks in September 2000. During this time 1,188 people, or 7 per cent of the Kalix population, answered the questions put to them. It seems that the Internet option was an import ant factor, as 86 per cent chose to vote via the Internet, from computers at home, at work, or in public places such as libraries, homes for the elderly and Internet cafés in the villages.

The overrepresentation of the 11–25 year age bracket (Table 10.3) partly reflects the fact that many pupils participated in the consultation as part of their schoolwork. More surprising, perhaps, and positive is that the consultation was quite representative for the population up to the age of 65. Furthermore, the data suggests that the voting population was somewhat skewed in terms of socio-economic factors, if not gender. The unemployed and pensioners were underrepresented.

Table 10.3   Internet voting by age

Age	Kalix age structure(%)	Participation(%)
0–11	9	0
11–25	19	38
26–35	11	12
36–45	13	14
46–55	14	16
56–65	13	11
66–	21	9

The second deliberation with voting concerned local taxes in the municipality. The purpose was to deepen citizens' knowledge and understanding of the tasks and duties of the municipal local authorities, and to increase citizen participation in local government issues. This time the consultation attracted 51 per cent of those entitled to vote. A very similar exercise took place in Nyköping from the 12–18 November 2001, where all the citizens of Nyköping over 18 years of age had the opportunity to vote on a proposition for a tax increase that would give the municipality another 26 million SEK to be used for more personnel mainly in schools and retirement homes. Fifty-three per cent of the people in Nyköping participated and the result was a clear 'No' as 75 per cent voted against the tax raise. Unfortunately, no comprehensive post-poll survey has been conducted to assess the socio-economic and demographic composition of the electorate in these two elections.

Party-run elections

The emergence of new technologies and their potential impact on politics has further heightened the interest in the future of political parties. Some radical commentators have seen the rise of new media leading to further weakening and erosion of traditional political institutions. Others have argued that the new media as a communications and participation tool has the potential to deepen internal party democracy (Gibson and Ward 2000; Löfgren 2001). The demise of parties as membership organizations has also sparked a debate about opening party structures for non-members and improving the chances for inner-party participation in the form of trial memberships. Already party websites are open for interested citizens and do not require party membership. Visiting party websites, browsing digital archives, participating in online discussions or single-issue debates much resembles the idea of trial memberships. What has been missing are authentic opportunities for participation in intra-party decision-making (Bieber 2000).

In September 2001, the Swedish Conservative Party (*Moderaterna*) conducted their first open primary election. The Conservative Party was the first party in Swedish history to invite the general public, and not just its members, to participate in deciding which party representatives would be on the Parliament (the *Riksdag*) list at the next election. All citizens, regardless of their political affiliation, were given the opportunity to cast a vote for a member of the Conservative Party for the Riksdag list, and as many as 7,258 individuals participated via the Internet. The result of the open primary election is advisory, and will together with the party-member primary election constitute the basis for the Riksdag lists compiled by the Conservative Party.

To summarize this section about Swedish I-voting experiments, we can first say that there are several activities of different kinds going on. However, even though these experiments give us important information, they are usually not systematically structured and evaluated in such a way that they allow us to develop more research-based knowledge. One obvious reason for this, at least in some of the cases, is that experiments are often implemented to try to legitimize an existing organization with democratic renewal initiatives. Projects focusing on extensive participation are really valuable and can strengthen the position of elected politicians and their organizations.

Conclusions

In this chapter we have seen that there is a Swedish electoral tradition of stressing values of security and reliability rather than extensive participation. This cautious way of balancing has mainly been the position of Swedish governments. There are of course important variations in Swedish society. As we have seen, state investigations, local authorities and other actors have been more open-minded to experiments using ICT. They tend to stress participatory values to a higher degree than Swedish governments have done. However, the short-term priority of security and reliability may at the same time be a long-term priority of community feeling and democratic duty, thanks to a common Election Day with a lot of public arenas. That is probably the heart of the matter for Swedish governments, trying to retain the electoral traditions. However, conservatism is sometimes about making 'necessary' reforms due to structural and contextual change. The Social Democratic Swedish government has opened up for overseas mail voting, on the one hand, and closed the door for Internet voting, on the other. Thus, the government seems to have two different strategies of balancing between security and participation. Perhaps this is not an example of logical inconsistency, but rather an expression of conservatism. That is, the newest technological equipment is the most threatening, but after experiments and testing during a decade or two a more positive attitude towards a major reform may develop. This was the case for overseas mail voting and the future will tell if I-voting will follow the same process of change.

The important differences in policies between Swedish governments and other actors in Swedish society are an interesting feature for the years to come. Using ICTs as an important ingredient for economic growth is a generally accepted strategy in Sweden. For commercial actors, such as private consultants, democracy is just another market, while the government upholds a division between ICT as an offensive instrument for growth and a possibility for democratic renewal. However, a relevant issue is whether the position of the Swedish government is rational in the long run in relation to its own values and preferences. It is fair to ask: what is leadership in this complex and dynamic area? Can passiveness be a rational strategy at all? The interest for Internet voting is growing and will probably continue to grow. Firstly, there is a risk that the Swedish government will lose influence by leaving experiments and learning processes to others (local authorities, private consultants and so on). It is not self-evident that they safeguard values that the government wants to secure and strengthen. Secondly, the current voting process has the advantage of being based on commonly understood systems. The Internet, while people are rapidly learning how to use it, is still unknown for many. People do not understand all of the information that is moving in and out of their computers while they are online, nor do they understand the underlying infrastructure or technology of the Internet. These are legitimate, important issues that must be addressed in order to lower the barriers to Internet voting technology (Dictson and Ray 2000). If Sweden is to take a lead, or at least contribute, in developing strategies and reforms towards a system of I-voting, a more active governmental policy will probably be needed. Thus, we should not expect Sweden to be a European forerunner in I-voting, being best in class in combining old and new. We can rather talk of a Swedish conservatism, with the government being reluctant to change democratic institutions that still seem to work quite well. In I-voting the Swedish government moves like a tortoise, while a lot of other actors in Swedish society often run quickly like hares.

References

Bieber, C. (2000) 'Revitalizing the Party System or, Zeitgeist on-line? Virtual Party Headquarters and Virtual Party Branches in Germany', in P. Ferdinand (ed.), *The Internet, Democracy and Democratization*. London: Frank Cass.

California Internet Task Force (2000) *A Report on the Feasibility of Internet Voting*. Sacramento, CA: Office of the Secretary of State for California.

Davis, R. (1999) *The Web of Politics. The Internet's Impact on the American Political System*. Oxford: Oxford University Press.

Dictson, D. and Ray, D. (2000) *The modern Democratic Revolution: An Objective Survey of Internet-Based Elections*,<www.SecurePoll.com>

Gibson, R. (2001) 'Elections Online: Assessing Internet Voting in Light of the Arizona Democratic Primary', *Political Science Quarterly*, 116: 4.

Gibson, R. and Ward, S. (2000), British Party Activity in Cyberspace: New Media, Same Impact? in R. Gibson and S. Ward (eds), *Reinvigorating Democracy? British Politics and the Internet*. Aldershot: Ashgate.

Government bill (1972) 105 *Proposition med förslag till vallag, m.m.*

Government bill (1981/82) 224 *Om försöksverksamhet med brevröstning i Förbundsrepubliken Tyskland.*

Government bill (1984/85) 119 *Om ändring I vallagen, m.m.*

Government bill (1996/97) 70 *Ny vallag.*

Government bill (2001/02) 53 *Ändringar i vallagen, m.m.*

Government bill (2001/02) 80 *Demokrati för det nya seklet.*

Grönlund, Å. and Hällgren, M. (2002) *Internetval – succé eller fiasko? Försöket vid Umeå kårval.* Umeå: Umeå Universitet.

Internet Policy Institute (2001) *Report of the National Workshop on Internet Voting: Issues and Research Agenda*, <www.Internetpolicy.org>

Lindholm, B. (2001) *Sammanställning av remissvar på Demokratiutredningen*, <www.demokratitorget.gov.se>

Lundqvist, L. J. (1980) *The Hare and the Tortoise: Clean Air Policies in the United States and Sweden.* Ann Arbor: University of Michigan Press.

Löfgren, K. (2001) *The Political Parties and Democracy in the Information Age. The Cases of Denmark and Sweden.* Copenhagen: University of Copenhagen.

Norris, P. (2001) *Digital Divide? Civic Engagement, Information Poverty, and the Internet Worldwide.* Cambridge: Cambridge University Press.

Olsson, A. R. (2001) *E-röstning. En lägesbeskrivning. Observatorierapport 35/2001.* Stockholm: IT- kommissionen.

Solop, F. I. (2000) 'Digital Democracy Comes of Age in Arizona: Participation and Politics in the First Binding Internet Election'. Paper presented at the American Political Science Association national conference, Washington, DC. 31 August–3 September, 2000.

SOU (1969) 19 *Ny valteknik. Betänkande III av 1965 års valtekniska utredning.*

SOU (1971) 72 *Maskinell teknik vid de allmänna valen. Betänkande IV av 1965 års valtekniska utredning.*

SOU (1980) 45 *Översyn av vallagen 2. Delbetänkande av 1978 års vallagskommitté.*

SOU (1992) 108 *Val, organisation, teknik, ekonomi. Delbetänkande av vallagsutredningen.*

SOU (1994) 30 *Vallagen. Slutbetänkande av 1993 års vallagskommitté.*

SOU (2000) 1 *En uthållig demokrati. Slutbetänkande av demokratiutredningen.*

SOU (2001) 125 *Teknik och administration i valförfarandet.*

Statistiska Centralbyrån (2001) *IT i hem och företag. En statistisk beskrivning.* Örebro: SCB.

Statskontoret (2001) *Utvärdering av kårvalet vid Umeå studentkår.* Rapport 2001: 26.

Åström, J. (2001) 'Digital Democracy: Ideas, Intentions and Initiatives in Swedish Local Governments'. Paper presented at the ECPR joint sessions of workshops, Grenoble, 6–11 April, 2001.

11
Electronic Voting in the United Kingdom: Lessons and Limitations from the UK Experience

Lawrence Pratchett and Melvin Wingfield

The United Kingdom aims to be in the vanguard of the e-government revolution generally, and in the development of electronic voting (e-voting) in particular. The government has already promised the UK's 44 million registered voters that they will all be able to vote electronically in a General Election before the end of the decade. A programme of research and implementation is already underway, ranging from national projects aimed at establishing a standard basis (for example, a standardized electoral register) through to a consultation programme and implementation strategy. In addition, electoral law has been altered to allow local governments to experiment with different forms of e-voting. Government-funded pilots that tested different types of e-voting (among other experiments) first took place in the local government elections of 2000 and were greatly extended in the local elections of May 2002 to include remote electronic voting. Further pilots, that broaden local government experience of e-voting, took place in the local election of 2003 and are expected in subsequent years.

This chapter examines the issues surrounding the e-voting pilots and the long-term plans for developing e-voting in the UK. Its starting point is the research undertaken for the government and other organizations by the authors and their colleagues into *The Implementation of e-Voting in the UK* (Pratchett *et al.* 2002). However, its primary focus is upon the 17 e-voting pilots that took place in the English local elections of May 2002 and, particularly, the five multi-channel experiments that tested a combination of Internet, telephone, SMS (short message service) text and remote kiosk voting in their areas. As well as drawing upon interviews with key actors in many of these pilots, the chapter also analyses the evidence offered in the formal evaluations of the pilots (Electoral Commission 2002). In so doing, it juxtaposes the significant barriers to implementation identified in the government-sponsored research with the lessons offered from the pilots. It argues that while the pilot approach offers some considerable experience in organizing and managing e-enabled elections, it does little to address the key implementation issues that need to be overcome before e-voting can become a mainstream feature of the electoral system. In short, the argument is that despite expensive pilots that tested a range of technical options, the lessons from current pilots are extremely limited and do not address the substantive policy problems facing implementation. Moreover, proposals for extending the pilot schemes in future years, and other aspects of the implementation strategy, seem unlikely to address these problems.

To develop this argument, four sections follow this introduction. First, the broader political and constitutional context of e-voting in the UK is briefly summarized. This section sets out the main features of the e-voting policy in the UK and its limitations. Second, the main issues and barriers to e-voting are elaborated. These barriers range from substantive legal problems to a range of normative and cognitive arguments against e-voting. Third, the 2002 pilots are described and analysed in some detail. As well as describing the process followed for the pilot programme, this section also analyses the differences between various pilots and their relative achievements towards the long-term aim of national implementation. Finally, a fourth section analyses the lessons from the pilots in the context of the substantive issues raised in the earlier sections and considers the opportunities and threats facing the further development of e-voting in the UK.

The e-voting policy context

Like many countries, Britain faces a significant problem of declining electoral turnout and the crisis of democratic legitimacy that low turnouts cause for politicians. In 1950, turnout at General Elections peaked at 83.6 per cent of the registered voters. Since then it has been in gradual decline. When New Labour was elected in 1997, turnout was the lowest since the Second World War, at just 71.4 per cent. This turnout, in itself, was deemed to be problematic and the newly elected government embarked upon an ambitious programme of constitutional reform and modernization, which included a significant attempt at democratic renewal. 'Modernizing' elections was one feature of this agenda. However, in the subsequent General Election of 2001, the turnout crisis deepened substantially, with just 59.4 per cent of registered voters bothering to go to the polls. While the causes of this substantial drop in turnout have little to do with voting mechanisms and much more to do with problems of a decline in civic responsibility, voter apathy and a broader mistrust of politicians (see, for example, Clarke *et al.* 2001), reform of the voting process is still high on the government's agenda.

Low turnout is not only a problem in national elections. Local government elections in Britain have always had notably lower turnouts, with most councils receiving fewer than 40 per cent (see, for example, Rallings, Temple and Thrasher 1996). In recent years, however, even this low base has declined. For example, the May 2002 local elections had a turnout of just 32.8 per cent and this was despite the fact that a high profile set of experiments did boost turnout in some areas (Electoral Commission 2002). European elections are even worse. Britain holds the dubious honour of having the lowest turnout in European elections of all member states: less than a quarter of Britain's registered voters go to the polls for European elections. Again, however, the cause of such low turnout is more generally associated with apathy towards or dislike of the particular institutions rather than with the method of voting, although a change from a plurality to party-list system in European elections is deemed to have worsened the UK situation.

Within the context of this electoral crisis, e-voting appears to offer something of a panacea. Most proponents of e-voting, however, now acknowledge that it is unlikely to have a significant effect upon turnout without a broader change to the political process. Indeed, this point is made starkly by the government's consultation paper on e-democracy (Office of the e-Envoy 2002) which devotes a substantial proportion of its time to promoting e-voting. Why, then, is there such a push for e-voting within the UK? For the government, the argument appears to be one of choice and flexibility. As the opening paragraphs in the e-voting section of the consultation paper state:

> Electronic voting will not solve the problem of low turnout in elections... The way in which we go about casting our votes in this country has hardly changed over the last century and yet our lifestyles have changed beyond all recognition from those of our 19th century predecessors. A 21st century democracy should provide a variety of ways of voting that reflect modern lifestyles. (Office of the e-Envoy 2002: 41)

Modernizing the voting process through the use of ICT may broaden participation in elections. It may, for example, make voting more attractive to those young people who are competent in ICT but who find traditional methods of voting unattractive or inconvenient. (Office of the e-Envoy 2002: 42).

Richard Allen MP, one of the strongest advocates of e-voting within the UK Parliament, sums up the argument more simply by suggesting that 'for a democracy to command respect it must operate in the same way as people do everything else in their lives' (cited in Pratchett *et al.* 2002). His belief is that if people can bank and shop online and, indeed, vote in interactive TV programmes, then they will expect the institutions of democracy to keep pace with such developments. Old fashioned voting procedures do not sit comfortably with modern economies. While there may be some credence to this assertion, there remains a substantial sub-text to the debate that is implicitly concerned with turnout. The belief that e-voting will appeal especially to young people is particularly instructive in this context. Even if those promoting e-voting do not explicitly expect it to resolve the turnout crisis, they nevertheless hope that it will halt its decline.

Within this context, e-voting is gaining a considerable momentum in the UK. The government has made a number of commitments towards its implementation, backed up by significant financial support for research and experimentation in the area. The Representation of the People Act 2000 was the first step in this direction, providing local authorities with the opportunity for experimentation with different voting methods, including various electronic methods. This Act also allowed all UK voters to opt for a postal vote if they preferred one: until this Act, postal voting was only allowed in exceptional circumstances. The principle of remote voting, therefore, is already established within UK experience and some 1.4 million electors voted in this way in the 2001 General Election (Electoral Commission 2001). For many, remote e-voting is simply an extension of this emerging practice.

The government has made a number of policy commitments which add to this momentum. First, there are the e-government targets, initially framed in the 1999 Modernizing Government White Paper and later modified by a strategic statement from the Office of the e-Envoy (2000), that require all public services to be available electronically by 2005. Somewhat curiously, elections are considered to be a 'service' in this context and registration and electoral processes are, therefore, included within the targets. Consequently, the 2005 targets can be seen to have a strong influence on the speed with which public authorities in the UK are seeking to take up e-voting systems. Second, the government has made a formal commitment to hold an 'e-enabled General Election' sometime after 2006: probably the General Election after next, which is likely to occur sometime between 2008 and 2010. The commitment to e-voting in future elections, therefore, is firmly in place. Third, and possibly most importantly, however, the government has already begun the implementation of e-voting in the UK through a large programme of experimentation and core project developments.

The experimentation is the main subject of this chapter and will be covered in more detail in a later section. In short, it has involved e-voting on a limited scale in a number of local government elections in 2002, each of which used different technological platforms and offered different opportunities for voting. In many instances, these systems were combined with other experiments such as postal voting and extended voting hours. The experimentation programme will continue and be expanded in subsequent local government elections. The lessons from these experiments are important for framing the implementation programme for e-voting more generally in the UK.

Core project developments are the nationally-led programmes that underpin and facilitate widespread e-voting in the future. Two are particularly important. First, the Local Authorities Secure Electoral Register (LASER) project seeks to provide a national network of locally maintained electoral registers that will be seamlessly linked. In the UK, the electoral register is traditionally maintained at local council level and no national system exists. While the registers and their use are governed by national standards and legislation, local authorities have adopted different computer systems and different processes for managing their registers. These systems range from some widely adopted and relatively sophisticated commercial packages through to in-house developed systems and even one local authority that maintains its register on a word-processing package. This project aims to provide a common infrastructure for local electoral registers based around standard addresses and linked to a national land and property gazetteer. It is widely deemed to be fundamental to allowing real-time online voting from anywhere. Second, and related to the problems of linking systems based on different platforms, the government is committed to developing, in collaboration with a number of other European countries, an Election Mark-up Language (EML). This project seeks to ensure that different e-voting systems will be able to communicate and transfer information between each other. Again, such infrastructure is fundamental to the 'vote from anywhere' principle.

The sum of these initiatives is a strategy for e-voting in the UK, some of which has been explicitly stated (see especially Office of the e-Envoy 2002) but other parts of which remain implicit. The explicit components of the strategy include: a commitment to multi-channel voting which will include but not be restricted to e-voting; the 'vote from anywhere' principle that includes registered voters participating in elections from overseas; and the notion of a phased implementation of e-voting based around gradually extended experiments at the local level. The implicit components of the strategy are more complex but include: a commitment to commercial exploitation of e-voting to ensure that best value is achieved by each local authority by exposing voting systems to the market; an emphasis upon multiple platforms being offered by competing suppliers; and the continued emphasis upon local control of election activities using a centrally prescribed but essentially bottom-up implementation process. This strategy sits at odds with many other countries that are seeking to implement e-voting. Other countries are seeking to define the components of their desired e-voting system and then inviting tenders for a supplier to deliver such a system. Within such processes, the assumption is that the state will take ownership of the final system. Within the UK implementation strategy, developments are more likely to be led by commercial suppliers and ownership of systems is likely to remain in commercial hands. Of course, opportunities for one commercial organization to unfairly exploit their ownership of e-voting systems will be limited by the existence of a competitive market. However, this very different strategy does mean that, at any given time, the UK is likely to have a variety of different systems in place to support e-voting and will be operating with a range of different suppliers. While the commercial sector will bear more of the financial risk in relation to e-voting in the UK, they will also have much greater control over how it will be developed.

Issues and barriers to e-voting

Realizing the strategy and implementing e-voting is dependent upon overcoming a number of obstacles to implementation. Some, such as the development of a suitably competitive market for delivering e-voting systems are fairly obvious. Others, however, present more intractable barriers to implementation. Based upon the research undertaken by the authors and their colleagues,* five main barriers need to be addressed before widespread e-voting can be implemented. These are: security and integrity of the vote; secrecy and privacy in voting; technological penetration and access; voter capacity and citizen confidence in e-voting; and organizational and market capacity. There are a number of other potential barriers, including acceptance by political parties of e-voting processes and the funding and financing of implementation. However, these five main barriers, we argue, form a framework through which the programme of e-voting pilots can be evaluated. In the following section we will first set out the barriers in some detail before going on to describe and evaluate the 2002 pilots against this framework. While the pilots do allow some lessons to be learned (for example, in relation to organizational capacity), they do not begin to address many of the bigger issues that the research has identified.

Security and integrity of the vote

Much has been written on the security and integrity of e-voting (cf. California Internet Voting Task Force 2000; Coleman *et al.* 2002; Internet Policy Institute 2001; Mercuri 2001; Schneier 2000, inter alia). While the range of potential threats is wide, however, their nature can be distilled into three main problems for those who would implement e-voting (for a comprehensive treatment see Fairweather and Rogerson 2002). First, there are concerns that technologically mediated voting may enable individuals or organizations to steal or alter votes in order to influence the outcome of an election. Various technological interventions may be possible in this context. Viruses may be propagated that steal or alter votes either on the machine at which the citizen casts the vote, or at some point in its transmission to the host machine. There is also the complication of ensuring that any host machine is free of such malicious viruses. Alongside viruses, there is the added risk that voting systems may incorporate some form of 'malware' that automatically biases outcomes towards particular results. These types of attacks, of course, assume that there are those who want to bring about a particular

---

* The research team consisted of Lawrence Pratchett, Melvin Wingfield, N. Ben Fairweather and Simon Rogerson from De Montfort University; Sarah Birch and Bob Watt from Essex University; and Sarah Candy and Vanessa Stone from the British Market Research Bureau. The research was sponsored by the Department for Transport, Local Government and the Regions, the Local Government Association, the Electoral Commission, the Improvement and Development Agency, the Society of Local Authority Chief Executives and the Office of the e-Envoy.

result. However, even where individuals or organizations are not seeking to deliberately distort an election in a particular direction, votes may still be stolen through spoofing: that is, through the creation of voting sites, particularly on the Internet, that give the appearance of being the official voting site but are, in reality, a false location. Where such sites are created, individuals may be tricked into believing that they have voted when they have not. In short, there are a number of ways in which votes can be stolen or altered, either to deliberately effect particular election results or simply 'to play around' with the election process.

Second, and related to the first, technologically dependent elections also face the risk of disruption through the prevention of voting. Viruses, of course, may have this effect. However, there is also a wide range of other ways in which voting may be prevented. A favourite method for malicious intervention on the Internet is a denial of service attack, in which the server is deliberately overloaded so that genuine service users cannot gain access. Such a denial of service can also occur unwittingly. For example, when the UK's 1901 census data was first made available on the Internet in January 2002 demand for access far outstripped the resource made available, locking the system up for several weeks. Low-tech interference in elections is also possible through the targeting of electricity supplies and so on, or even through industrial action by those responsible for ensuring that the infrastructure is working. Again, technological dependence creates new vulnerabilities for elections.

Finally, and possibly most importantly, however, there is a significant issue around confidence. Perhaps the most effective way of disrupting an electronic election is not so much by achieving an attack but in claiming that such an attack has taken place. Anecdotes of voters being unable to gain access to the system or of individuals gaining unauthorized access are likely to have a negative effect upon public perception, far in excess of the reality of the potential attacks. Dot.com companies have experienced this phenomenon with many people fearing the security that such companies offer their credit cards. In an election context there are already anecdotes and, indeed, evidence that postal and proxy voting has been abused in recent elections. Anecdotes of this nature could easily be exploited by losing candidates or parties, especially where the election outcome is unexpected or particularly close. Such confidence attacks could do more damage to an election than an actual attack because they would undermine the credibility of the election and, ultimately, the legitimacy of those representatives elected in this way.

Secrecy and privacy in voting

The legal context of voting in the UK is complex, with no single piece of legislation defining the whole position. The main legal challenge to e-voting, however, especially where it occurs outside of polling stations (that is, remote e-voting), is in relation to the secrecy of the ballot. Bob Watt has argued forcibly that remote e-voting contravenes a number of international laws and conventions to which the UK is a signatory and by which, therefore, it is bound (Watt 2002). He is not alone in making this argument. Hubertus Buchstein (see his chapter in this book), separately, has expressed both normative and legal concerns over the secrecy of the ballot. The legal concerns revolve around such international conventions as the European Convention on Human Rights (protocol 1, article 3) which requires signatory states to hold democratic elections in which the ballot is cast in secret. Remote e-voting by the Internet, telephone or digital television is potentially in contravention of this and other similar conventions because, clearly, secrecy of individual votes cannot be ensured by the state. There are a whole range of domestic and, possibly, employment situations where voters may have influence exerted on them from third parties. From a legal position, the as yet untested question is whether these conventions place a duty upon the state to ensure that all votes are cast in secret (in which case, remote e-voting will be illegal) or whether the state merely needs to take reasonable steps to allow secret voting (in which case there are a number of potential remedies to the problem). The normative dimension of this issue is more intractable. If remote e-voting is accepted, it seems inevitable that some citizens will have their vote unduly influenced by domestic partners or employers.

Of course, this problem also occurs through other forms of remote voting such as the already universal postal vote that has occurred in some local elections in the UK and was available to all voters in the 2001 General Election. However, the argument that Watt and others make is that remote e-voting greatly exacerbates this problem, particularly because much of the equipment through which e-voting will take place, such as on computers or televisions, is in open space within a domestic context rather than wholly private. Whereas with a postal vote, the individual can retire to a corner to cast their vote, on a computer or television, privacy is much harder to ensure and is often socially unacceptable.

There is an empirical dimension to this problem. First, there needs to be a legal challenge to e-voting to ascertain its lawfulness or otherwise. Second, and more importantly, however, there needs to be some sophisticated research into the social and political risks associated with remote voting. Such research needs to ask questions about who is most likely to have their votes influenced, how likely it is and what are the implications of this occurring? It is only from such an empirical base that the secrecy threats of e-voting can be balanced against the potential advantages that it offers many groups in society. Whether small-scale voting experiments in local government elections can provide answers to this issue is questionable.

Technological penetration and access

The digital divide remains a concern for those who promote e-voting. Access to the technologies on which e-voting can potentially be implemented is differentially distributed among citizens. Taking 2002 as an example year, access to different technologies varied considerably in the UK. Telephone access was the most ubiquitous technology, with 93 per cent of households having one (and a further 6 per cent holding a mobile phone instead). Overall, some 73 per cent of UK adults had a mobile phone. Internet use was also quite widespread, with around 40 per cent of households having direct access and 53 per cent of adults claiming to have used it in the previous year. Digital television is also popular in the UK, and 37 per cent of households in 2002 had access to this technology (by far the highest in Europe) although only half had used its interactive facilities. From an optimistic point of view, therefore, many of the technologies required for e-voting are already in a broad state of adoption in the UK.

The problem, however, is that the distribution and access to these technologies is systematically biased towards certain demographic and geographic groups and against others. Households in the bottom two income deciles are almost eight times less likely to have Internet access than those in the top income decile. At the start of 2002, 39 per cent of women had used the Internet compared with 52 per cent of men. Only 6 percent of those over 65 had access to the Internet compared with 45 per cent of 35–44 year olds. Regional variations are also marked, with the prosperous London and south-east region having 45 per cent of households with Internet access compared with 26 per cent in the former industrial heartland of the north-east of England. The danger is that in implementing e-voting, existing biases in voter behaviour are reinforced and non-voters are given no additional incentive to participate. It is widely known within political science that more prosperous and educated people are more likely to participate politically, including voting, than those from more disadvantaged backgrounds (see, for example, Parry, Moyser and Day 1992). Given that the technologies are systematically skewed in favour of the more wealthy sections of society, it is not difficult to conclude that e-voting is likely to benefit current voters but do little to assist non-voters. There is a danger that it will further privilege the already privileged.

Voter capacity and citizen confidence in e-voting

Linked to the issue of differential penetration and access to technology is the issue of voter capacity to use the technology on offer and citizen confidence in the outcome of an election conducted by electronic means. As part of the research that this chapter draws upon, the British Market Research Bureau (BMRB) conducted a series of focus groups with citizens across the UK on behalf of the research team (for details see BMRB 2002; Pratchett *et al.* 2002). This research found that there are significant cognitive barriers to the use of e-voting technology among sections of society. For those who are familiar with new technologies it is easy to overestimate the cognitive capacity of citizens and their ability to understand an e-voting process. Such an argument is not one of intellectual or cultural superiority – it is much simpler and more profound in its implications than that. Quite simply, those who have no experience of using a computer in their daily lives (and that is a relatively large proportion of the population, at least in the UK), find the implicit rules and norms embedded within computerized systems difficult, if not impossible to comprehend. This cognitive capacity, and the limitations it imposes upon universally available voting systems, was painfully exposed during the focus groups. As part of the discussion, participants were invited to log on to a mocked-up voting system, enter a password and then cast a vote for a preferred candidate. While some had no difficulty in undertaking the task, others found it difficult first of all to log on to the system and subsequently to enter passwords. Some gave up after several repeat attempts in which the system refused to allow them to proceed because of errors in entering a number. Others were clearly embarrassed by their inability to make sense of what was required of them.

The problem of cognitive capacity appears to have little to do with the general aptitude of participants. Many of those who were unable to access the e-voting mock-up were otherwise strong contributors to the focus groups, demonstrating a good understanding of the broader issues under discussion and making valuable contributions where relevant. Rather, cognitive capacity appears to have more to do with the general life experiences of the individual. In order to understand the rules of an e-voting system it is necessary to have had some prior experience of using the type of technologies on which it is based. Of course, these life experiences are closely linked to education and employment patterns. Once again, it is the already privileged who have the experience and confidence to use e-voting systems while those from disadvantaged social backgrounds are least likely to have the cognitive capacity, skills and confidence to use the technology.

Organizational and market capacity

This final set of obstacles concerns those that are most directly respons-ible for implementing e-voting in the UK. Elections are a highly decen-tralized process in the UK, and as stated earlier the implementation strategy for e-voting appears to sustain this decentralized process within a national framework of standards and expectations. Consequently, each local authority will remain responsible, under the current strategy, for determining which systems it puts in place and which suppliers to contract with. Central government has entered into a framework agreement with selected suppliers to ensure that central requirements are met and local authorities are restricted to contracting with these suppliers. Indeed, in the 2002 pilots, the contracts were made with central government on behalf of local authorities. In the long term, however, local authorities can expect to take on responsibil-ity for developing such relationships themselves, albeit within a central government framework agreement.

This process raises questions about whether there is sufficient organ-izational capacity within local government to manage such implemen-tation and whether the market is sufficiently developed to support implementation across the 400 or so authorities responsible for elec-tions in their areas. Many of the more rural authorities have limited technological and financial resources and may also lack the inclination to champion radical technology projects. It cannot be assumed that each authority has the expertise and knowledge to successfully procure appropriate technologies to support e-voting. The official evaluation of the 2002 pilots (Electoral Commission 2002) emphasizes the close rela-tionship between the individual authorities and the suppliers as a key feature of their success. It seems unlikely that if e-voting is 'rolled-out' in time for a General Election sometime around 2009 or 2010, that the organizational capacity and market will exist to sustain complete implementation, without some substantial intervention from central government.

The 2002 pilots

On 2 May 2002, a range of voting experiments took place in the local government elections of that day. These ranged from all postal ballots in mayoral elections (for example, Middlesbrough) through to multi-channel e-voting pilots using a combination of polling stations, kiosks, Internet, telephone and, even, SMS texts from mobile phones in some areas. While there had been some limited e-voting experiments in the May 2000 local government elections (see Local Government Association 2000), these experiments were far more sophisticated in their approach, for the first time offering UK voters (in selected areas) the opportunity to vote using electronic means, from their homes or other chosen location. In total there were 30 pilots across England, of which 17 involved some form of electronic voting or counting. Of these, five are particularly interesting, because they involved some combination of remote e-voting technology. These were:

- Crewe and Nantwich Borough Council that used Internet voting combined with traditional voting mechanisms (polling station and postal voting) in two wards.
- Liverpool City Council that used real-time Internet, telephone and SMS text messaging combined with traditional voting mechanisms (polling station and postal voting) in two wards.
- St Albans that used Internet and telephone voting combined with traditional voting mechanisms (polling station and postal voting) in two wards.
- Sheffield City Council that used real-time Internet, telephone and SMS text messaging combined with traditional voting mechanisms (polling station and postal voting) in three wards.
- Swindon Borough Council that used Internet and telephone voting combined with traditional voting mechanisms (polling station and postal voting) in all 19 wards that were involved in elections.

These were generally small-scale pilots that enabled a few thousand voters in each town to participate (with the exception of Swindon, which covered a much wider number of wards). However, they do allow some comparative experience of the different channels to be observed. Table 11.1 shows the proportion of voters in each of these areas opting to use the different channels available to them.

The pilots involved 11 different commercial suppliers who were selected by central government from an initial tender of 48 interested

Table 11.1   The five multi-channel pilots

	Polling stations/ postal votes		Internet		Telephone		SMS	
	No.	%	No.	%	No.	%	No.	%
Crewe & Nantwich BC (2 wards)	1,839	83.5	364	16.5	n. a.	n. a.	n. a.	n. a.
Liverpool City (2 wards)	3,957	59.4	1,093	16.4	1,162	17.4	445	6.7
St Albans (2 wards)	1,539	49.5	825	26.5	744	23.9	n. a.	n. a.
Sheffield (3 wards)	8,881	67.7	2,904	22.1	n. a.	n. a.	1,327	10.7
Swindon (19 wards)	33,329	84.1	4,293	10.8	2,028	5.1	n. a.	n. a.
Total	49,545	76.5	9,479	14.6	3,934	6.1	1,772	2.7

Source: Electoral Commission (2002): 44.

parties. These 11 suppliers included a cross-section of organizations from specialist companies with an established background in e-voting (for example, Powervote and Elections.com) through to large ICT companies with a vested interest in becoming involved in this new initiative (such as British Telecom). The total cost of the 17 e-voting pilots was around €6 million, of which, the five multi-channel pilots cost about €3.5 million. Somewhat ironically, the systems that allowed e-voting from within polling stations and which, consequently, only marginally increased voter convenience, were among the most expensive to implement.

Each pilot developed different processes for voting, including different advertising arrangements as well as different procedures for ensuring the security and integrity of the ballot. One of the key distinctions between the pilots, however, was between those that operated multi-channel voting in real time and those that operated them separately. Liverpool and Sheffield operated all of their different channels in real time. Registered voters could cast their ballot by any means right up until the close of polling. By contrast, others, such as Swindon, allowed remote electronic voting before the traditional polls opened, or conventional polling station voting on the day. The former were much more technologically sophisticated, requiring an interactive link to be maintained with the electoral register throughout the polling period.

By contrast, Swindon used a low-tech solution, by producing marked registers of all of those who had voted in advance of the polling day.

There can be little doubt that the pilots were a success for e-voting. As the official evaluation of the experiments states:

> Overall, the Commission believes that the May 2002 pilots successfully widened the choice of voting method available to those interested in participating in the election and secured significant increases in turnout in some pilot areas; the process was generally well managed by the local authorities and there were no significant technical problems. Although there were concerns in some areas about possible increased risk of fraud, the Commission has identified no evidence that these fears were realised in practice. (Electoral Commission 2000: 4)

Turnout increased in the pilot areas, although not as much in the e-voting areas as in the all-postal ballot areas. Survey work after the elections showed that very few voters objected to the new methods although a large majority (72 per cent) said that it had had no effect upon them. The commercial companies involved were at pains to emphasize that no security breaches had been recorded and that all had passed off smoothly. Furthermore, important lessons were learned. Technical lessons included some minor problems with the delays that can occur with SMS texting, which means that some votes cast shortly before the close of poll may not necessarily have been recorded by the system. Similarly the extent and nature of technical support necessary for effective implementation was also clarified. In terms of process, the political parties identified the issue of developing electronic marked registers that would enable them to tell who has voted (but not how they have voted) in order to help with vote mobilization: this is a common practice in the UK, normally achieved by tellers outside of the polling station asking those attending to identify themselves. The electronic exit polls conducted by some authorities even enabled them to identify by age and gender who had voted by which channel and when in each case. Indeed, the official evaluation highlights a wide range of useful lessons from the pilots and makes detailed recommendations on how these can be built on for future pilot programmes in 2003 and beyond. Important lessons have been learned that will support the development of more extended pilots and, eventually, full-scale implementation of e-voting. However, there remain questions over whether the pilots have successfully addressed or offered lessons for the larger barriers to implementation developed in the previous section.

Lessons and limitations

Returning to the evaluatory framework developed in the earlier section it is possible to explore the limits of the lesson building that the pilots can offer. In terms of organizational and market capacity, there probably have been significant lessons that will inform future developments. In relation to the other four barriers, however, lessons are much more limited.

First, the security and integrity of the vote has not really been tested in the pilots. It is true that no security breaches were identified during the pilots, although it is equally clear that an absence of identification does not mean that there can be absolute confidence in the process. Successful electoral fraud surely depends upon it not being spotted by the authorities. However, this point aside, the very limited scale of the elections means that they have not tested the security of the system effectively. There is a big difference between allowing a few thousand voters access to e-voting systems and putting a potential 44 million voters online. It is only when there is a big system in place that serious attempts to hack or defraud the system are likely to occur. Equally, it is only in the context of a large-scale implementation that the resource capacity of the system can be tested (including technical support and organizational capacity). The acid test for security and integrity can only really come when a General Election or other equally significant vote, such as a referendum, is widely exposed to e-voting. Even then, security will only be as good as the last election and will not promise indefinite protection against attack.

Second, an understanding of the secrecy and privacy of voting has not been addressed by the pilots. A legal challenge to postal voting was pursued by a City of Birmingham councillor in the aftermath of the 2002 elections, but this was rejected on a technical motion. No real legal challenge has yet been tested to establish the legality or otherwise of remote electronic voting. More significantly, the normative risks of remote voting, in which some social groups will have undue pressure exercised on them to vote in particular ways, has not really been explored in the context of the pilots. Indeed, some of the publicity surrounding the pilots showed groups of young people sitting together to cast their votes on mobile phones. If anything, the pilots appeared to endorse 'family' or 'collective' voting. It is notable that the official evaluation does not even make reference to this potential problem. It seems that pilot schemes cannot address this form of barrier: other approaches to understanding the problem are required.

Third, the issue of technological penetration and access is only tangentially addressed by the pilots. In some areas, such as Sheffield, kiosks distributed around the city allowed voters without direct access to the technology to still participate in the experiment. Similarly, some of the wider policies being adopted by the Office of the e-Envoy, such as the 6,000 UKOnline centres being made available, will help provide widespread and free access to the technologies. However, such schemes only begin to address the fourth problem of voter capacity and citizen confidence in e-voting. As we argued above, the ability to use e-voting systems is closely linked to day-to-day experience of using new technologies. This experience is, itself, linked to education and employment. The pilots and, indeed, the broader schemes to widen technological access, do little to increase voter capacity. As Table 11.1 shows, the majority of voters in the multi-channel areas still prefer traditional means of voting. The pilots, while popular among a few technologically literate and time-conscious individuals, have not really begun to challenge the more systemic biases that exist.

Overall, therefore, it is difficult to avoid the conclusion that the pilots tested and offered lessons for some of the small problems but made little contribution towards addressing the more substantive barriers that e-voting presents. The UK strategy for implementing e-voting is premised upon an expanding programme of pilots. While these pilots will offer significant lessons in such areas as organizational and market capacity, they will do little to address the more deep-rooted problems that face e-voting. If these more deep-rooted problems are not addressed, however, then e-voting could have a negative impact upon elections in the UK, rather than the hoped for renaissance. Pilots can and should only be one part of the implementation strategy.

References

BMRB (2002) *Public Attitudes Towards the Implementation of Electronic Voting: Qualitative Research Report*, <www.odpm.gov.uk/egov/e-voting>

California Internet Voting Task Force (2000) *A Report on the Feasibility of Internet Voting*, <www.ss.ca.gov>

Clarke, H., Sanders, D., Stewart, M. and Whiteley, P. (2001) *Britain (not) at the Polls, 2001*, <www.essex.ac.uk/bes/papers/pollsrev.doc>

Coleman, S. (2002) *Elections in the 21st Century: From Paper Ballot to e-Voting*. London: Electoral Reform Society.

Electoral Commission (2001) *Election 2001: The Official Results*. London: Electoral Commission.

Electoral Commission (2002) *Modernising Elections: A Strategic Evaluation of the 2002 Electoral Pilot Schemes*. London: Electoral Commission.

Fairweather, B. and Rogerson, S. (2002) *The Implementation of Electronic Voting in the UK: Technological Issues*, <www.odpm.gov.uk/egov/e-voting>

Internet Policy Institute (2001) *Report of the National Workshop on Internet Voting*, <www.nsf.gov>

Local Government Association (2000) *Elections – the 21st Century Model: An Evaluation of May 2000 Local Electoral Pilots*. London: Local Government Association.

Mercuri, R. (2001) 'Electronic Vote Tabulation Checks and Balances', PhD thesis: University of Pennsylvannia.

Office of the e-Envoy (2000) *e-Government: A Strategic Framework for Public Services in the Information Age*. London: Stationery Office.

Office of the e-Envoy (2002) *In the Service of Democracy: A Consultation Paper on a policy for Electronic Democracy*. London: Cabinet Office.

Parry, G., Moyser, G. and Day, N. (1992) *Political Participation and Democracy in Britain*. Cambridge: Cambridge University Press.

Pratchett, L., Birch, S., Candy, S., Fairweather, B., Rogerson, S., Stone, V., Watt, B. and Wingfield, M. (2002) *The Implementation of Electronic Voting in the UK*. London: Local Government Association.

Rallings, C., Temple, M. and Thrasher, M. (1996) 'Participation in Local Elections', in L. Pratchett and D. Wilson (eds), *Local Democracy and Local Government*. Basingstoke: Macmillan – Palgrave.

Schneier, B. (2000) *Secrets and Lies: Digital Security in a Networked World*. Chichester: John Wiley.

Watt, B. (2002) *The Implemnattion of Electronic Voting in the UK. Legal Issues*. London: Local Government Association.

Part III

Studies on Electronic Participation and Digital Divides

12
Will New Technology Boost Turnout? Evaluating Experiments in UK Local Elections

Pippa Norris

As access to the new communication and information technologies have diffused throughout post-industrial societies, the idea of using electronic tools to modernize electoral administration has been widely debated, with potential benefits of greater efficiency, speed and accuracy (for further details see Norris 2001a, 2002a, 2004). Perhaps the most important and influential argument concerns the claim that remote electronic voting will make the process more convenient and thereby strengthen electoral turnout and civic engagement, especially for the wired younger generation (see Stratford and Stratford 2001; Borgers 2001). If citizens will not come to the polls, it is argued, why not bring the polls closer to citizens? In Britain, after all, like horse-hair wigs on the judiciary, and men-in-tights in the House of Lords, the traditional method of expressing voting preferences by writing crosses on ballots, depositing them in black boxes in local polling stations, then counting the piles of paper in public halls, has essentially not changed since the 1888 Secret Ballot Act.

Much speculation and industry-generated hype surround the virtuous of remote electronic voting, yet until recently almost no systematic evidence derived from actual elections was available to evaluate this issue. Given the vital importance of maintaining public confidence in the legitimacy and fairness of the electoral process, and the potential for even small details to cause disruption (exemplified by Floridian hanging 'chads' and butterfly ballots), policy-makers need careful cautious and critical evidence-based evaluations throwing light on the pros and cons of implementing remote e-voting.

Evidence to evaluate this question is drawn here from the results of a series of innovative experiments conducted by the UK Electoral Commission using 59 pilot voting schemes available to 6.4 million citizens (14 per cent of the English electorate) in the 1 May 2003 English local elections. These contests are characteristically low-salience campaigns, determining control of local town halls up and down the land, but commonly stirring minimal interest among the media and the public. Turnout is usually fairly low; for example only one-third of the electorate voted in the previous year's contests. The most recent range of pilot schemes used by the UK Election Commission provide an exceptionally good test of the effects of modernizing electoral administration and voting facilities. Implications can be drawn well-beyond the particular context, as the electorate in each district cast legal votes with the outcome determining the election of local representatives and the partisan control of councils.

These studies built upon the experience of the more limited pilot schemes tried in 2000 and 2002. In the May 2003 elections, 59 different English local districts tested alternative ways of facilitating electronic voting, including use of the Internet from home and public access sites, interactive digital television, SMS text messaging and touch-tone telephones. Pilots also used all-postal ballots, getting electronic information to voters, extended voting periods, and electronic counting.

The evidence from the election results, and from the survey conducted after the contest, confirms that use of all-postal voting facilities generated a turnout of about 50 per cent, compared with average turnout of about 35 per cent in the same districts. All-postal voting also improved public satisfaction with the electoral process, as intended. Nevertheless there are good reasons to be skeptical about claims that electronic technologies can automatically resuscitate electoral participation. Remote e-voting, in particular, may expand citizen choice, but it proved far less effective in improving turnout than the implementation of old-fashioned snail-mail (all-postal ballots). The age profile of who used different voting mechanisms provides an important clue to their effects.

The UK Electoral Commission (2003) has evaluated the results of the trials and this analysis will contribute towards the government's proposed reforms of voting procedures in future UK elections. The July 2003 report issued by the UK Electoral Commission, *The Shape of Elections to Come*, recommended rolling out all-postal votes as standard practice for all local elections, with further evaluation before this practice is extended to other types of election. With regard to electronic voting, the Commission reached far more cautious conclusions, suggesting these should continue to be tested, with the overall aim of using electronic voting as a way of providing citizens with more choice about how they cast their ballots, rather than of improving turnout.

To consider these issues, the following section summarizes what we know about the technological, social and practical barriers to electronic voting and about electoral engineering and turnout. I shall then set out the context of the UK local elections and describe the pilot schemes, followed by a consideration of the macro and micro-level evidence about the impact of modernizing voting facilities on electoral turnout, comparing all-postal ballots with the use of a variety of electronic technologies. The conclusion summarizes the results and considers their broader implications for the impact of new technologies on citizen participation and civic engagement.

The pros and cons of remote e-voting

The modernization of electoral administration is often regarded as a logical extension of technological developments widely used in communications, commerce and government. One of the most common forms of modernization concerns electronic voting, which can be sub-divided into two categories:

- *Remote electronic voting* (or remote e-voting for short), is understood here as the transmission of a secure and secret official ballot to electoral officials via various electronic information and communication technologies at a site located away from the polling station, whether from home, the workplace or a public access point. Remote e-voting is sometimes thought to refer only to Internet voting, but in this study we can compare many electronic devices which are capable of transmitting an electronic ballot, including computers, touch-tone terrestrial telephones, cell (mobile) phones, text messaging devices and digital televisions.
- By contrast, *on-site electronic voting* technologies are used to vote within the traditional physical location of a polling station, exemplified by touch-activated screens, dedicated computer terminals or electronic counting devices, as debated after the Florida debacle.

Proponents suggest many advantages that may come from implementing remote e-voting:

- The most important is the added convenience for citizens. By using a telephone, computer, palmtop device or digital television to cast a ballot from home or the workplace, citizens could reduce the time and effort traditionally required to participate in person at the polling station. This may help overcome problems of social exclusion, especially for those with limited mobility such as the elderly, caregivers confined to the home by dependent relatives, or employees and shift-workers with little flexibility in their work hours, as well as for those who are travelling away from home and for overseas residents. The implementation of remote e-voting can be regarded in many respects as an extension of the use of other familiar and well-tested voting facilities already widely available in many countries, including the use of postal, absentee, oversees or advance ballots (see IDEA 2003). In the June 2001 UK general election, for example, 1.3 million postal votes were cast, representing 5.2 per cent of all ballots (House of Commons 2003).
- Moreover both remote and on-site electronic voting could potentially reduce the information costs of participation, and allow citizens to match their preferences more accurately to their electoral decisions, by providing relevant information at the time that people are casting their ballot, for example by incorporating an optional webpage display of photos and standardized biographies linked to each candidate, or by providing a briefing synopsis explaining each side of a referendum issue.
- For officials, well-designed and effective electronic technologies, either remote or onsite, could potentially improve and streamline the process of electoral administration by increasing the efficiency, speed and accuracy of recording and counting votes (Arterton 1987; Budge 1996; Rash 1997; Rheingold 1993; Barber 1998).

For all these reasons, the idea of e-voting has been hailed by advocates, particularly those in the industry, as an automatic 'magic ballot' that could entice more people to vote, make citizens more informed, and improve vote-counting.

Against these arguments, skeptics counter that many contemporary limitations – technological, socioeconomic and practical – combine to create substantial barriers to the effective implementation of e-voting.

Technological barriers

Democratic electoral systems must meet certain stringent standards of security, data-protection, secrecy, reliability, accuracy, efficiency, integrity and equality. Public confidence in the integrity of the electoral system must be maintained to ensure the legitimacy of the outcome, which makes the administrative challenges of e-voting more difficult than the implementation of many common forms of electronic government or commerce, even banking. If poorly implemented, citizens could be discouraged from voting via new technologies, for example the design could prove difficult for the disabled, those with low literacy skills, or the elderly. Electronic votes cast in a general election could be a high-profile target for malicious publicity-seeking hackers. The bursting of the dot.com bubble, combined with the recent spate of disruptive viruses and the inundation of e-mail spam, may have depressed public confidence in the security of the Internet. Critics claim that the technology required to authenticate voters, and to assure the accuracy and integrity of the election system, either does not exist at present, or is not sufficiently available to prove equitable and effective. Task forces reviewing the evidence, such as the US NSF and the UK Electoral Reform Society, have proved doubtful about the technological, security and legal issue surrounding e-voting, suggesting that further exploratory pilot studies are required before adoption (see IPI 2002; Electoral Reform Society 2002).

When remote e-voting has been tried in small-scale pilot studies, so far the security and technological issues involved in casting hundreds of votes electronically have often proved problematic. In October 2001, for example, the residents of the Dutch towns of Leidschendam and Voorburg were given the chance to vote via the Internet on the choices for the merged towns' new name. The vote was abandoned when it became obvious that more votes had been cast than there were electors.[1] The Arizona Democratic primary election, which also experienced many technical glitches, has been widely quoted, although it remains difficult to assess how far we can generalize from the particular circumstances surrounding this unique contest (Gibson 2002; Solop 2001). Government schemes for remote e-voting in official elections have been developed in the Swiss cantons of Geneva, Zurich and Neuchatel, and first implemented officially in a Geneva referendum in January 2003 (Auer and Trechsel 2001). Internet voting has also been employed as an option for shareholder elections by companies such as Chevron, Lucent Technologies and Xerox, as well as in student elections (Dictson and Ray 2000).

It remains unclear whether the purely *administrative* problems revolving at present around the practical issues of security, secrecy and integrity might eventually be resolved in future by suitable technological and scientific innovations. Potential problems of voter fraud might be overcome by advances in biometric voice, retina scanning and fingerprint recognition, for example, or by the widespread use of 'smart cards' as identifiers with a computer chip and unique digital certificates.

Social barriers

Setting aside these important technical and security matters for the moment, another fundamental issue concerns the potential problems that could arise if remote e-voting serves to exacerbate existing structural inequalities in electoral participation. In democracies the electoral process has to be equally available to every citizen, without discriminating against any particular group. This important principle is widely recognized in locating traditional polling stations throughout local communities, or in translating the instructions for registration and voting into the languages spoken by minority populations. Critics charge that implementation of remote e-voting from home or work could violate the equitable principle, given the widespread existence of the familiar 'digital divide' in Internet access. Making remote voting easier for those with access to electronic technologies could further skew who participates, and therefore politically influence more affluent and wired socioeconomic groups. While not actively harming poorer neighborhoods, remote e-voting could still potentially privilege some social sectors.

This argument holds less force when it comes to remote voting through special dedicated public terminals located in the community, such as any voting facilities established in libraries, schools or even supermarkets, where similar principles would apply to those determining the location of traditional polling stations. But the argument becomes relevant if remote e-voting is available from any home or workplace computer terminal, which is the most radical and exciting application of this principle.

Official estimates suggest that by spring 2003 about half of the British population (54%) had used the Internet in the previous three months, and 60 per cent had used the Internet at some time (National Statistics Omnibus Survey 2003). About 40 per cent of households had an Internet connection, a higher proportion than the European average (see Table 12.1). Other common communication technologies remain far more widespread, however, including the availability of mobile phones, found in 65 per cent of households. Other technologies are also widely available throughout Britain, including digital TVs (in 35 per cent of households), VCRs, Teletext TV, Satellite TV, and fax machines.

Many have expressed concern about the 'digital divide', the substantial differential in Internet access between the information haves and have-nots, including among rich and poor, as well as between graduates and those with minimal educational qualifications, between the younger and older generations, as well as among countries (Norris 2001). The European digital divide in the mid-1990s presents a similar picture to that found in the United States; in 1996, access was concentrated among the younger generations, more affluent households, university graduates, managers and white-collar workers (as well as students), and, to a lesser extent, among men (see Gönlund in this volume). By spring 2000 the social profile in Europe has not changed that much as the strongest rise in access has been among the most affluent households, the well-educated, and among managerial professionals, although use has spread rapidly among the early-middle aged, as well as the youngest age group. Multivariate analysis confirms that

Table 12.1 Trends in household access to communication technologies, UK 1970–2002

	Telephone	Mobile phone	Video recorder	Satellite receiver[a]	Home computer	Internet connection
1970	35	—	—	—	—	—
1975	52	—	—	—	—	—
1980	72	—	—	—	—	—
1985	81	—	30	—	13	—
1990	87	—	61	—	17	—
1994–95	91	—	76	—	—	—
1995–96	92	—	79	—	—	—
1996–97	93	16	82	19	27	—
1997–98	94	20	84	26	29	—
1998–99	95	26	86	27	32	9
1998–99	95	27	85	28	33	10
1999–2000	95	44	86	32	38	19
2000–01	93	47	87	40	44	32
2001–02	94	65	90	43	49	40

Note: Percentage of UK households with durable goods 1970 to 2001-02. [a]Includes digital and cable receivers.
Sources: UK Expenditure and Food Survey <www.statistics.government.uk/StatBase>

by 2000 the digital divide remains significant by age, gender, education, income and class, as well as showing the marked contrasts in access among the countries of Northern and Southern Europe. The age effects turn out to be very important for turnout, as discussed later.

This familiar pattern suggests that if remote e-voting, via computer terminals in the home or workplace, were introduced into UK elections within the next few years,[2] then the digital divide will probably reinforce, or even widen, many of the familiar socioeconomic disparities in electoral participation that already exist, including those of social class, education, gender and income (Norris 2002). Yet there is one important qualification to this conclusion, as remote electronic voting could encourage younger people to take advantage of this opportunity. Of course this argument does not apply to other forms of remote e-voting, such as via public kiosks at traditional polling stations, or in public access locations such as libraries, town halls, schools and community centres. On the other hand, the real advantages of using electronic voting are reduced through these channels, because people would still have to travel to a public location, while the disadvantages of electronic over paper ballots for administrative security remain.

Practical barriers

For the purposes of exploring the arguments further let us assume for the moment that the familiar digital divide in society is in the process of shrinking, as access to the wide range of new communication and information technologies, including text-messaging mobile phones, teletext digital television and the Internet, gradually diffuse throughout affluent societies. If the issues of technological security and of socioeconomic equality are resolved, the key question then arises whether the introduction of remote e-voting would actually facilitate participation.

There are many reasons to remain skeptical about this claim. The theory that we can use to understand electoral participation, developed more fully elsewhere, suggests that the incentives motivating citizens to cast a ballot represent a product of three factors (see Norris 2002, 2004 chapter 5): *electoral costs* involved in registering to vote, sorting out relevant information, deciding how to vote, and then actually casting a ballot; *electoral choices,* determined largely by the range of parties, candidates and issues listed on the ballot paper; and, *electoral decisiveness,* influenced by how far votes cast for each party, candidate or issue are thought to determine the outcome.

1 *Electoral costs.* The theory assumes that rational citizens will be less likely to vote if they face major electoral costs of participating. This includes registering as electors, becoming informed about the issues, parties and candidates, and finally casting a ballot to express their voting choice. Standard rational-choice theories suggest that, all other things being equal, the deterrent of higher costs reduces electoral participation.

Holding elections on a weekend or holiday, or over a series of days, rather than on a workday can reduce costs. Registration procedures also are often believed to be an important hurdle. In many countries, including Britain, Sweden and Canada, registration is the responsibility of the government, conducted via a door-to-door canvas or annual census, so most eligible citizens are automatically enrolled to vote. In others including the United States, France and Brazil citizens have to apply to register, often well-ahead of the election, and complicated, time-consuming or restrictive practices can depress participation levels (Katz 1997: Table 13.2).[3]

In this regard, the use of remote e-voting can be seen as essentially similar in principle to other remote voting facilities in common use for casting a ballot, exemplified by the widespread availability of special arrangements for mobile populations, including the use of mail, proxy, absentee or overseas votes, as well as polling facilities for the elderly and disabled in nursing homes and hospitals (see IDEA 2003; Maley 2000, Blais and Masciotte 2000; Crewe 1986; Powell 1086; Jackman 1987; Jackman and Miller 1995; Blais and Dobrzynska 1998; Lijphart 1997). But casting the ballot is only the last step in the electoral decision-making process, and not necessarily the most significant one if people lack the sense that they have electoral choices matching their preferences, and that voting counts towards the outcome.

2 *Electoral choices.* These are determined by broader characteristics of the political system including the options available on the ballot, notably the range of parties and candidates contesting elected offices, and the policy alternatives listed for referenda issues. In turn, these options can be related to the type of electoral system, the party system, and other basic political institutions such as parliamentary or presidential executives.

Rational-voter theories suggest that in general, all other things being equal, the greater the range of choices available on the ballot, the more the public will find an option (a party, candidate or referendum issue) that reflects their own viewpoint, preferences and interests, and therefore the stronger the incentive to vote. Remote e-voting is unlikely to have an impact on any of these factors.

3 *Electoral Decisiveness.* Electoral decisiveness is also important, meaning the political benefits anticipated from casting a ballot in determining the composition of parliament, of government, and the public policy agenda. In elections that are anticipated to be close (on the basis of past results, opinion polls or media commentary), citizens are likely to feel a greater incentive to get to the polls than in those where the outcome appears to be a foregone conclusion. Of course the actual benefits of casting a single vote may, on purely rational grounds, be illusory, because one vote is unlikely to decide the outcome of an election, but this is not to deny the psychological belief that in close elections, each vote is believed to count for more than in safe contests. Hence, for example, British studies have found that the closer the difference in the national shares of the vote between the two major parties, the higher the level of electoral participation during the postwar era (Heath and Taylor 1999). The marginality of British constituencies has also commonly been found to be one of the best predictors of turnout in each seat (Whiteley 2001).

There are trade-offs between electoral choices and electoral decisiveness. Widening the range of choices on the ballot paper may allow citizens to find a closer match to their interests, but if the party system becomes too fragmented with multiple choices, then the outcome of casting a vote for smaller parties will be even less likely to influence the outcome, whether for parliament, government or the policy agenda. Moreover a wider range of choices also simultaneously increased the costs of becoming informed about alternative candidates, parties and issues.

Given this understanding, this study hypothesizes that the introduction of remote e-voting from the home or workplace would probably marginally reduce the costs of casting a ballot at a polling station. But e-voting would be unlikely to affect other important costs, such as the significant cognitive demands required to sort out the relevant information in deciding how to vote, nor would it influence electoral choices and electoral decisiveness. As such the Internet cannot be regarded as a magic panacea for all the ills of electoral participation, which are the result of many deep-seated forces, particularly how far citizens feel that they have a genuine choice that matches their prior preferences, and that casting a ballot influences the outcome.

Turnout, political institutions, legal rules and voting facilities

To examine some of the available evidence on these issues, drawn from a broader forthcoming study examining patterns of activism worldwide (see Norris 2002), Table 12.2 compares levels of turnout (measured as the number of valid votes cast as a proportion of the voting-age population)[4] in 70 national parliamentary or presidential elections held during the 1990s in 25 established democracies.[5] Model A examines the impact of *voting facilities*, including the use of automatic or voluntary registration processes, the number of polling days, the use of rest days or workdays for polling, postal voting, proxy voting, special polling booths, transfer voting and advance voting. In contrast, model B examines the role of *political institutions* for elections, which have commonly been found to influence patterns of turnout,[6] including the basic type of electoral system, the mean district magnitude, the frequency of elections, whether a parliamentary or presidential contest, and the level of fragmentation in the party system (for the full theoretical reasons for the inclusion of these items, as well as their operationalization and measurement, see the discussion in Norris 2002a: chapter 4). Model B also examines the impact of the *legal rules* including the use of compulsory voting, the age of voting eligibility, and the length of women's enfranchisement. Model C presents the combined impact of all the factors under consideration. All the regression models control for socioeconomic level and degree of democratization, which are important in worldwide comparisons although these factors prove largely insignificant predictors of voter participation among affluent post-industrial societies sharing similar levels of economic development and an established tradition of political rights and civil liberties.

The result of the analysis in model A in Table 12.2 shows that, after controlling for levels of development among voting facilities, only polling on a rest day proved to provide a significant boost to turnout in established democracies; in contrast the use of proxy voting and the number of days that the polling stations were open proved to be significant but *negatively* associated with turnout, perhaps because countries concerned about low turnout try to increase the opportunities to get to the polls. Other special voting facilities, such as the availability of postal or advance voting, as well as the use of automatic or voluntary registration procedures, proved to be unrelated to levels of electoral turnout. Overall the results suggest that the role of voting facilities (in model A) proved to explain far less variance in electoral participation than the role of institutions and legal rules (in model B). Among institutional variables, voting participation is most likely to be

Table 12.2 Explaining turnout in 25 older democracies in national elections held during the 1990s

	Model A				Model B				Model C			
	b	(s.e.)	St. beta	Sig.	B	(s.e.)	St. beta	Sig.	B	(s.e.)	St. beta	Sig.
Constant	98.6	(40.70)		**	40.5	(44.2)			11.707	(79.18)		
Development												
Human development	-.051	(.040)	-.12		-.076	(.036)	-.39	*	-.071	(.037)	-.35	
Level of democratization	2.23	(2.26)	.17	3.576	.28		.50			(2.23)	.04	
Political institutions												
Electoral system					2.952	(1.87)	.19		8.34	(2.68)	.55	**
Population per MP					-.0262	(.00)	-.56	**	-.044	(.000)	-.11	
Frequency of election					-1.386	(.871)	-.18		-4.00	(1.33)	-.53	**
Presidential election					4.042	(2.95)	.11		3.81	(2.79)	.10	
Fragmented party system					3.546	(4.16)	.09	-4.00		(5.07)	-.11	
Legal rules												
Age of voting eligibility					3.630	(2.14)	.14		5.71	(3.99)	.22	
Length of women's enfranchisement					.416	(.078)	.54	***	.322	(.095)	.42	***
Use of compulsory voting					10.413	(2.75)	.34	***	14.87	(3.53)	.49	***
Voting facilities												
Automatic registration	6.32	(3.33)	.22						-4.37	(5.49)	-.16	
Number of polling days	-12.19	(3.49)	-.65	***					.696	(6.03)	.04	
Polling on rest day	7.20	(3.44)	.24	*					-8.94	(5.08)	-.30	

Table 12.2 Explaining turnout in 25 older democracies in national elections held during the 1990s *continued*

	Model A				Model B				Model C			
	b	*(s.e.)*	*St. beta*	*Sig.*	*B*	*(s.e.)*	*St. beta*	*Sig.*	*B*	*(s.e.)*	*St. beta*	*Sig.*
Postal voting	1.22	(3.21)	.04						−5.43	(3.38)	−.20	
Proxy voting	−11.55	(3.50)	−.40	**					5.60	(4.98)	.19	
Special polling booths	1.070	(3.92)	.03						6.90	(3.11)	.23	*
Transfer voting	3.67	(3.34)	.13						5.03	(3.00)	.18	
Advance voting	1.78	(3.44)	.06						−3.59	(3.13)	−.12	
Number of elections	70				70				70			
Adjusted R2	.339	(11.16)			.687	(7.68)			.735	(7.06)		

Notes: Vote/VAP is measured as the number of valid votes as a proportion of the Voting Age Population in 70 parliamentary and presidential national elections in 25 older democracies during the 1990s. The figures represent unstandardized regression coefficients, standard errors, standardized beta coefficients, and significance, with mean vote/VAP as the dependent variable. *=p<.05 ** p<.01 ***p<.001; Human Development:* Human Development Index 1998 combining literacy, education and income; UNDP. *Level of Democratization:* Freedom House Index in the year of the election. Combined reversed 14-point scale of political rights and civic liberties; Freedom House, <www.freedomhouse.org> *Electoral system:* Majoritarian/plurality (1), semi-proportional (2), PR (3). *Party System:* Fragmented party system where the party in 1st place gets 30 per cent of the vote or less. *Compulsory Voting:* Australia, Belgium, Costa Rica, Cyprus, Greece, Italy, Luxembourg. *All Voting Facilities:* Coded Yes (1) No (0). *Source:* Calculated from International IDEA database *Voter Turnout from 1945 to 2000,* <www.idea.int>. For full technical details see Norris (2002a).

maximized in national elections using proportional representation, with small electoral districts, regular but relatively infrequent national contests, competitive party systems, and in presidential contests. The final equation in model C, including all structural and developmental factors, successfully explains almost three-quarters of the variance in turnout among established democracies. In the final model, the most important factors concern the type of electoral system (whether PR or not), the frequency of elections (where more frequent contests depress turnout through voter fatigue), the length of women's enfranchisement, the use of compulsory (see p. 00) voting (in worldwide comparisons including consolidating democracies the use of compulsory voting was not significant, probably due to differences in implementation), and after introducing all the controls, among voting facilities only the provision of special polling booths proved significant at conventional levels.

This limited analysis only briefly examines a few of the structural factors that can be expected to influence the costs, choices and decisiveness of elections, and survey analysis is necessary for a fuller examination of the social psychology of voting participation (see Norris 2002 chapter 5). Nevertheless if we can draw a valid analogy between the provision of existing voting facilities like postal ballots and the proposed use of the Internet to register and vote from home or work, then this evidence suggests that e-voting would have only little or no effect on turnout. Elections need to matter, and there need to be an effective range of real choices on the ballot for citizens to believe that they can make at least a symbolic difference to the outcome through casting a vote. If European elections are widely regarded as largely irrelevant to the policy outcome, or if people do not feel that they are presented with choices which represent their interests, then no matter if casting a vote becomes as easy as clicking a mouse, participation levels will, unfortunately, probably remain miserably low.

Evidence for evaluating remote e-voting

What evidence would allow us to evaluate these issues? Here we can turn to the British case, which has gone further than any other country in testing the impact of a wide variety of remote e-voting technologies using official ballots cast during actual elections.

Concern about electoral participation has risen in Britain. During postwar general elections, UK turnout (measured as the proportion of the voting-age population casting a valid vote) has seen a broad picture of trendless fluctuations (see Kersting and Baldersheim in this volume). But the 2001 UK general election saw turnout plummet, from 71.5 per cent to 59.4 per cent of the electorate, the lowest level since the 'khaki' election of 1918. Moreover, this followed a series of local elections from 1998 to 2000 that witnessed historically low levels of turnout, reaching the nadir of one-quarter (27%) of the electorate bothering to vote in 2000 (see Figure 12.1). If unchecked, this pattern is worrying for democracy as the legitimacy of the electoral process, and the mandate of the government, might eventually be undermined.

The Labour government has proposed modernizing electoral administration in an attempt to reengage the electorate. Recent changes enabled by the Representation of the People Acts 2000 and 2001 include universal postal voting (available on request without needing a reason), an extension of the traditional polling hours, and more modern methods of how citizens can cast their ballots, including the possible use of telephone and Internet-based voting.

The UK Electoral Commission is the official agency charged with implementing the process of modernization and advising the Deputy Prime Minister about the most effective options in electoral administration. Innovations in polling places, polling hours, and all-postal

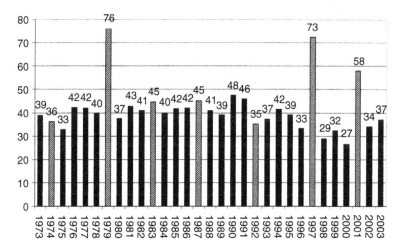

Figure 12.1 Turnout in UK local elections, 1973–2003
Note: Turnout is defined here as valid votes cast as a percentage of the eligible electorate. The highlighted (striped) columns are general election years. When both contests are held simultaneously, local election turnout rises sharply. When held separately, turnout is closer to the local election average.
Source: Rallings and Thrasher (2000).

ballots were tested in 38 pilot schemes used among 3.5 million eligible electors in the May 2000 local elections. All-postal ballots remove the need for citizens to apply for a mail ballot; instead local authorities provide all citizens on the electoral register in an area with the automatic ability to cast a mail ballot during an extended period of about two weeks prior to Election Day. These initiatives were followed in the May 2002 local elections by 30 more pilots tried among 2.5 million eligible electors with a greater range of innovations directed at improving turnout, counting and the provision of information. The Commission concluded that these generated interesting preliminary results, with significant increases in voting turnout (particularly from all-postal voting schemes), no significant technical problems of implementation or electoral management, and no evidence of fraud. Following evaluation, the government signalled its desire to use electronic voting by the next general election after 2006 (Office of the e-Envoy 2002), and the Spending Review allocated substantial resources to fund further pilot studies conducted at local government level. Nevertheless, many significant questions remained concerning variations in turnout among wards, the best methods of avoiding electoral fraud, and issues of scalability across whole councils. The Commission concluded that the initial lessons needed to be tested more extensively, especially facilities for remote e-voting using multiple technologies (UK Electoral Commission 2002).

The May 2003 pilot schemes

Accordingly a further series of 59 pilot schemes were conducted in the May 2003 local elections, the focus of this chapter (see also Pratchett and Wingfield in this volume). In total, 17 of the 2003 pilot schemes explored innovative ways of remote electronic voting using a range of technologies including mobile phone text-message services, touch telephones, local digital television, online Internet voting using home computers, terminals in local libraries, and council-run information kiosks. For comparison, the Electoral Commission also continued to examine the use of all-postal ballots in over half the pilot schemes (see Karp and Banducci 2000). Examples of the May 2003 initiatives included:

- Chorley offered electors all-postal ballots, Internet and telephone voting throughout their area, and used electronic counting.
- Ipswich offered citizens Internet, telephone and SNS text-messaging ballots.

- Shrewsbury and Atcham used all-postal voting, Internet, telephone and digital TV voting, as well as electronic counting.
- Sheffield used voting via public kiosks, Internet, telephone and mobile phone text-messaging.
- Medway, and Windsor and Maidenhead, extended traditional voting hours.

Other pilots used electronic counting, mobile polling stations and extended polling hours. Timing is believed to be important: most countries hold their elections on a single day, usually at the weekend that makes it easier for employed people to visit a polling station. In a few countries, however, elections are spread over more than one day. Franklin (2002) compared average turnout 1960–95 in parliamentary elections in 29 countries and found that compulsory voting, Sunday voting and postal voting facilities all proved important predictors, along with the proportionality of the electoral system, although not the number of days that polls were open.

The political context of the May 2003 local elections

The political context of the UK local elections in May 2003 concerned a mid-term contest with elections to the Scottish Parliament and the Welsh Assembly, as well as local government elections in Scotland and England (outside of Greater London). The last time the English councils came up for election, in 1999, the Conservatives gained 1,300 seats, many from Labour, despite these results failing to translate into any substantial progress for the Conservative party in the 2001 general election. In May 2003, in a low-key campaign, it was widely expected that Labour would experience some electoral damage, after being in power for six years and during a period of public disquiet about the perceived lacklustre delivery of public services, as well as massive opposition to Blair's support for the Iraq war. The question before the election was which opposition party would benefit most from Labour's mid-term blues in terms of gains in the share of votes, seats and councils.

On election night, the Conservatives won 35 per cent of the local council vote, a modest (+1%) rise from 2002. Nevertheless, they enjoyed net gains of 566 seats, winning control of an additional 31 councils. The Liberal Democrats also had a successful night, with an estimated 27 per cent of the vote, making net gains of 193 seats and five councils (House of Commons 2002). The far-right anti-immigration British National Party achieved a controversial local triumph by fielding a record 221 candidates (many in the north-east and north-west), gaining 11 seats, becoming the second largest party in Burnley. Labour were the main losers in the English council elections, with 30 per cent of the vote (down 3 per cent from 2002), suffering a net loss of 883 seats and 28 councils. This was a substantial loss, although not outstanding historically for a mid-term period. At the same time Labour retained a working majority in the Welsh Assembly, and they were returned again as the biggest party in the Scottish Parliament.

Two sources of evidence are available to analyse the patterns of turnout. First we can examine the change in the macro levels of turnout in the local authority districts using the pilot schemes in May 2003 compared against the level of turnout in the last benchmark election in these same areas.[7]

Moreover, to understand the micro-level behaviour of voters, and the reasons behind patterns of electoral participation, we can analyse the post-election survey conducted by MORI on behalf of the Electoral Commission in these districts. MORI interviewed a representative sample of approximately 200 adults aged 18+ in 29 of the 59 authorities which were piloting new voting arrangements at the May 2003 elections. A total of 6,185 interviews were conducted. Quotas were set by age, gender and work status with approximately 100 voters and 100 non-voters interviewed in each authority. Data were weighted by age, sex and working status to the known profile (using 2001 census data), and by turnout on 1 May 2003. Aggregate data were also weighted by the population size of each pilot authority. Fieldwork took place between 2–12 May 2003.[8]

The impact of e-voting

There were many reasons, both long-term and short-term, to expect that electoral participation would fall further in these contests. In Britain power has gradually drained away from town halls, as more and more attempts have been made by both Conservative and Labour administrations to curtail local fiscal autonomy and control the standards of public service delivery in local areas. People may also be suffering increasingly from voter fatigue and 'election overload': compared with previous decades, there are now a regular series of European elections, Mayoral elections, and Scottish/Welsh regional elections, and occasional referenda, as well as general elections and local elections. As with other new assemblies, the first elections to the Scottish Parliament and Welsh Assembly could also be expected to attract higher than average turnout through a 'honeymoon' effect, and participation would be likely to fall in subsequent contests.

The particular May 2003 election was also a low-key affair. Since they came to power in 1997, Labour had enjoyed a continuous lead over the Conservatives in the national monthly opinion polls (with one minor blip). Usually in British elections, the safer the government's lead, the lower the turnout (Heath and Taylor 1999). In addition, since Labour moved back into the centre of the political spectrum in the mid-1990s, British party competition has moderated. Voters today perceive few major contrasts between the main parties on most issues, with Labour under the leadership of Tony Blair bang in the centre of the political spectrum, the Liberal Democrats under Charles Kennedy close by to the centre-left, and the Conservatives flailing away under Iain Duncan Smith somewhere towards the right (Norris and Lovenduski 2004). The local election campaign also had fairly fuzzy issues: there was little conflict over the issues of taxes and spending, education and health, and nothing like the way that the issue of the Conservative Poll Tax mobilized voters during the early 1990s. The public and the news media had paid even less attention than usual to the local campaign in the run-up to polling day, with events in Iraq dominating the headlines. In the run-up to the election, most of the editorial speculation about domestic politics had surrounded who might replace the Conservative leader, Iain Duncan Smith, in the event of a poor result for Tory Central Office, and whether the nationalists would do well in Scotland.

Given this context, not surprisingly the overall level of turnout in May 2003 was 49 per cent in Scotland (down 9 per cent from 1999, the inaugural election for the Scottish Parliament), and 38.2 per cent in Wales (down 8%). In England, however, despite expectations, local government turnout was 37 per cent, a rise of 5 per cent from 1999 and a rise of 3 per cent from 2002. How far was the increase in the English local elections due to the pilot initiatives?

Table 12.3 shows the districts where all-postal voting was used, the most comparable previous election, the turnout in May 2003, and the change in turnout. The results illustrate the outstanding success of all-postal ballots: on average turnout increased from one-third (34%) to almost half (49.3%) of the electorate in these districts. The increase was even more remarkable in some of the northern areas that had been lowest in turnout, almost doubling voting participation in Blyth Valley, for example, as well as Rotherham, Sunderland and Blackpool. By contrast, there were more modest increases registered in most councils, and only three cases with any slight fall. The fact that a 15 per cent increase in turnout was also found in the 2002 all-postal pilots confirms the consistency and robustness of these results. The Electoral Commission also found very limited evidence that the use of all-postal ballots led to any increase in fraud or electoral offences. Of course part of the rise in turnout there could be due to a one-off 'Hawthorne effect', if local authorities mounting these initiatives publicize the opportunities to vote by mail more actively than usual, and if voters respond to the publicity and to the novelty-value. On the other hand, the fact that the rise in turnout was fairly substantial and reasonably consistent across many different types of urban and rural areas, as well as parts of England, suggests that at least some of the benefits of postal voting are likely to persist if used more widely in future local elections.

By contrast, the districts using electronic voting showed a far more mixed picture of turnout, as illustrated in Table 12.4 and Figure 12.2. Overall only about 9 per cent of the electorate in these districts used the electronic technologies to cast a ballot, with most of the public opting for traditional methods of voting. Three districts using electronic voting (South Salisbury, Shrewsbury and Atcham, and Vale Royal) did experience a rise in turnout of 9–12 per cent, but two of these also used all-postal voting as well. Overall, two-thirds of the areas experimenting with electronic voting registered a modest fall in turnout, not any rise, disappointing the hopes of the reformers.

Both all-postal voting and remote electronic voting share certain important features, both offering voters additional convenience over traditional in-person visits to the polling station. So why should areas using these facilities generate such different patterns of macro-level turnout? Here we need to turn to the micro-level survey data to understand more fully how the public responded to these opportunities, and which social groups used the all-postal and electronic voting facilities. In particular, even if the electronic facilities generated no positive effects in aggregate turnout that were evident at district level, there could still be differential patterns in which certain social groups took greatest advantage of the new voting facilities. In particular it is important to monitor whether younger people – who are both the most wired generation and also the group least likely to turn out using conventional methods – might prove more likely than average to use electronic voting facilities. Figure 12.3 shows the familiar curvilinear pattern of reported voting by age (in years): as a multitude of studies have found, younger people are persistently less

Table 12.3 Impact of all-postal voting in the 1 May 2003 UK local election pilot schemes

Name of authority	Year of last comparable election	% Turnout at last comparable election	Type of election this time (full/3rd)	Start of polling date	% Total turnout May 2003	Change in % turnout since last comparable election
Blyth Valley BC	1999	27	Whole	15 April	52.00	25
Rotherham MBC	2002	27	Thirds	17 April	51.30	24
Sunderland City C	2002	22	Thirds	17 April	46.46	24
Herefordshire CC	1999	38	Whole	15/17 April	61.00	23
Blackpool BC	2000	29	Whole	17 April	50.43	22
St Helens MBC	2002	26	Thirds	17 April	48.00	22
Stockton-on-Tees BC	1999	31	Whole	13 April	52.00	22
Derwentside, Chester le Street & Wear Valley	1999	31	Whole	17 April	52.40	21
Lincoln City C	2002	26	Thirds	17 April	47.33	21
Telford & Wrekin	1999	28	Whole	10 April	48.65	21
DarlingtonBC	1999	34	Whole	14 April	51.54	18
Doncaster C	2002	29	Thirds	16 April	47.00	18
Newcastle City C	2002	32	Thirds	17 April	49.83	18
North Lincolnshire	1999	33	Whole	15/16 April	51.28	18
Wansbeck DC	1999	32	Whole	17 April	50.20	18
Chesterfield BC	1999	35	Whole	18 April	51.69	17
Copeland BC	1999	39	Whole	14 April	55.70	17
Guildford BC	1999	37	Whole	11 April	54.00	17
Hyndburn BC	2002	36	Thirds	17 April	51.47	16
Salford City C	2002	25	Thirds	14 April	41.00	16
Redcar & Cleveland BC	1999	37	Whole	17/21 April	51.50	15
Rushcliffe BC	1999	40	Whole	19/22 April	54.00	15
Sedgefield BC	1999	30	Whole	14 April	44.15	14

Table 12.3 Impact of all-postal voting in the 1st May 2003 UK local election pilot schemes *continued*

Name of authority	Year of last comparable election	% Turnout at last comparable election	Type of election this time (full/3rd)	Start of polling date	% Total turnout May 2003	Change in % turnout since last comparable election
Corby BC	1999	31	Whole	12/14 April	43.00	12
East Staffordshire BC	1999	34	Whole	10/11 April	44.97	11
Kings Lynn & West Norfolk BC	1999	36	Whole	15 April	47.66	11
North Shropshire DC	1999	33	Whole	17 April	43.80	11
Bolton MBC	2002	32	Thirds	15 April	42.00	10
Brighton & Hove City C	1999	38	Whole	15 April	45.96	8
St Edmundsbury BC	1999	38	Whole	19/22 April	38.50	1
Stevenage BC	2002	53	Thirds	16 April	52.20	-1
Trafford MBC	2002	53	Thirds	14 April	52.39	-1
Gateshead MBC	2002	57	Thirds	17 April	54.65	-2
Average		34			49.34	15

Note: Turnout is based on the number of votes cast as a proportion of the eligible electorate. The most comparable election depends upon whether whole (1999) or one-third (2002) elections are used in each district. BC=Borough Council. MBC=Metropolitan Borough Council. DC=District Council. C=Council.

Source: The UK Electoral Commission (2003).

Table 12.4 Impact of remote electronic voting in the 1st May 2003 UK local election pilot schemes

Name of authority	Year of last comparable election	% turnout at last comparable election	Type of election this time (full/3rd)	Total number of votes cast	% total turnout in May 2003	Change in % turnout from last comparable election	Number votes cast using e-channels	% electorate using e-channels	% turnout using e-channels
Vale Royal	1999	30.8	Whole	40,904	43.6	**12.8**	9,752	10	23.8
Shrewsbury & Atcham	2002	43.2	Thirds	22,039	54.5	**11.3**	4,090	10	19.0 (i)
South Somerset	1999	38.0	Whole	53,311	46.9	**8.9**	8,428	7	15.8 (i)
St Albans	2002	38.1	Thirds		43.4	**5.3**			
Basingstoke & Deane	2002	29.0	Thirds	28,317	30.9	**1.9**			
Norwich	2002	35.3	Thirds	33,866	35.8	**0.5**	3,442	4	10.7
Sheffield	2002	29.7	Thirds	110,988	29.5	-0.2	20,845	12	37.0
Swindon	2002	31.2	Thirds	40,812	29.8	-1.4	10,189	7	25.0
Chester	2002	35.5	Thirds	22,482	34.0	-1.5	6,699	10	29.1
Epping Forest	2000	30.0	Thirds	15,431	28.4	-1.6	14,683	27	95.0
Rushmoor	2002	34.7	Thirds	18,345	31.0	-3.7	2,760	6	15.0
Kerrier	1999	32.2	Whole	17,662	28.3	-3.9	3,374	5	15.0
Stroud	2002	42.6	Thirds	20,441	36.7	-5.9	4,176	8	20.4
Ipswich	2002	39.0	Thirds	28,516	31.9	-7.1	6,183	9	21.7
South Tyneside	2002	54.7	Thirds	52,368	46.1	-8.6	6,008	5	11.5 (i)
Stratford-on-Avon	2002	44.6	Thirds	21,669	35.6	-9.0	4,176	7	19.0
Chorley	2002	61.5	Thirds	32,900	49.9	-11.6	3,072	6	9.0 (i)
Average		38.2			37.4	-0.8	22,270	8.8	24.5

Notes: Turnout is based on the number of votes cast as a proportion of the eligible electorate. (i) Includes all-postal ballots.
Source: The UK Electoral Commission (2003).

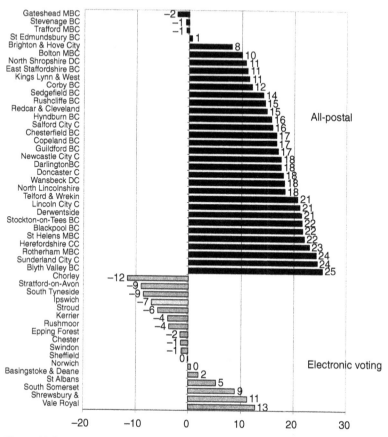

Figure 12.2   Percentage change in turnout in the May 2003 UK local election pilot schemes

Notes: Turnout is defined here as valid votes cast as a percentage of the eligible electorate. For details, including the date of the previous election used for calculating the % change in turnout in each district, see Tables 12.4 and 12.5.

Source: The UK Electoral Commission (2003).

likely to participate, with voting rising to a peak in late middle age, until there is a fall among the over 70s who often have difficulty in getting out to the polls.

The sample is not large enough to be able to reliably monitor each of the specific technologies used, such as text messaging or the Internet, but respondents in the MORI survey can be divided into three major categories according to whether the type of pilot scheme used in their district was either combined, any electronic pilot, or all-postal pilot.

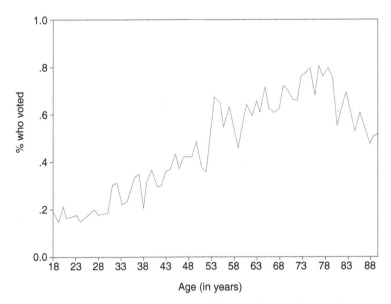

Figure 12.3   The age profile of voters in UK local authority election pilot areas
Note: Reported voting by age (in years) in all UK local authority pilot areas.
Source: MORI post-election survey of 6,185 electors 2–12 May 2003 in 29 UK local authorities piloting new voting arrangement. The survey results were weighted by wtfinal. For more details see http://www.mori.com/polls/2003/electoralcommission.shtml

Table 12.5 shows the breakdown of reported voting by the type of pilot areas and by major age groups.

The combined pilot areas allowed people to vote automatically by a postal ballot, or alternatively by some form of electronic technologies (whether by telephone, internet, text messaging or digital TV). In these areas there were enormous disparities in reported voting participation by age group: 84 per cent of young people said that they did not vote, compared with only one-quarter of the over-60s. Just fewer than one in ten in each of the age groups used the electronic channels of voting, and this pattern was fairly similar among young and old. But postal voting proved by far the most popular among the older group, who often have limited mobility.

The all-postal ballot pilots generated similar age differentials to the combined pilot areas: only one-fifth of the younger group reported voting compared with almost three-quarters of the elderly.

The last category of pilot schemes allowed people to cast a ballot either electronically or at traditional in-person polling stations. In

Table 12.5   Reported voting participation by age group

Type of pilot	Age group	Did not vote	Reported voting			
			Voted at a polling station	Voted electronically	Voted by post	Total
Combined pilots	Younger	84	n/a	8	8	100%
Middle aged		61	n/a	9	30	100%
Older		25	n/a	7	68	100%
All-postal pilots	Younger	81	n/a	n/a	19	100%
Middle aged		58	n/a	n/a	42	100%
Older		29	n/a	n/a	71	100%
Electronic pilots	Younger	84	10	5	1	100%
Middle aged		70	20	8	3	100%
Older		47	38	8	8	100%

Note: Younger = 18–29 years old; middle-aged = 30–59; older = 60+ years old. N/a not applicable in pilot area.
Source: MORI post-election survey of 6,185 electors 2–12 May 2003 in 29 local authorities piloting new voting arrangements. The survey results were weighted by wtfinal. For further details see <http://www.mori.com/polls/2003/electoralcommission.shtml >

these areas, electors could also opt for postal vote by application, but this process was not automatic. This category saw an intriguing pattern: as we have seen, aggregate levels of turnout actually fell in some of these areas, and overall across all these pilot schemes turnout did not increase. One of the main reasons uncovered by this analysis is that without all-postal voting (where the local authority *automatically* sends everyone the option to cast a mail ballot) the elderly are less likely to vote either in person at polling stations or electronically through new technologies. And in these areas, while younger people do use the new electronic voting channels, nevertheless they remain less likely to vote than the older generation. Figure 12.4 confirms this pattern, where age (in years) is regressed on reported turnout in each category of pilot schemes. Compared with other pilots, the strength of the age regression coefficient is reduced in the electronic pilot schemes, but this effect occurs mainly by depressing the participation of the elderly, rather than by boosting the participation of the young.

Multivariate analysis, introducing controls for gender, race and class into logistic regression models of voting participation in each category of pilot schemes, confirmed that the effect of age remained consistently significant even after applying controls, and that the age effect diminished most under the electronic pilot schemes (see Table 12.6). This suggests that the use of electronic voting technologies combined with in-person voting in traditional polling stations alone, *if they are not supplemented by the simultaneous employment of automatic postal ballots*, would not bolster turnout. Quite simply, the elderly generation remain the least comfortable using new technologies, having not grown up in the world of microchips, mobiles, and text messaging that

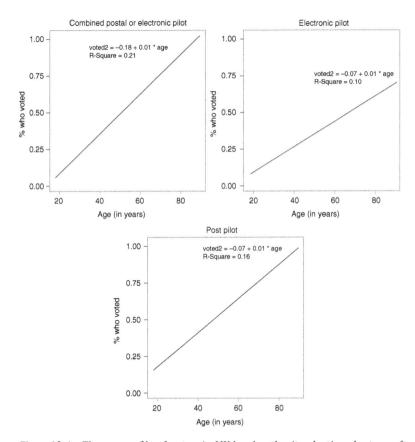

Figure 12.4   The age profile of voters in UK local authority elections by type of pilot scheme

Note: The lines represent the linear regression of age (in years) by reported voting.

Source: MORI post-election survey of 6,185 electors 2–12 May 2003 in 29 UK local authorities piloting new voting arrangement. The survey results were weighted by wtfinal. For more details see <http://www.mori.com/polls/2003/electoralcommission.shtml>

is now ubiquitous among the younger generation. And the older generation is the social sector with the strongest habits of voting, and yet the least physical mobility, who are therefore most motivated to take advantage of opportunities to cast a ballot by mail. The theory developed earlier suggests that reducing the costs of voting helps, but in order to participate citizens also need the sense that they have genuine electoral choices, and that casting a ballot will have an important impact through electoral decisiveness. Convenience in casting a ballot therefore only facilitates action if citizens are motivated through broader political considerations.

Table 12.6   Regression models predicting turnout in UK local elections

Type of pilot scheme in area		*B*	*S.E.*	*Sig.*
Combined postal + electronic pilots	Gender (male = 1)	–0.88	0.18	0.000
	Ethnicity (white = 1)	0.64	0.82	0.434
	Logged age (years)	**6.65**	**0.65**	**0.000**
	Class (4-cat)	0.09	0.08	0.257
	Constant	9.89		
	Nagelkerke R^2	0.31		
	% correctly predicted	72.80		
	No. of cases	1125		
Electronic pilots	Gender (male = 1)	0.30	0.10	0.002
	Ethnicity (white = 1)	0.17	0.29	0.554
	Logged age (years)	**4.59**	**0.33**	**0.000**
	Class (4-cat)	0.17	0.04	0.000
	Constant	7.87		
	Nagelkerke R^2	0.15		
	% correctly predicted	70.00		
	No. of cases	2416		
Postal pilots	Gender (male = 1)	–0.45	0.08	0.000
	Ethnicity (white = 1)	0.12	0.20	0.552
	Logged age (years)	**5.35**	**0.26**	**0.000**
	Class (4-cat)	0.09	0.04	0.012
	Constant	8.35		
	Nagelkerke R^2	0.21		
	% correctly predicted	68.70		
	No. cases	2444		

Note: Binary logistic models predicting reported turnout in the UK local elections, May 2003.
Source: MORI post-election survey of 6,185 electors 2–12 May 2003 in 29 local authorities piloting new voting arrangement. The survey results were weighted by wtfinal. For further details see <http://www.mori.com/polls/2003/electoralcommission.shtml>

Conclusions and discussion

Modern lifestyles mean that younger generations have become increasingly comfortable with the security of online banking, shopping and stockmarket trading, so advocates of e-voting hope that this process could generate similar levels of trust and confidence. The use of electronic technologies in elections can be regarded as building upon other increasingly common electoral and political uses of the Internet for information and communications, such as the use of websites and e-mail by parties, candidates and interest groups, the publication of election results online, the provision of voter registration facilities, and the use of the Internet for the submission, collection and disclosure of campaign finance.

Nevertheless, the evidence presented in this study suggests that at present, even if the technical and social equality issues could be overcome, there are few grounds to believe that adopting remote e-voting from home or work on a wide-scale basis would radically improve turnout. The introduction of remote e-voting would probably have a modest impact upon the younger generation, if judged by the available evidence from the British pilot studies, but automatic postal ballots are far more effective in improving participation among the older generation, as well as being cheaper and more efficient to administer. Remote e-voting is therefore unlikely to prove a 'magic ballot'. Technological quick fixes, while superficially attractive, cannot solve long-term and deep-rooted civic ills. Yet this does not mean that we should abandon all hope of modernizing elections; the impact of all-postal voting proved positive and highly significant. For the simple price of a postage stamp, snail-mail proved very effective at boosting turnout, and the MORI survey of attitudes showed that postal voting also generated high levels of trust, satisfaction and a sense of security among citizens (UK Electoral Commission 2003).

This is not to argue that the Internet fails to serve many other important functions during election campaigns, including for civic engagement. Content analysis of party websites suggests that the Internet provides a more level playing field for party competition, serving information and communication functions that are particularly important for minor and fringe parties (Norris 2002b). American surveys show that online communities can serve both 'bridging' and 'bonding' functions strengthening social capital (Norris 2002c). Experimental evidence demonstrates that party websites on the Internet do indeed promote civic learning, and in this regard information on the Internet is analogous to campaign information from newspapers or television news (Norrsi and Sanders 2004). Nevertheless, survey evidence from those Americans who use the Internet during campaigns in the United States strongly suggests that e-voting would be used most heavily primarily by people who are already most likely to participate, thereby still failing to reach the apathetic and disengaged (Norris 2001c).

Perhaps the primary impact of the Internet on democratic life concerns its ability to strengthen the public sphere by expanding the information resources, channels of electronic communication, and the networking capacity for many organized interest groups, social movements, NGOs, transnational policy networks, and political parties and candidates (such as Howard Dean's run for the presidency) with the technical know-how and organizational flexibility to adapt to the new medium (Norris 2001b). The impact of new technologies on intermediary organizations is evident from the way that they facilitate networks of activists concerned to challenge the decision-making processes in global governance, as well as most recently generating the 'flash-mob' phenomenon in popular culture. As such the debate about remote e-voting may well fail to identify the primary political impact of new information and communication technologies on democracy. How political leaders respond to these new demands, and thereby use the potential of new technologies to widen and deepen the democratic processes, remains one of the key challenges of governance for the twenty-first century.

Notes

1   See <http://news.bbc.co.uk/hi/english/in_depth/sci_tech/2000/dot_life/newsid_1746000/1746902.stm>
2   Of course none of this provides any evidence concerning the potential use of voting electronically via text messaging, using conventional or mobile telephones, since this is not measured in the Eurobarometer surveys under comparison. The widespread access of telephones in European societies could mitigate some of the social inequalities of Internet voting, although of course this does not necessarily overcome, and may even exacerbate, the concerns about security.
3   It should be noted that under other less democratic regimes, citizens face far more serious barriers, such as in the recent presidential election in Zimbabwe where electors stood in line at polling stations despite delays of up to 50 hours, and the serious threat of intimidation, violence and coercion.
4   It should be noted that the same models were run with turnout measured by vote as a proportion of the registered electorate (Vote/Reg), and no significant differences were found in the overall results.

5 *Established democracies* are defined as nation states with average Freedom House ratings of political rights and civil liberties of 2.0 or less in 1999–2000 (plus India rated at 2.5), and with at least 20 years continuous experience of democracy (1980–2000) based on the mean Freedom House rating 1972–1999. For the complete list see Norris 2002a, appendix A.

6 Previous studies have commonly found that the type of electoral formula shapes participation, with proportional representation systems generating higher voter participation than majoritarian or plurality elections. See Powell (1986); Jackman (1987); Jackman and Miller (1995); Blais and Dobrzynska (1998); Ladner and Milner (1999).

7 It should be noted that the particular benchmark year varies by the type of authority, with some councils elected in whole and others by thirds.

8 It should be noted that there were serious limitations in what could be analysed using the MORI survey data because of a number of design flaws. In particular there was no 'control' sample of voters in non-pilot districts. There were none of the standard attitudinal measures used for analysing turnout, such as political efficacy and partisanship. Many of the questions were filtered so that they were only asked of sub-samples in different pilot areas, preventing comparison across areas. Moreover, the way of classifying 'pensioners' into the DE class skewed the age profile in this category, making class analysis unreliable. There were also too few ethnic minorities to allow reliable analysis by racial group.

References

Arterton, C. F. (1987) *Teledemocracy*. Newbury Park, CA: Sage.

Auer, A. and Trechsel, A. H. (2001) 'Voter par Internet? Le projet e-voting dans le canton de Geneve dans une perspective socio-politique et juridique', www.helbing.ch

Barber, B. R. (1998) 'Three Scenarios for the Future of Technology and Strong Democracy', *Political Science Quarterly*, 113(4): 573–90.

Blais, A. and Dobrzynska, A. (1998) 'Turnout in Electoral Democracies', *European Journal of Political Research*, 33(2): 239–61.

Blais, A. and Massicotte, L. (2000) 'Day of Election', in R. Rose (ed.), *The International Encyclopedia of Elections*. Washington, DC: CQ Press.

Borgers, T. (2001) 'Is Internet Voting a Good Thing?' *Journal of Institutional and Theoretical Economics*, 156(4): 531–47.

Budge, I. (1996) *The New Challenge of Direct Democracy*. Oxford: Polity Press.

Craig, L. B. and Grofman, B. (1999) 'When Registration Barriers Fall, Who Votes? An Empirical Test of a Rational Choice Model', *Public Choice*, 21: 161–76.

Crewe, I. (1981) 'Electoral Participation', in A. Ranney and D. Butler (eds), *Democracy at the Polls*. Washington, DC: AEI Press.

Dictson, D. and Ray, D. (2000) 'The Modern Democratic Revolution: An Objective Survey of Internet-Based Elections', <www.Securepoll.com>

Electoral Reform Society (2002) *Elections in the 21st Century: From Paper-Ballot to e-Voting*. Electoral Reform Society. The Independent Commission on Alternative Voting Methods, <http://www.electoral-reform.org.uk/sep/publications/books/exec.pdf>

Fenster, M. J. (1994) 'The Impact of Allowing Day of Registration Voting on Turnout in U.S. Elections from 1960 to 1992', *American Politics Quarterly*, 22: 74–87.

Franklin, M. (2002) 'Electoral Participation', in L. LeDuc, R. G. Niemi and P. Norris (eds), *Comparing Democracies 2: Elections and Voting in Global Perspective*. London: Sage.

Franklin, M. *et al.* (1996), The Institutional Context: Turnout', in C. van der Eijk and M. Franklin (eds), *Choosing Europe? The European Electorate and National Politics in the Face of Union*. Ann Arbor, MI: University of Michigan Press.

Gibson, R. (2002) 'Elections Online: Assessing Internet Voting in Light of the Arizona Democratic Primary', *Political Science Quarterly*, 116(4): 561–83.

Heath, A. and Taylor, B. (1999) 'New Sources of Abstention?' in G. Evans and P. Norris (eds), *Critical Elections: British Parties and Voters in Long-term Perspective*. London: Sage.

House of Commons (2003) House of Commons Library Research Paper, July 2003, in *UK Elections Statistics 1945–2003*. 03-59: 17.

Independent Commission on Alternative Voting Methods (2002) *Elections in the 21st Century: From Paper-Ballot to e-voting*. Electoral Reform Society, January 2002, <http://www.electoral-reform.org.uk/sep/publications/books/exec.pdf>

IPI (Internet Policy Institute for the National Science Foundation) (2001) Report of the National Science Foundation *2001: Workshop on Internet Voting*. March 2001, <http://www.Internetpolicy.org/research/e_voting_report.pdf>

Jackman, R. W. (1987) 'Political Institutions and Voter Turnout in Industrialized Democracies', *American Political Science Review*, 81: 405–23.

Jackman, R. W. and Miller, R. A. (1995) 'Voter Turnout in Industrial Democracies during the 1980s', *Comparative Political Studies*, 27: 467–92.

Karp, J. A. and Banducci, S. (2000) 'Going Postal: How All-Mail Elections Influence Turnout', *Political Behavior*, 22(3): 223–39.

Katz, R. S. (1997) *Democracy and Elections*. Oxford: Oxford University Press.

Knack, S. (1995) 'Does "Motor Voter" Work? Evidence from State-level Data', *Journal of Politics*, 57: 796–811.

Knack, S. and White, J. (2000) 'Election-Day Registration and Turnout Inequality', *Political Behavior*, 22(1): 29–44.

Ladner, A. and Milner, H. (1999) 'Do Voters Turn Out More under Proportional than Majoritarian Systems? The Evidence from Swiss Communal Elections', *Electoral Studies*, 18(2): 235–50.

Lijphart, A. (1997) 'Unequal Participation: Democracy's Unresolved Dilemma', *American Political Science Review*, 91: 1–14.

Maley, M. (2000) 'Absentee Voting', in R. Rose (ed.), *The International Encyclopedia of Elections*. Washington, DC: CQ Press.

Martinez, M. D. and Hill, D. (1999) 'Did Motor Voter Work?' *American Politics Quarterly*, 27(3): 296–315.

MORI polls (2003) 'New Ways to Vote', <http://www.mori.com/polls/2003/electoralcommission.shtml>

National Statistics Omnibus Survey (2003) *Individuals Accessing the Internet. Access to Internet from Home – Expenditure and Food Survey* (January to March 2003).

Norris, P. (2001a) *Digital Divide: Civic Engagement, Information Poverty and the Internet Worldwide*. New York: Cambridge University Press.

Norris, P. (2001b) 'Who Surfs? New Technology, Old Voters and Virtual Democracy in US Elections 1992–2000', in E. Kamarck (ed.), *democracy.com*, revd edn. Washington, DC: Brookings Institute.

Norris, P. (2002a) *Democratic Phoenix: Political Activism Worldwide*. New York: Cambridge University Press.

Norris, P. (2002b) 'Preaching to the Converted? Pluralism, Participation and Party Websites', *Party Politics*, 9: 21–45.

Norris, P. (2002c) 'The Bridging and Bonding Role of Online Communities', *The Harvard International Journal of Press-Politics*, 7(3): 3–8.

Norris, P. (2004) *Electoral Engineering: Electoral Rules and Voting Choices*. New York: Cambridge University Press.

Norris, P. and Lovenduski, J. (2004) 'Why Parties Fail to Learn: Electoral Defeat, Selective Perception and British Party Politics', *Party Politics*, 10(1).

Norris, P. and Sanders, D. (2001) *Knows Little, Learns Less? An Experimental Study of the Impact of the Media on Learning During the 2001 British General Election*. Annual Meeting of the American Political Science Association, San Francisco.

Norris, P. and Sanders, D. (2004) 'Medium or Message? Campaign Learning During the 2001 British General Election', *Political Communications* (forthcoming).

Office of the e-Envoy (2002) *In the Service of Democracy*. July, <www.edemocracy.gov.uk>

Powell, G. B. Jr. (1986) 'American Voter Turnout in Comparative Perspective', *American Political Science Review*, 80(1): 17–43.

Rallings, C. and Thrasher, M. (2000) *British Electoral Facts 1832–1999*. Aldershot: Ashgate.

Rash, W. Jr. (1997) *Politics on the Net: Wiring the Political Process*. New York: W. H. Freeman.

Rheingold, H. (1993) *The Virtual Community: Homesteading on the Electronic Frontier*. Reading, MA: Addison Wesley.

Schwartz, E. (1996) *Netactivism: How Citizens Use the Internet*. Sebastapol, CA: Songline Studios.

Solop, F. (2001) 'Digital Democracy Comes of Age: Internet Voting and the 2000 Arizona Democratic Primary Election', *Political Science and Politics*, 34(2): 289–93.

Stratford, J. S. and Stratford, J. (2001) 'Computerized and Networked Government Information', *Journal of Government Information*, 28(3): 297–301.

UK Electoral Commission (2002) *Modernising Elections: A Strategic Evaluation of the 2002 Electoral Pilot Schemes*. London: UK Electoral Commission, <www.electoralcommission.org.uk>

UK Electoral Commission (2003) *The Shape of Elections to Come*. London: UK Electoral Commission, <www.electoralcommission.org.uk>

Whiteley, P. (2001) 'Turnout', in P. Norris (ed.), *Britain Votes 2001*. Oxford: Oxford University Press.

Wolfinger, R. E., Glass, D. P. and Squire, P. (1990) 'Predictors of Electoral Turnout: An International Comparison', *Policy Studies Review*, 9: 551–74.

Wolfinger, R. E. and Rosenstone, S. J. (1980) *Who Votes?* New Haven: Yale University Press.

13
Support for Online Voting in the United States

Ramona S. McNeal and Caroline J. Tolbert

The timeline representing the policy area of e-voting (Internet voting) in the United States has not been a long one. A generous individual casting his/her 'net' far afield may argue that the roots of this policy area may have started back as far as 1992 when presidential candidate Ross Perot proposed the concept of electronic town-hall meetings – suggesting the potential of the Internet for increasing citizen participation in the electoral process. A more conservative and systematic approach might date to the Clinton/Gore presidential administration, which placed a strong emphasis on public policy to bring the nation into the information age. The Clinton/Gore administration spent much of the 1990s promoting the idea of 'reinventing government', using technology as well as other administrative reforms to improve government efficiency and citizen participation (see Osborne and Gaebler 1992). During this administration, programmes such as the Technology Opportunities Programme (TOP) under the Department of Commerce and the Community Technology Centre (CTC) initiative and the E-rate administered by the Department of Education were put into place to increase Internet access among American citizens, particularly disadvantaged groups. A purist, however, might start this timeline in January 2000. During this month the California Internet Voting Task Force established by Secretary of State Bill Jones in January 1999 released its report on the viability of online voting, and the Brookings Institution and Cisco Systems, Inc. cosponsored the symposium, *The Future of Internet Voting.* The two events generated considered enthusiasm for and debate over the prospect of online voting.

Regardless where we start the Internet voting timeline, the road it has followed has been far from straight – a random walk might be the best description. The road travelled, so far, has been a hodge-podge of false starts, high hopes, great leaps forward, steps backwards, a move towards oblivion followed by renewed interests. Both optimism and concerns preceded the Internet Task Force Report and the symposium (20 January 2000). John Chambers, keynote speaker of the symposium and President and CEO of Cisco Systems, demonstrated great faith in the Internet, predicting that most states would have Internet voting by the 2004 presidential election. Further, based on experiences from business, he predicted that the Internet would lead to an improved democratic process through a more educated electorate. He argued that the Internet has given employees greater access to information that has allowed them to make knowledgeable decisions. So too, with elections, the Internet may augment citizen knowledge about politics allowing for a greater deliberative process. While Chambers expressed hope for the future of Internet voting, other member of the symposium and the California task force took a more moderate stand.

Ann McGeeham, panel member and director of elections for the state of Texas, pointed out that while Texas has made great effort to make voting more accessible, there is no real proof that these efforts are increasing turnouts. In 1987, the state legislature passed a system that permits voters to cast their ballots 17 days before the election in central locations such as K-Marts, Wal-Marts and grocery stores. While these measures are quite popular among individuals who use them, voter turnout in Texas is no better than the rest of nation. In the 1998 mid-term election, Texas could only muster a 32.5 per cent turnout for the governor's race. This raises the concern of whether increased access made available by the Internet would encourage political participation.

While McGeeham raised the issue that the Internet may not increase voter turnout to the extent hoped, the Internet Task Force Report (and others since then) focused on the issue of security. Although the task force recognized that Internet voting might encourage greater turnout through convenient ballot access and flexibility, it also expressed concern over threats to both security and privacy. Security concerns included authenticity – how can it be guaranteed that Internet voters are who they claim they are? Privacy – how can it by ensured that the ballots remain secret? Finally, tamper-proof – how can it be guaranteed that viruses such as the so-called 'trojan horse' viruses, which are capable of changing votes, do not interfere with election outcomes? Similar concerns are raised about electronic voting machines and the need for a verifiable paper trail.

Weighting these pros and cons, the task force recommended a gradual process to implementing online voting. The first step would be to only allow Internet voting in polling places. This would allow for maximum security and give individuals the opportunity to become comfortable voting online in an environment where they can ask questions should they have trouble using the technology. Once the public has become comfortable with the technology, the second phase would be to install county-controlled kiosks in public places such as malls and supermarkets. Kiosks would permit greater access than polling places but yet still allow for security measures such as cameras. The final stage (known as remote voting) would be Internet voting where individuals could vote from anywhere including their home or office. It was believed that a gradual approach would both allow the public to adapt to the new technology while permitting security measures to develop to the point where hackers could be thwarted and anonymity of ballots could be ensured.

The task force and the symposium do not represent the only voices or the last word on the topic. A body of literature on the general impact of the Internet and Internet voting began to surface. Many voices were pessimistic about the possible impact of the Internet on participation, and many did not share Chambers' belief that increased information and accessibility made possible by the Internet would result in a more informed electorate and increased turnout. Researchers and pundits alike argued that individuals are not passive receivers of information but actively determine what media they will consume based on a number of needs including surveillance, pleasure and affection. They also actively avoid certain media messages. Past studies (Blumler and McQuail 1969; McLeod and Becker 1974; Wenner 1983) examining factors that have impacted media use and political participation found that lack of interest, disagreement with the media message and the prospect of being bored were important factors in avoiding political news. This earlier research was based on television news, but by extending the findings to the Internet one could argue that the Internet might widen the gap between those who do and do not participate (see Norris 2001; Mossberger *et al.* 2003; Alvarez and Hall 2004). Those interested in politics may find further motivation to participate as a result of the additional political information on the Internet and the convenience of Internet voting, while those disinterested in the political process might avoid online political information and not take advantage of greater voting sites.

Inequality in access to the Internet is a major obstacle to Internet voting in the United States. Leading behavioural theories of political participation have shown that socioeconomic characteristics of voters–education and income – are the most important variables in explaining whether one votes in the United States (Campbell *et al.* 1960; Wolfinger and Rosenstone 1980; Verba, Schlozman and Brady

1995). Existing disparities in access to the Internet based on income, education and race/ethnicity (US Department of Commerce 2002) mean that technology resources are far from equally distributed and online politics may therefore magnify existing gaps in participation (Davis and Owen 1998; McChesney 1999; Mossberger, Tolbert and Stansbury 2003; Norris 2001; Wilheim 2000). This disparity in Internet access might result in a greater chasm between those who do and do not vote, particularly if policy was to result in a remote voting option instead of providing Internet access at polling places or in kiosks.

Experiences with mail and e-voting

The state of Arizona was the first to allow remote Internet voting during the Democratic primary in 2000 in addition to traditional polling booth voting. Alvarez and Nagler (2002) argue one way to assess Internet voting is to compare the group of citizens currently voting to those that would vote if online balloting were implemented. Sharp differences in the demographics of these two groups would be evidence of a change in political representation caused by Internet voting. Alvarez and Nagler use aggregate census and election-return data from Arizona's 15 counties and ecological inference methods (King 1997) to estimate white and non-white Democratic turnout rates. They compare turnout in the 1998 statewide Democratic primary with the 2000 Democratic presidential primary, where Internet voting was introduced. While overall statewide turnout was significantly lower in the 2000 primary (10.59 per cent) compared to average primary turnout of 23.94 per cent in the past three elections, the authors found that the average rate of decrease for non-white voters was six times greater than the average rate of decrease for white voters. White turnout actually increased from 1998 levels in two counties, but non-white turnout declined from 1998 to 2000 in every Arizona county. Multivariate regression analysis suggests elderly, non-white, unemployed and rural residents were also statistically less likely to engage in Internet voting, controlling for other factors.

The research on Internet voting suggests its potential to mobilize new sectors of the population, particularly the young, but also to expand existing disparities in unequal participation rates based on race/ethnicity and socioeconomic status. The findings in part support both sides of the argument over online voting. The Internet may mobilize the young, a group known for low voter turnout; only about 32 per cent of the age group 18–24 voted in 1996, and 17 per cent turned out for the 1998 election (Gibson 2001: 571). While the turnout among the young was encouraging, concerns that e-voting may have disenfranchized poor individuals led to a court case that was eventually dismissed. There was also concern over possible breaches of security. Personal identification numbers (PIN) allowing individuals to vote were sent through the mail and were not always received; there were instances of landlords receiving the PIN numbers of previous tenants. In addition, people with older browsers with Y2K problems and machines with disabled cookies were locked out of the system. There were other breaches of security such as an hour-long breakdown of service on the first day of voting (Gibson 2001: 580).

Initial findings about Internet voting are suggestive, but online voting may not be a widespread reality in the proximate future. Controversies over e-voting include concerns about election fraud and online privacy, and the construction of secure voting systems would represent considerable expense (Clift 2000). The California Secretary of State banned e-voting during the 2004 presidential elections in four counties because of security concerns. The Arizona Democratic primary suggested for many that a slow approach may be the best policy. Despite the concern over online voting, numerous states are moving forward by allowing online voter registration. The experience in Arizona may have slowed the spread of Internet voting in the United States. Michigan was the only state to experiment with remote Internet voting during the 2004 presidental primary elections. Michigan Democrats were permitted to vote by mail, online and in person. A little more than 46,000 (28%) voted online. The turnout was considered a success with few technology-related problems. Nevertheless, it is difficult to project from this experience because of strong interest in the 2004 presidential election (Range 2004).

State experiments with mail voting provide a useful analog to Internet voting, and suggest that election reforms can increase political participation. Absentee mail-in voting is encouraged in many states, with a third or more of the ballots being cast in advance of Election Day in Western states (Bowler and Donovan 2004). In 1988 Oregon voters eliminated neighbourhood polling places, requiring all state voters to cast ballots exclusively by mail beginning with the 2000 elections. Research on the impact of conducting elections entirely through the mail found that mail ballots significantly increase turnout in both local and statewide elections. All-mail elections tend to produce the most dramatic increases in low-stimulus elections at the local level or in primaries where turnout is relatively low (Karp and Banducci 2000). Southwell and Burchett (2000b) suggest that the all-mail format is a major stimulus to voter participation, second only to the impact of a presidential contest.

The increase in turnout, however, is not uniform across demographic groups, tending to rise among those who are already predisposed to vote, such as those with higher socioeconomic status (Karp and Banducci 2000). Karp and Banducci suggest that like other reforms designed to make voting easier (such as Internet voting), the expanded pool of voters will likely be limited to those already inclined to vote but find it inconvenient to go to the polling place. They argue that mail voting is not a panacea for low turnout among the disenfranchised. Others (Southwell and Burchett 2000a) find that 'vote-by-mail' voters in Oregon differed only slightly from 'traditional' voters who went to the polls in previous elections, in that they were older, more urban and less partisan, but were similarly informed, educated and involved as traditional voters. Rather than magnifying existing disparities in the composition of the electorate, they suggest that all-mail elections provide a method of converting peripheral voters into core voters. A citizen initiative on the Colorado 2002 ballot proposed creating mail-ballot elections but was defeated (Initiative and Referenda Institute 2002).

While a few studies were conducted following the Arizona Democratic primaries and a number of reports issued, there remains a dearth of research devoted to online voting in the United States. A limited but developing body of research has explored the relationship between Internet use and varying forms of civic participation, including voting (Bimber 2001; Norris 2001; Alvarez and Hall 2004; Shah, Kwak and Holbert 2001; Solop 2000; Tolbert and McNeal 2003). Yet few have explored citizen *attitudes* towards the use of the Internet to conduct elections, rather than to obtain political information. No national survey in the United States, to our knowledge, has included a question regarding public support for Internet voting. Attitudes are important, because of their potential to affect public policy. While e-voting may be convenient, it may not increase turnout if concerns about the new technology, such as security, keep individuals from taking advantage of increased access. The following study will examine citizen willingness to use online voting procedures. Independent variables include race, income, age, gender and education to determine if they influence the willingness to use the new technology – an important concern if we hope to close existing gaps in voter turnout instead of increasing them.

Public opinion about online voting and registration

The source of data for this study is a national random telephone survey conducted in July 2001 by Kent State University's Computer Assisted Telephone Interviewing (CATI) lab. The data used in this analysis was originally conducted for a project exploring dimensions of the digital divide. The results of the complete survey are reported in *Virtual*

Inequality: Beyond the Digital Divide, Georgetown University Press (2003) by Karen Mossberger, Caroline Tolbert and Mary Stansbury. The original survey data was merged with 2000 county-level US census data to control for contextual effects. We focused exclusively on four questions asked about Internet voting and registration. The authors thank Karen Mossberger and Mary Stansbury for allowing us to use the survey data. One national random sample of 1,190 respondents was drawn from all high-poverty census tracts in the 48 states, excluding Alaska and Hawaii. High-poverty tracts were defined as those with 50 per cent or more of the households living at or below 150 per cent of the federal poverty level. The response rate for individuals in the high poverty tracts was 92 per cent. Federal data show that telephone services now reach 94 per cent of the population (US Department of Commerce 1995), so telephone surveys are a reasonable methodology for obtaining sample data even in low-income communities. A second national random sample of 655 respondents served as a control group, with a response rate of 88 per cent. There were 1,837 valid responses overall.

Telephone numbers were dialed daily through the months of July (37 days in the field) by trained interviewers. Up to 524 callbacks were attempted to contact potential respondents for the general population sample and 371 for the poverty sample. Answering machines were treated as 'no answer' and called back on a regular no-answer rotation, a minimum of three hours later. After securing cooperation, interviewers used Computer-Assisted Telephone Interviewing systems to administer questions and record responses. The telephone survey included 50 items and averaged 8.5 minutes to complete (see Mossberger, Tolbert and Stansbury 2003: 17–18).

Because the survey targeted high-poverty areas, the sample included a relatively large proportion of racial and ethnic minorities, compared to standard surveys. Of the 1,837 respondents, 70 per cent were white non-Hispanic, 19 per cent were African-American, 9 per cent Latino and 1.5 per cent Asian American. Thus, Latinos and Blacks comprised 28 per cent of the sample population, compared to 25 per cent of the US population in the 2000 census. Thirty-eight per cent of our sample had household incomes below $30,000. This allowed us to make accurate inferences to minority and low-income populations as a whole, and the survey generated data that was comparable to large-sample studies. Sixty-one per cent of our respondents reported having access to a home computer, and 54 per cent reported having home Internet access. This closely tracks the figures in the US Department of Commerce study conducted in August of 2001 – 66 per cent and 54 per cent respectively.

We use multivariate regression models to predict the impact of demographic and partisan factors on attitudes towards Internet voting and registration. We also report some descriptive statistics (frequencies of responses to survey questions).

Findings from our survey

Analysis of the survey data demonstrates that innovations, like online voting, are controversial among the American public, but technology innovations in the polling place are generally supported. Respondent support for Internet voting was almost evenly split. When asked, 'How do you feel about voting in a government election online?' 48 per cent agreed, while 52 per cent were opposed. This could indicate public qualms about security or privacy, or more general disinterest in voting. The survey revealed more support for online voter registration; when asked, 'How do you feel about registering to vote online?' support rose to 58 per cent.

Because limited access to computers and the Internet may have biased responses to the questions, we repeated the questions asking if the respondent supported online voting and registration using a computer in a public place, where access would be provided and election fraud could be more easily controlled. When asked, 'Would you use a computer located in a public place to vote in an election?' support rose by more than 10 per cent, with 59 per cent agreeing. Of the respondents, 67 per cent supported using a computer is a public place to register to vote. Respondents were considerably *more willing* to use new technology for voting and registration at a public place rather than at home. Moreover, even with a representative sample of low-income individuals, a majority of respondents were supportive of Internet voting, at least when public access (and security) is provided (Mossberger, Tolbert and Stansbury, 2003: 98–9).

Support for online voting, holding other factors constant

Since voting is the most basic component of participation in a democracy and previous surveys have not explored attitudes towards online voting and registration, we felt the responses to these questions had special importance. Percentages are useful for understanding general trends, but they can't sort out the relative significance of different factors in the same way that statistical methods such as multivariate regression can. Using these methods, we can distinguish the causes of disparities in attitudes, or the differences that matter. Using multivariate logistic regression, we compared the results of four models, created to explain support for each of the following four questions: Do you support: (1) voting in a government election online; (2) registering to vote online; (3) voting in a government election online in a public place; and (4) registering to vote online in a public place. The responses for each question were coded 1 for agree and 0 for disagree.

Explanatory or independent variables measured individual-level demographic and attitudinal factors. Dummy variables were included to measure gender, race, ethnicity, partisanship and income. This means that they are coded as categories, with female, African-American, Latino, Asian American, Democrat, Republican and those with an annual income less than $30,000 coded 1 and 0 otherwise. For race and ethnicity whites were the reference group, or the left-out group that was not coded. For partisanship, those without strong partisan identification – independents – were the reference group that was not included. Education was measured on a 5-point scale with responses ranging from 1= less than a high school degree to 5= postgraduate work. Age was recorded in years. We also measured traditional political participation where 1 indicates that the individual was both registered and voted in the 2000 presidential election, and 0 otherwise. This measure was created by combining two survey questions, and used instead of voting to help control for the problem of over-reporting in survey data. The problem with using self-reported voting alone is that the per centage of people who ostensibly vote usually far outstrips actual turnout. Finally, we control for Internet access, given the importance of access for remote online voting. Respondents with home access to the Internet were coded 1, with all others coded 0.

In addition to the individual-level factors, we merged the survey data with county-level data from the 2000 US Census to control for contextual effects. For each respondent in the survey we recorded data about the county in which they reside. Environmental data were used to measure racial diversity and socioeconomic condition, factors important in not only access to technology but political participation. We measured racial diversity by the percentages of African American, Latino or Asian American at the county level. We measured socioeconomic conditions by the percentages of high-school graduate or higher and median income at the county level (US Census 2000).

What matters

The only statistically significant differences are reported below (also in Table 13.1):

1 **Who is more likely to support online voting?**
   Young; educated; Democrat; voted in 2000 election; home Internet access; reside in county with larger Latino populations.

2 **Who is more likely to support online voter registration?**
   Young; educated; Democrat; males; non-Hispanic white; voted in
   2000 elections; home Internet access; reside in county with larger
   Latino populations.
3 **Who is more likely to support online voting in a public place?**
   Young; educated; affluent; voted in 2000 elections.
4 **Who is more likely to support online voter registration in a
   public place?**
   Young; educated; affluent; Democrats; home Internet access; voted
   in 2000 elections.

Table 13.1 presents the results from the statistical analysis. Since the
dependent variables are binary, logistic regression coefficients are
reported. To our surprise, most of the contextual or county-level variables
were not significant. The exception is the per cent Latino population in a
county; individuals residing in areas with more Latinos are more supportive of voting in an election online and registering to vote online. But the
coefficient for Latino respondent is negative and statistically significant;
Latinos are less likely than non-Hispanics to support online voter registration. This suggests that other cultural or regional characteristics of areas
with large Latino populations are associated with higher support for
e-voting. Latino populations are concentrated in the south-west, states
with the highest per cent of high-technology industries.

Of the individual-level variables, age is an important predictor of
support for e-voting. The young are more supportive of online voting and
registration, as well as using new information technology to participate in
a public place. Consistent with previous research (Solop 2000; Mossberger'
Tolbert and Stansbury 2003), this suggests online voting may provide a
stimulus to increase participation levels of the young. Education is important in support of Internet voting in America. Individuals with more education are more likely to support online voting and registration at a
remote site or in a public place, such as a polling booth. Previous participation in elections, measured by voting in the 2000 elections – is also positively related to support for Internet voting. Those with incomes over
$30,000, however, were only more likely to support online voting or regis-
tration in a public place, suggesting that privacy and security concerns are
important to the middle and upper class.

Partisanship emerges as a critical factor and is consistently related to
support for Internet voting in three of the four models. Democrats are
significantly more supportive of reforms to allow online voting, voter registration and voter registration in a public place than Republicans or
those without strong partisanship – independents. There is no difference

Table 13.1 Voting and support for Internet registration: logistic regression

Variables	Would you vote in an election online?		Would you register to vote in a government election online?		Would you use a computer located in a public place to vote in an election?		Would you use a computer located in a public place to register to vote?	
	B(se)	P>|z|	B(se)	P>|z|	B(se)	P>|z|	B(se)	P>|z|
Environmental[1]								
Per cent Black	.00(.00)	.546	.00(.00)	.634	.00(.00)	.531	.00(.00)	.501
Per cent Latino	.02(.01)	.001	.01(.01)	.063	.00(.01)	.363	.01(.01)	.263
Per cent Asian	-.01(.01)	.283	-.01(.01)	.374	.00(.01)	.898	-.01(.01)	.529
Per cent of H.S. Graduates	.11(.48)	.818	-.14(.39)	.726	-.13(.33)	.694	-.30(.37)	.410
Median income	.00(.00)	.782	.00(.00)	.934	.00(.00)	.469	.00(.00)	.440
Individual								
African American	-.04(.20)	.846	-.03(.21)	.885	-.07(.20)	.712	.02(.22)	.913
Latino	-.35(.31)	.252	-.60(.31)	.051	-.07(.30)	.821	.16(.34)	.638
Asian	-.50(.81)	.533	-.71(.89)	.426	-.34(.79)	.663	-.34(.86)	.696
Age	-.02(.01)	.000	-.03(.05)	.000	-.02(.01)	.000	-.02(.01)	.000
Education	.29(.07)	.000	.37(.07)	.000	.17(.07)	.074	.12(.07)	.091
Poor	-.02(.16)	.913	.07(.17)	.679	-.38(.16)	.017	-.38(.17)	.026
Republican	-.03(.20)	.886	.09(.20)	.667	-.04(.19)	.829	.10(.21)	.633
Democrat	.51(.19)	.008	.54(.20)	.007	.17(.19)	.367	.38(.20)	.059
Male	.12(.15)	.417	.29(.15)	.060	-.09(.14)	.513	.24(.16)	.123
Home Internet	.71(.16)	.000	1.00(.16)	.000	.22(.15)	.147	.49(.17)	.003
Voted in 2000 election	.34(.19)	.071	.41(.19)	.038	.43(.19)	.019	.42(.20)	.034
Constant	-.99(.42)	.019	-.43(.42)	.303	.53(.41)	.194	.87(.43)	.043

Table 13. 1 Voting and support for Internet registration: logistic regression *continued*

Variables	Would you vote in an election online?		Would you register to vote in a government election online?		Would you use a computer located in a public place to vote in an election?		Would you use a computer located in a public place to register to vote?	
	B(se)	P>|z|	B(se)	P>|z|	B(se)	P>|z|	B(se)	P>|z|
N	1464		1464		1464		1464	
LR chi-square	131.382	.000	201.980	.000	53.453	.000	77.128	.000
Pseudo R square	.174		.253		.075		.112	

Source: Tolbert, Mossberger and Stansbury, July 2001. 'Defining the Digital Divide Survey'. National random digit-dialed telephone survey from high poverty US Census tracks and a representative control group, N=1837, conducted by the Sociology Department Computer Assisted Telephone Interviewing Lab at Kent State University. Unstandardized logistic regression coefficients, standard errors in parentheses, probability based on 2-tailed test. County-level data from the 2000 US Census Bureau's State and County Quickfacts.

in support for using a computer in a public place to vote in an election between Democrats, Republicans and Independents. As expected, those with home Internet access favour online voting and registering to vote online. But Internet access does not affect support for electoral reforms involving registering to vote in a public place, such as a polling station. This makes sense, as home Internet access would not be an asset if voting continued to occur in neighbourhood polling places. Gender is significant in only one model, with males more likely to support online voter registration than females. Race and ethnicity do not appear to be important in support for e-voting, with no statistically significant differences between whites, African Americans, Asian Americans and Latinos, with the one exception mentioned earlier.

Conclusion

From the survey analysis, one might conclude that online voting in the United States is just around the corner, especially if privacy and security concerns could be abated with voting continuing at traditional polling places. Of the respondents in our nationally representative survey, almost 60 per cent supported voting in an election online in a public place, and nearly 70 per cent supported using a computer to register to vote online in a public place. The prospect of remote Internet voting and voter registration was more controversial, with support falling roughly 10 percentage points. While security and privacy issues are common concerns raised by opponents of Internet voting, the more intractable problem lies with unequal access to technology and the skills needed to use them.

In *Virtual Inequality: Beyond the Digital Divide*, Mossberger, Tolbert and Stansbury (2003) attempt to redefine the issue of the digital divide in broader terms. They argue that the problem has been too narrowly conceived in public debate, research and programmes as primarily an issue of access. In reality, there are multiple information technology divides – an access divide, a skill divide, an economic opportunity divide, and a democratic divide. Access without skill is insufficient. In the age of the Internet, this includes basic literacy skills and 'information literacy', or the ability to locate and evaluate information. Information technology access and skills merit policy attention (and may be considered public goods) because of their implications for economic opportunity and democratic participation. Individuals with access to computers and skills to use them will be better able to use technology for economic opportunity and political participation.

Our findings are consistent with those reported in *Virtual Inequality*. The multivariate statistical analysis exposes a democratic divide; the educated, affluent and those with home Internet access are more supportive of Internet voting and registration. This suggests that online political participation may exacerbate existing disparities in voter participation based on income and education found in traditional elections. Interestingly, income is only a predictor of support for online voting and registration at a polling pace where access and instruction is provided. At the same time, the young are considerably more supportive of using technology for political participation, suggesting the mobilizing potential of this electoral reform. Partisanship emerges as an important factor, with self-identified Democrats significantly more supportive of online voting and registration compared to Republicans or those without party ties (independents). Despite public support for computerized voting, party politics may serve as a major obstacle to electoral reform in the United States, as it has in the past.

This chapter has shown that the American states have led the way in innovating with Internet voting and other electoral reforms, such as mail voting. The statistical analysis reveals that individuals living in geographic areas with significant Latino populations (concentrated in the western states) are more supportive of online political participation than those residing in other areas of the country. For the past century, the western states have been innovators in political reform. Many Progressive-era electoral reforms (1890–1917) – direct democracy (initiative, referendum and recall), direct election of US senators, direct primary, home-rule for municipalities, secret ballot, long-ballot, women's suffrage, at-large vs. ward districts, civil service system, and many other procedural policies – were first adopted in the western states (Schmidt 1989; Smith and Tolbert 2004). Many of these electoral reforms diffused across the states and were later adopted at the national level.

Research suggests states with direct democracy, where citizen act as legislators by voting on policy questions, are an important mechanism for early adoption of both historical and contemporary (term limitations, campaign finance reform, mail ballots) political reform in American states (Tolbert 1998, 2001; Schmidt 1989). Direct democracy is especially important when a proposed policy faces opposition by state lawmakers. Two unsuccessful citizen initiatives to permit Internet voting circulated for the 2000 California ballot. Because of the expense related to constructing secure voting systems, Clift (2000) argues that such an innovation is most likely to occur in states that have ballot initiatives, giving voters a direct mechanism to demand change. Will future statewide ballots focus on election reform, including Internet voting? Will the states pave the way for reform of the American electoral system at the national level, as has occurred in the past? What type of twenty-first century electoral reforms will parallel the secret ballot, direct election of US senators and women's suffrage adopted at the turn of the twentieth century?

References

Alvarez, M. and Hall, T. (2004) *Point Click and Vote*. Washington, DC,: The Brookings Institution Press.

Alvarez, M. and Nagler, J. (2002) 'The Likely Consequences of Internet Voting for Political Representation', *Loyola University Law Review*, Los Angeles, California.

Bimber, B. (2001) 'Information and Political Engagement in America: The Search for Effects of Information Technology at the Individual Level', *Political Research Quarterly*, 54(1): 53–67.

Blumler, J. and McQuail, D. (1969) *Television and Politics: Its Uses and Influence*. Chicago: University of Chicago Press.

Bowler, S. and Donovan, T. (2004) *Reforming the Republic*. Upper Saddle River, NJ: Prentice Hall.

Bowler, S., Donovan, T. and Tolbert, C. J. (eds) (1998) *Citizens as Legislators: Direct Democracy in the United States*. Columbus: Ohio State University Press.

California. Office of the Secretary of the State (2000) *California Internet Voting Task Force Report*, <http://www.ss.ca.gov/executive/ivote/>

Campbell, A., Converse, P. E., Miller, W. E. and Stokes, D. E. (1960) *The American Voter*. Chicago, Ill.: University of Chicago Press.

Clift, S. (2000) *The E-Democracy E-Book: Democracy is Online 2.0*, <http://www.e-democracy.org.>

Future of Internet Voting (2000) 'A Symposium Co-Sponsored by the Brookings Institution and Systems, Inc.', <http://www.brookings.org/comm/ tran-scripts/20000120.htm>

Gibson, R. (2001) 'Elections Online: Assessing Internet Voting in Light of the Arizona Democratic Primary', *Political Science Quarterly*, 116(4): 561–83.

Initiative and Referendum Institute (2000) 'California Initiative Review Report: Analysis of Internet Voting Proposals', http://www.iandrinstitute.org/

Initiative and Referendum Institute (2002) Washington, DC, 'Ballot Watch', <www.ballotwatch.org>

Internet Policy Institute (2001) *Report of the National Workshop on Internet Voting:Issues and Research Agenda*, <http://www.Internetpolicy.org/research/ results.html>

Karp, J. and Banducci, S. (2000) 'Going Postal: How All-Mail Elections Influence Turnout', *Political Behavior*, 22(3): 223–39.

King, G. (1997) *A Solution to the Ecological Inference Problem*. Harvard, Mass: Cambridge University Press.

Livingston, B. (2001) 'First Congressionally Mandated Internet Vote Points The Way to Technology of the Year', *InfoWorld*, 23(5): 78.

McChesney, R. (1999) *Rich Media, Poor Democracy: Communication Policy in Dubious Times*. Urbana, Ill. University of Illinois Press.

McLeod, J. and Becker, L. B. (1974) 'Testing the Validity of Gratification Measures Through Political Effects Analysis', in J. Blumler and E. Katz (eds), *The Uses of Mass Communication: Current Perspectives on Gratification Research*. Beverly Hills, CA: Sage.

Morrow, J. (1999) 'The Mouse That Voted', *U.S. News and World Report*, 126(24): 30.

Mossberger, K., Tolbert, C. J. and Stansbury, M. (2003) *Virtual Inequality: Beyond the Digital Divide*. Washington, DC: Georgetown University Press.

Norris, P. (2001) *Digital Divide: Civic Engagement, Information Poverty, and the Internet Worldwide*. Cambridge: Cambridge University Press.

Osborne, D. and Gaebler, T. (1992) *Reinventing Government: How the Entrepreneurial Spirit is Transforming the Public Sector*. Reading, Mass.: Addison-Wesley.

Range, S.(2004) 'Internet Voting Wins Praise of Party Leadership' *Lansing State Journal*, <http://www. lsj.com/news/local/040208internet_9a.html>

Schmidt, D. D. (1989) *Citizen Lawmakers: The Ballot Initiative Revolution*. Philadelphia: Temple University Press.

Shah, D., Kwak, N. and Holbert, L. (2001) '"Connecting" and "Disconnecting" with Civic Life: Patterns of Internet Use and the Production of Social Capital', *Political Communication*, 18: 141–62.

Smith, D. and Tolbert, C. (2004) *Educated by Initiative: The Effects of Direct Democracy on Citizens and Political Organizations in the American States*. Ann Arbor MI: University of Michigan Press.

Solop, F. I. (2000) 'Digital Democracy Comes of Age in Arizona: Participation and Politics in the First Binding Internet Election'. Presented at Annual Meeting of the American Political Science Association, Washington, DC, 31 August–3 September 2000.

Southwell, P. and Burchett, J. (2000a) 'Does Changing the Rules Change the Players? The Effect of All-Mail Elections on the Composition of the Electorate', *Social Science Quarterly*, 81: 837–45.

Southwell. P. and Burchett, J. (2000b) 'The Effect of All-Mail Elections on Voter Turnout', *Social Science Quarterly*, 82: 72–9.

Storey, T. (2001) 'In Search of a Perfect Election', *State Legislature*, 27(2): 17–18.

Tolbert, C. (1998) 'Changing the Rules for State Legislatures: Direct Democracy and Governance Policy', in S. Bowler, T. Donovan and C. Tolbert (eds), *Citizens as Legislators: Direct Democracy in the United States*, Columbus: Ohio State University Press.

Tolbert, C. (2001) 'Rethinking Lowi's Constituent Policy: Governance Policy and Direct Democracy', *Environment and Planning C: Government and Policy*, 20(1): 75–93.

Tolbert, C. and McNeal, R. (2003) 'Unraveling the Effects of the Internet on Political Participation', *Political Research Quarterly*, 56(2): 175–85.

US Department of Commerce. National Telecommunication and Information Administration (1995) *Falling Through the Net: A Survey of the 'Have Nots' in Rural and Urban America*, <http://www.ntia.doc.gov/ntiahome/fallingthru. html>

US Department of Commerce. National Telecommunication and Information Administration (2002) *A Nation Online: How Americans are Expanding their Use of the Internet*, <http://www.ntia.doc.gov/ntiahome/dn/anationonline2.pdf/>

Wallace, B. (2000) 'Payyourparkingtickets.gov – Coming to a Town Near You', *PC World*, 18(6): 70–1.

Wenner, L. A. (1983) 'Political News on Television: A Reconsideration of Audience Orientation', *Western Journal of Speech Communication*, 47: 380–95.

Verba, S., Schlozman, K. L. and Brady, H. E. (1995) *Voice and Equality: Civic Voluntarism in American Politics*. Cambridge, MA: Harvard University Press.

Wolfinger, R. and Rosenstone, S. J. (1980) *Who Votes?* New Haven: Yale University Press.

14

Digital Democracy Comes of Age: Internet Voting and the 2000 Arizona Democratic Primary Election*

Frederic I. Solop

The Internet has recently become an important part of the democratic process (Wilhelm 2000; Kamarck and Nye 1999; Rash 1997; Firestone and Corrado 1996). It was only a matter of time until democracy and politics entered the digital world, and now we are moving towards holding elections over the Internet. A major step in this direction took place early in the 2000 presidential election when the Arizona Democratic primary featured the first binding Internet election for public office (Solop 2000; Alvarez and Nagler 2000).

This research examines participation in the Arizona Democratic primary. The article discusses demographic and attitudinal differences between Internet voters and voters who cast ballots either by mail or by going to the polls and submitting traditional paper ballots on election day. Information is drawn from three telephone surveys: a 1,200 person cross-sectional survey of Arizona adults, a 1,200 person survey of registered Democrats in Arizona, and a post-election panel study with 783 registered Democrats, 318 of whom participated in the primary election.

Digital democracy comes of age in the 2000 presidential election

'Digital democracy' refers to the integration of Internet technologies into the functions of government and the apparatus of democracy.

* This research was supported by the National Science Foundation (NSF 0001401).

This involves making governmental information accessible through websites, online political mobilization and, now, Internet voting. Federal, state and local agencies in the United States provide substantial information online to the body politic. Political parties, interest groups and other organizations have created sophisticated and easily accessible, websites. Candidates for public office make position papers, family biographies and solicitations for campaign donations available at the click of a mouse button. Legislative voting records can be easily downloaded. In some communities, web users can pay municipal fines online, while errant drivers attend online traffic school in other communities. Web enthusiasts can receive regular updates on the news, research issues online, and discuss politics in numerous Internet chat groups.

Internet voting is the latest innovation in digital democracy and interest in it is growing rapidly. Many multinational corporations such as Chevron, Lucent Technologies, Xerox and TIAA/CREF already use Internet voting as an option for shareholder elections (Nathan 2000). In March 2000, striking Boeing engineers used Internet voting to ratify a new contract ending their walkout (Rohde 2000). Many universities, including Stanford University and the University of Arizona, have employed Internet voting for student elections. Additionally, a handful of non-binding Internet voting experiments has taken place, most notably in Iowa and Washington. California convened an Internet Voting Task Force in 1999 to investigate the feasibility of binding Internet elections for public officials (Jones 2000). The commission recommended moving slowly in this direction with onsite Internet voting first being available at polling locations on election day.[1] Several other states such as Florida and Ohio are considering proposals to introduce Internet voting in statewide elections. Amidst this growing interest, the first instance of statewide binding Internet voting took place in the 2000 Arizona Democratic primary election.

Public opinion supports the introduction of Internet voting. A July 2000 national survey of registered voters by Anderson Consulting found that 71 per cent of survey respondents would be 'comfortable' casting their vote online (Meeks 2000). Sixty-one per cent of respondents said they would vote by Internet in the 2000 presidential election if the choice was available. A Medill News Service survey found that 41 per cent of Election 2000 non-voters believed Internet voting would improve turnout (Medill News Service 2001). Many people believe Internet voting will make voting easier and cheaper, and that it is also an accurate and verifiable method for recording votes.

Internet voting supporters believe voter turnout will increase when elections go online, but critics argue that current technology does not yet support widespread implementation of Internet voting. Security issues have yet to be conquered (Rubin 2000), and the 'digital divide' may lead to discriminatory access for specific groups within the population (United States 1999, 2000; Hoffmann and Novak 1999; Hoffmann, Novak and Venkatesh 1997).

The impact of Internet voting on the electoral system is still not understood. Are Internet voters different from other voters? Does Internet voting encourage particular types of people to participate more often than others? Will Internet voting advantage one set of ideas over another? This article presents findings from the first empirical study of participation in a public Internet election and focuses on the choice voters confronted in the Arizona primary election to use the Internet to vote from either remote or onsite locations, or to use another method of voting, such as mail balloting, or simply to use a paper ballot at the polls.

History of the Arizona Internet election

Arizona Democrats' decision to integrate Internet voting into their 2000 primary election emerged from unique political circumstances. At the time of the primary, Republicans dominated Arizona state politics, holding four of five top statewide offices and controlling both houses of the state legislature. From this position, Republican lawmakers maneuvered the Democratic Party into holding a private, rather than public, primary election. The Republicans selected a February date for Arizona's public primary election knowing that the Democratic National Committee would not certify a primary held sooner than the first week of March. Thus, the Arizona Democratic Party needed to schedule its primary for a later date and to fund the election itself.

Because the Democrats sponsored their own primary, they maintained almost total control over the election process. Betsey Bayless, Arizona Secretary of State, was not responsible for overseeing and certifying election procedures. This anomalous situation created the opportunity for the Democrats to think creatively. Arizona Democrats signed a contract to conduct the primary election with election.com,[2] a company specializing in Internet elections. Prior to the primary, Internet voting instructions and personal identification numbers were sent to all 821,000 registered Democrats in Arizona, along with an application to receive a mail ballot. Arizona Democrats could thus participate in the election using one of four voting methods: votes could be cast prior to Election Day by mailing in a ballot or by accessing an electronic ballot from any remote Internet connection four days prior to election day (7–10 March); on election day, Internet voting was available onsite from 124 official Democratic Party primary polling locations in Arizona; or voters could also cast a traditional paper ballot from any polling site on election day.

Shortly after Internet voting was announced, Voting Integrity Project of Virginia (VIP) filed a lawsuit seeking an injunction against Internet voting. They argued that even though the Democratic primary in Arizona was a private election, preclearance from the Justice Department was required to conduct the election over the Internet.[3] They also argued that the digital divide in America occurs along racial lines thereby making Internet voting a discriminatory election practice in violation of the 1965 Voting Rights Act.

Arizona Democrats consented to the first point and submitted their election plan to the Justice Department for preclearance, which was received in February 2000. A federal judge heard the remainder of the VIP case in February of the same year. The court decided that Internet elections were not inherently discriminatory given the current state of knowledge about the digital divide. The panel left open the possibility of rehearing the case after the election and, if a violation of the Voting Rights Act of 1965 could be proven to have occurred, nullifying election results.[4]

Participation dynamics

Before election day, there was substantial support throughout Arizona for Internet voting (Solop 2000, 1999). Fifty-six per cent of Arizona adults supported adding Internet voting as an option for all future Arizona elections. Among supporters of Internet voting, 12 per cent thought Internet voting should only be available before election day, 29 per cent thought Internet voting should only be available on election day, and 58 per cent thought Internet voting should be available both before and on election day.

Support for Internet voting is best understood by examining the number of people who cast a ballot over the Internet in the 2000 Arizona Democratic primary election. In this election, a total of 86,907 ballots were cast (10.6 per cent of registered voters), with almost half (46 per cent) of all votes cast over the Internet (see Table 14.1). Forty-one per cent of votes were cast from remote Internet sites and 5 per cent of votes were cast from onsite Internet connections on election day. According to survey findings, more than four out of five voters casting a ballot from a remote Internet site voted from their homes, 8 per cent voted from work, 1 per cent voted from a public library, and 6 per cent voted from somewhere else.

Turnouts in Arizona Democratic presidential primary elections are historically small. In the 2000 primary, however, turnout was 579 per cent larger than turnout in the 1996 Arizona Democratic Party primary election. Some could say that because the 1996 and 2000 Arizona Democratic primary elections were only presidential nominating contests and 1996 was an uncontested year for the Democrats, the difference in turnout is really not impressive. Turnout in 2000 would naturally increase if turnout in 1996 was used as the point of reference. However, this argument does not stand up to empirical testing.

To place the turnout figures within a broader context, among the 30 states holding a Democratic primary election in both 1996 and 2000, 15 experienced increased turnout in 2000 while 15 experienced lower turnout.[5] Excluding Arizona, the mean difference in turnout for Democratic primary elections between 2000 and 1996 was a 40.6 per cent increase. The median rate of turnout was −3.2 per cent. Arizona had the highest percentage increase in turnout in the Democratic primary election, followed by Rhode Island (419 per cent), Massachusetts (260 per cent), and Georgia (200 per cent).

Turnout in the Republican primary elections was similar in that among the 38 states holding Republican primaries in both 1996 and 2000; the mean increase in turnout was 7.1 per cent and the median rate of turnout was −6.2 per cent. Slightly less than half of these states (18) had increased rates of turnout in 2000 and 20 states experienced a decline in primary participation.

Table 14.1 Voting methods in the 2000 Arizona Democratic primary election (percentages of votes cast)

		Voters
Internet voting	Remote-site Internet	41
	On-site Internet	5
Other forms of	Mail-in	38
voting	Polling place paper	16
		100

Source: <www.azdem.org/breakdown.html>

The growth in turnout experienced by Arizona Democrats is not simply a result of the unique characteristics of an uncontested 1996 primary election. Availability of Internet voting contributed to this increase. Other factors, including media attention focusing on the availability of Internet voting, may also have contributed to larger turnout. The relative contributions of these and other factors cannot be determined from the available data.

Interestingly, turnout in Arizona's 2000 Democratic Party primary would have been larger had Internet voting not been affected by technological problems (Raney 2000). Four per cent of registered Democrats tried to vote over the Internet but were unsuccessful and ultimately never cast a ballot. The most common problems were technical: would-be voters logged onto the website and the ballot did not appear, computers were not able to accept 'cookies' or small programs from Internet sites, or older Internet browsers were not able to connect to the secure website. Some people said they did not receive a PIN number in the mail, their personal information could not be verified once they were online, or directions were too confusing.

Profile of voter types

This section examines the demographic and attitudinal differences between Arizona Democratic primary voters casting ballots over the Internet compared to people voting either through mail balloting or by casting a paper ballot on election day. This section asks whether Internet voters are different from other types of voters, and explores the implications of these differences.

Demographic differences

According to descriptive statistics in Table 14.2, Internet voting was most popular among white, non-Latino voters, and more popular among males rather than females, and middle age voters (36–65) rather than younger or older voters.[6] Voters from the highest income households are almost three times as likely as voters from the lowest income households to have cast their ballot over the Internet (70 per cent versus 24 per cent, respectively). Internet voting also appears to be more attractive to well-educated rather than less well-educated voters, and liberal Democrats seem to prefer Internet voting more than conservative Democrats. There are no apparent differences in interest related to respondent location.

Table 14.2   Survey demographics by use of the Internet for voting or another method

	Internet voters (%)	Other voters (%)	Chi square	PRE statistic
Race (L)			.093	.000
White, non-Latino	47[a] (116)[b]	53 (130)		
Latino	44 (16)	56 (20)		
Sex (L)			2.237	.021
Male	51 (58)	49 (55)		
Female	42 (86)	57 (117)		
Age			23.144***	.413***
18–35	44 (4)	56 (5)		
36–55	68 (36)	32 (17)		
56–65	55 (56)	45 (46)		
66 +	33 (46)	67 (94)		
Income			20.1638***	–.459***
$0–$20K	21 (8)	79 (30)		
> $20K–$50K	45 (35)	55 (43)		
> $50K–$75K	51 (18)	49 (17)		
$75K +	69 (40)	32 (17)		
Education			47.703***	–.538***
< HS/HS degree	17 (15)	83 (71)		
Some college	47 (43)	53 (48)		
College Degree	53 (31)	47 (27)		
Post-college	69 (52)	31 (23)		
Ideology				
Liberal	54 (45)	46 (39)	2.478	.175
In-between	45 (86)	55 (107)		
Conservative	39 (9)	61 (14)		
Location (L)			1.977	.000
Urban	45 (58)	55 (70)		
Suburban	47 (57)	53 (64)		
Rural	49 (27)	51 (28)		
Remote	–	100 (2)		

[a] Represents percentage of demographic group who used the Internet to vote; [b] figures in brackets represent weighted sample size; * $p < .05$; ** $p < .01$; *** $p < .001$.

Table 14.2 also takes this analysis one step further by examining the strength of association between subgroup demographics of voters and voting methods and the significance of these relationships. In this analysis, only a few relationships stand out as significant. Voting methods are moderately associated with education, income and age, in that order. Internet voting tends to be attractive to better-educated voters, voters coming from higher income households, and younger voters. While ideology appears to be somewhat related to Internet voting, with liberal Democratic voters more likely to vote using the Internet than conservative Democratic voters, ideology fails the chi-square test of significance in this analysis. Within this sample of voters, one would have to conclude that ideology is not significantly related to Internet voting. Race, sex and location are unrelated to the choice to vote using the Internet or to use other options.

Extending this study, a logistic regression analysis is appropriate to investigate the predictive relationship between demographic variables significantly associated with Internet voting and the choice of whether to use the Internet to vote. This test develops a model of contributions each condition makes to the decision to vote using the Internet or to vote using other means. This test also analyses the predictive success of this model compared to a random distribution of the data. Age, income and education were entered into the model as interval-level variables. Table 14.3 displays the results of the binary logistical regression test. Age and education make significant contributions to the decision whether to use Internet voting. Income is not a significant predictor of vote-method choice. The overall predictive success of this model is 71 per cent.

Attitudinal differences

Understanding differential interest in voting over the Internet is an important first step towards knowing how Internet voting affects the political process. Another approach to understanding the impact of Internet voting on the political process comes from an analysis of attitudinal differences between Internet voters and other voters. Do Internet voters relate to the political system differently than other

Table 14.3 Binary logistical regression analysis of relationship between demographic variables and Internet versus non-Internet voting method

	B	S.E.	Wald	Sig.	Exp(B)
Age	.042	.013	11.235	.001	1.043
Education	− .316	.086	13.517	.000	.729
Income	.000	.000	.744	.388	1.000
Constant	− .620	.919	.456	.500	.538

Model Chi-square: 40.917***

voters? Would Internet voters still cast a ballot if Internet voting was not an electoral option? Do Internet voters vote differently than other types of voters?

It is important to know whether Internet voters would still cast a ballot if Internet voting was not available in an election. In the preelection survey of registered Democrats, the question that comes closest to this concern is the following: 'If Internet voting was available in all future elections, would you be more likely to vote in future elections, less likely, or would it make no difference?' Prior to the primary election, nearly one-quarter of people who eventually cast a ballot over the Internet said availability of Internet voting makes them more likely to vote, while only one in ten eventual non-Internet voters answered this way. Following the election, Internet voters were much more likely than non-Internet voters to say that availability of Internet voting would encourage them to vote more often in the future (see Table 14.4). Thirty-four per cent of Internet voters in the post-election period said they would be more likely to vote if Internet voting was an option compared to 9 per cent of non-Internet voters. This pre-election and post-election difference of 25 per cent is noteworthy. The experience of Internet voting was positively received with Internet voters more likely to express a commitment to voting in the future if Internet voting options were available.

An additional attitudinal concern involves whether Internet voters differ politically from other voters. We have already seen that ideology does not play a significant role in determining whether one votes over the Internet or via another method. It is also important to understand whether levels of efficacy differ between Internet voters and other voters. The survey of registered Democrats presented three

Table 14.4   If Internet voting was available in all future elections, would you be more likely to vote in future elections, less likely, or would it make no difference? (percentages)

	Pre-election			Post-election	
	Registered Democrats	Internet voters	Other voters	Internet voters	Other voters
More likely to vote	17	26	9	34	9
Less likely to vote	7	–	7	2	8
Doesn't matter	74	74	82	64	77
Don't know	2	1	2	–	5

standard efficacy questions drawn from the National Election Study.[7] Answers to the three efficacy questions were averaged and a mean efficacy rating was assigned to each respondent. A lower rating on the scale indicates that people tend more often to agree with these questions, thereby indicating a feeling of being less efficacious. Higher ratings are associated with higher levels of efficacy.

Registered Democrats, as a whole, had a mean efficacy rating of 2.77 on this scale. Internet voters, however, had a mean rating of 3.24, indicating a higher level of efficacy than the entire group of registered Democrats. Voters who selected either mail or paper balloting rated 2.73 on this scale. The non-Internet voter group has an efficacy profile that is very similar to registered Democrats as a whole. In sum, Internet voters share a greater belief that their participation in the political process matters.

Discussion

Circumstances surrounding the 2000 Arizona Democratic primary are unique, thus making it difficult to generalize from these findings to future Internet elections. However, this information provides a starting place for understanding the importance and impact of this next wave of election reform.

Arizona experienced a surge of participation in the 2000 Democratic primary. This surge exceeded increases in voter turnout in every state that had Democratic and/or Republican primary elections during that year. The availability of Internet voting contributed to Arizona's increase in political participation; it is likely that other factors such as media attention also contributed to that increase. Participation would have been even greater if all technical glitches had been anticipated and corrected before voting began.

Internet voting is attractive to both well-educated and younger voters. Well-educated voters reproduce biases already inherent in electoral processes as education is considered a critical variable for determining who participates and who does not. This study's finding that age is an important variable in Internet voting is particularly important. Younger voters are shown to have been more interested in using the Internet to cast their vote. It is difficult to make conclusions about election choices made by the youngest voters given the low number of 18–35-year-old voters in this study. However, it is well-known that young people have consistently low rates of election turnout. If Internet voting is shown to bring young voters into the electoral process, then significant long-term cohort effects could follow.

This research also shows that there are attitudinal differences between Internet voters and other voters, with Internet voters feeling more efficacious than both non-Internet voters and Arizona's registered Democrats.

Outside of the Arizona 2000 Democratic primary, five non-binding Internet voting experiments took place during the 2000 general election for president: four in California and one in Arizona. As well, a small number of military personnel living abroad cast their presidential votes over the Internet in an experiment organized by the Federal Voter Assistance Project. Young people participated in a national, non-binding, online presidential election.[8] Although the current state of technology does not support large-scale implementation of remote-site Internet voting,[9] widespread availability of Internet voting is not far in the future. The Florida recounts have raised national awareness about the need for an accurate and verifiable method of recording votes cast in the United States, and Internet voting could fulfill this need sometime in the future.

The analysis presented here is a starting point for development of a future research agenda examining the significance of Internet voting. Additional analyses of Internet voting should locate this reform within a larger movement towards digital democracy. As nations put more information online and citizens use the Internet more frequently to become politically involved, broader changes in patterns of participation will inevitably take place. Now is the time for political scientists to cast their gaze on the implications of the digital future.

Notes

* This chapter is based on F. Solop, 'Digital Democracy Comes of Age: Internet Voting and the 2000 Arizona Democratic Primary Election', *PS: Political Science and Politics*, 34(2), 289–93.

1   The National Science Foundation, in cooperation with the University of Maryland and the Internet Policy Institute, convened a commission in October 2001 to define a research agenda for Internet voting. This commission also concluded that Internet voting should be introduced slowly beginning with on-site Internet voting before moving to kiosk voting and, eventually, remote site voting. See Report of the National Workshop on Internet Voting: Issues and Research Agenda. http://www.Internetpolicy.org/research/ e_voting_report.pdf.

2   Formerly Votation.com

3   Several counties in Arizona are named in the Voting Rights Act of 1965 as requiring Department of Justice approval for modifications of electoral processes.

4 Following the primary election, VIP planned to continue pursuing their lawsuit in federal court. As of this writing, VIP has agreed to end the lawsuit.
5 Turnout figures for 1996 were drawn from Federal Election Commission statistics located at <http://www.fec.gov/pubrec/presprim.htm>. Turnout figures for 2000 are located at <http://www.cnn.com/ ELECTION/2000/primaries/>
6 Given the small number of 18–35-year-old voters in this study, it is difficult to draw definitive conclusions about relative interest in Internet voting between this group and 36–55-year-old voters.
7 The three efficacy statements used in this analysis include: €1) Public officials don't care much about what people like me think; €2) People like me don't have any say about what the government does; €3) Sometimes politics and government seem so complicated that a person like me can't really understand what's going on.
8 See the Youth Evote site <http://www.youthevote.com>
9 It is important to note that the first binding Internet election in the world took place free from computer hacking or concern about security breaches.

References

Alvarez, M. R. and Nagler, J. (2000) 'The Likely Consequences of Internet Voting for Political Representation', Paper presented at the Internet Voting and Democracy Symposium, 1 November, Loyola Law School.

Firestone, C. M. and Corrado, A. (1996) *Elections in Cyberspace: Toward a New Era in American Politics*. Aspen Institute Programme on Communications and Society. American Bar Association, Standing Committee on Election Law. Washington, DC: Aspen Institute.

Hoffmann, D. L., Novak, T. P. and Schlosser, A. E. (2000) 'The Evolution of the Digital Divide: How Gaps in Internet Access May Impact Electronic Commerce', *Journal of Computer-Mediated Communication*, 5(3).

Hoffmann, D. L., Novak, T. P. and Venkatesh, A. (1998) 'Diversity on the Internet: The Relationship of Race to Access and Usage', in A. Gramer (ed.), *Investing in Diversity: Advancing Opportunities for Minorities and the Media*. Washington, DC. The Aspen Institute.

Jones, B. (2000) 'A Report on the Feasibility of Internet Voting', California Internet Voting Task Force, <www.ss.ca.gov/executive/ivote/>

Kamarck, E. C. and Nye, J. S. (1999) *Democracy.com? Governance in a Networked World*. Hollis, NH: Hollis Publishing.

Meeks, B. N. (2000) 'Message From the People: Get Online!' MSNBC website, <http://www.msnbc.com>

Medill News Service (2001) 'Survey: Nonvoters Not a Lost Cause', in Inside Mediall News, <www.mediall.nwu.edu/inside/2001/nonvoters.html>

Nathan, S. (2000) 'More Investors Click to Cast Proxy Votes', *USA Today* (27 March): 13B.

Raney, R. F. (2000) 'After Arizona Vote, Online Elections Still Face Obstacles', in *The New York Times On-line*, <www.nytimes.com/library/tech/00/03/cyber/ articles/ 21vote. html>

Rash, W. Jr. (1997) *Politics on the Net: Wiring the Political Process*. New York: W. H. Freeman.

Rohde, L. (2000) 'Net Voting Resolves Boeing Labor Dispute', *The Standard*, <www.thestandard.com/article/display/0,1151,13112,00.html>

Rubin, A. (2000) *Security Considerations for Remote Electronic Voting Over the Internet*, <http://avirubin.com/e-voting.security.html>

Solop, F. I. (1999) 'Arizona Embraces Internet Voting', in *Social Research Laboratory*, <http://www.nau.edu/~srl/releases/rel15oct99.htm>

Solop, F. I. (2000) 'Public Support for Internet Voting: Are we falling into a "Racial Ravine"', Paper presented at The American Association of Public Opinion Research, 18–21 May, Portland, Oregon.

United States, National Telecommunications and Information Administration (1999) *Falling Through the Net : Defining the Digital Divide : A Report on the Telecommunications and Information Technology Gap in America*. Washington, DC: National Telecommunications and Information Administration, US Department of Commerce.

United States, National Telecommunications and Information Administration (2000) *Falling Through the Net: Toward Digital Inclusion: A Report on Americans' Access to Technology Tools*. Washington, DC: National Telecommunications and Information Administration, US Department of Commerce.

Wilhelm, A. G. (2000) *Democracy in the Digital Age*. New York: Routledge.

15
Internet Voting Behaviour: Lessons from a German Local Election

Norbert Kersting

During the direct election of the Landrat (the county's head of administration) in the county Marburg-Biedenkopf in September 2001, voters had the opportunity to vote by Internet. Because it was parallel to the binding election, it acted as a simulation. The project group 'Electronic Voting by Internet' (ESI) was founded in June 2001 and was a public–private cooperation with the goal of managing the technical and organizational implementation of Internet voting and to evaluate, aside from the technical aspects, the legal and political framework. The members were the Faculty of Computer Science and the Institute for Political Science at the University of Marburg, the local administration of the city of Marburg, the local administration of the county of Marburg-Biedenkopf, the electoral supervisor (*Landeswahlleiter*) of the state of Hessen (Ministry of the Interior), the commissioner for data protection (*Datenschutzbeauftragter*) of the state of Hesse, the regional computing centre (KIV) and a local private software company. This pilot project would be a first step towards developing Internet voting as an alternative to mail-in voting.

Four weeks before the election day the registered voters received voter notification. Voter registration in Germany is handled by the local administration and every adult is registered. The registered voters in the city of Marburg, which is part of the county of Marburg-Biedenkopf, received notification as to where they could apply as usual for voting by mail-in ballots. Furthermore they could apply for Internet voting. Of the total, 3,759 applied for absentee voting, mostly applying 2–3 weeks before election day. Of these, 3,226 (91%) of voted by mail. This group formed 21 per cent of all voters. The mail-in ballot consisted of a postal ballot paper and a declaration to say that they had filled out the ballot without external pressure or manipulation. There was also the possibility of casting the ballot at the town hall during this period.

Three hundred and fifty-six registered voters applied at the same time for Internet voting. They had to use the vote by mail ballot, which was binding, and could at the same time vote by Internet, which was not binding. The reason for this was that Internet voting was not yet incorporated in electoral law and a signed declaration (digital signature) was lacking. Two hundred and thirty-four citizens voted by Internet, 65 per cent of those who applied. So, 1.6 per cent of all voters used the new instrument.

The total turnout in the direct election of the Landrat was very low (31.1 per cent) and the Internet voters were not representative of the real outcome. In the Internet voting sample the candidate for the Social-Democrats won with 57.8 per cent, against the Christian-Democrat candidate (42.2%). However, in reality the Christian-Democrat representative got 52 per cent against 48 per cent for the Social Democrat candidate.

Empirical findings

Research on Internet voting at the Institute for Political Science combined quantitative and qualitative empirical approaches (opinion polls and focus groups). The main empirical instrument was a survey with a sample of 356 participants in the ESI project. The *Landeswahlleiter* (electoral supervisor) and the Ministry of the Interior state of Hessen gave a research allowance to implement a postal survey in October 2001 that allowed the construction of user profiles and so forth. Furthermore, in various focus groups participants and non-participants of the ESI project were interviewed intensively.

Research focused on the following aspects (see Buchstein in this volume; Buchstein 2000; Coleman 2001; Gibson 2001; Kersting 2002):

- *Constitutional regulations*: were these and the national electoral framework respected?
- *Equal election*: was there evidence of disproportion or digital divide regarding Internet voting? Was there free access to Internet voting?
- *Free and secret ballots*: was coercion or vote-selling prevented? What was the voting situation?
- *Influence on voting behavior*: did Internet voting influence voting behaviour? Does it increase the motivation to vote and therefore

enhance turnout? Does the percentage of voters by mail increase? What does the change in the voting process and in the social context of voting (building up social capital, identity etc.) mean?

- *Legitimacy and trust*: was there high confidence in Internet voting and did the electoral process influence political legitimacy? What about democratic control of the voting process (transparency, recount etc.)?
- *Time of voting*: did early voting influence the voting decision? Does this lead, according to democratic norms, to an unequal vote?

In September 2001 all voters who wanted to participate in Internet voting got the opportunity to evaluate the instrument in a mail-in opinion poll; 212 answered the questionnaire. The following results are based on this mail-in survey and focus on user profiles, digital divide, and so on. Of the sample, 182, that is 87 per cent, voted in the ESI project; 13 per cent (32) of the sample had applied for participation but, for various reasons, did not vote. The discrepancy between the voters and the groups who applied, resulted from technical problems (access denied, no computer at home), political disinterest and forgetfulness.

User profiles: socio-economic analysis

Socio-economic analysis shows some quite surprising results. Employees and public officials amounted to 39 per cent and, in relation to the social structure in Marburg, are overrepresented (Census 1987, and Table 15.1). Predominantly higher ranking employees and officials have used the new instrument. Also, the self-employed at 14 per cent are a proportionally big group. On the other hand only 20 per cent of students voted electronically, which is nearly 9 per cent below their demographic level. Workers (1 %) and the unemployed (31 %) are also underrepresented. Surprising is the high percentage of pensioners representing 13 per cent of the participants.

Internet voting found a greater interest within the population having a higher education; 47 per cent of the users had a university degree and a further 30 per cent a high-school diploma. Electronic voting was accepted in all age groups. Voters between 18 and 29 years made up 25 per cent of the users, but the age groups of 30–39, 40–49 and 50–59 also each represented approximately 20 per cent of the participants. Even people over 60 formed were 15 per cent of the participants in the ESI project.

Table 15.1 Socio-economic status of Internet voters (percentages)

Occupation		Age	
Employee/Official	39	18–29	25
Student	20	30–39	20
Self–employed	14	40–49	19
Pensioner	13	50–59	21
Worker	1	60 +	15
Housewife	7		
Unemployed	3		
Education		*Gender*	
University degree	47	Male	65
Highschool diploma	30	Female	35
GCSE (*'Mittlere Reife'*)	10		
Secondary school	11		

Rounded data, *N*=212.

However, Internet voting seems to reflect a gender bias; 65 per cent of the participants were male. The low percentage of female Internet users may have an influence on Internet voting.

Factors associated with Internet voting

The use of Internet voting depends on knowledge and use of the Internet, political interest and a preference for postal voting:

- *Postal voting.* The concept pursued in Marburg saw Internet voting as an additional instrument for postal voters, and the acceptance of this procedure within the group of postal voters is very interesting. According to the decisions of the Constitutional Court in Germany, postal voters should remain a minority. The question arises whether Internet voting could displace the classic election in the polling station. Participants in the Internet voting project in Marburg were recruited particularly from the group of postal voters; 41 per cent always use mail-in voting, a further 31 per cent use it frequently, and 18 per cent rarely. Nevertheless 10 per cent requested postal voting for the first time, but only a small percentage of these had voted for the first time. It cannot be clarified whether the possibility of Internet voting motivated this group to request for postal voting.
- *Internet use.* The Internet is becoming an important communication and information instrument, especially within the younger

generations; this was one reason for introducing online elections. The survey data show that the use of the Internet is dependent both on sex as well as age and education; a smaller percentage of women than men use the Internet. Furthermore, use of the new communication instrument decreases within the higher age groups and increases in the groups with a higher level of education. About 70 per cent of the online voters in Marburg use the Internet (nearly) daily; 18 per cent use this instrument frequently; 9 per cent use it rarely and 4 per cent had never used the Internet before.

- *Political interest.* A further factor in the use of online elections is political interest. This was operationalized in the questionnaire with the question about participation within local elections. Ninety-two per cent of the participants in the online election project always voted in local elections. 6 per cent frequently participated and 3 per cent only rarely participated. The survey data show that at the local level the voter turnout rises with age and that amongst students a high portion of non-voters can be found (see also Kersting 1997).
- *Citizen obligation and citizen right.* Through qualitative interviews in the focus groups of different age, gender and socio-economic status it emerged that interviewees regard elections as an important citizen obligation. Political disinterest and apathy in elections is explained by the existence of too many elections. But elections are still seen as special chance for political participation. It is obvious that there is social pressure on citizens, because it can be unpleasant to declare not having voted. According to the focus-group, elections are to some extent a citizen's obligation, since people who do not cast their vote have no right to criticize government policies. Nevertheless, electoral apathy can be regarded as a legitimate means to express political cynicism towards the political class and a lack of legitimacy of the political system. Thus Internet voting is not regarded as a remedy to solve political apathy and protest and to increase voter turnout. Voting behaviour also reflects the importance of the different types of election; general national elections are classified as more important than, for example, local elections. Second-order elections (local elections, European elections) can also be left out once in a while:

> I regard it as an obligation to cast my vote in order to influence politics. I can remember that I once didn't vote because of laziness and lack of interest, but that changed. Now, I regard elections as very important.

Internet elections and voting by mail

Internet elections and postal voting show a high resonance (see Table 15.2); 90 per cent vote for the introduction of Internet voting and find this instrument 'very good' and 'good', and only 3 per cent consider it 'bad' and/or 'very bad'. These opponents to Internet voting see the trustworthiness of the procedure as problematic and criticize the form of e-banking in Germany with well-known procedures using PIN and TAN numbers.

The possibility of absentee and postal voting are evaluated by 94 per cent as 'very good', with only 1 per cent regarding these as 'bad'. The critique focuses on the clarity of voter notification as well as fears that the secrecy of the vote cannot be guaranteed. This leads to a lower use of postal voting. Voter notification, which was sent out to all citizens, covers multiple information, so that the very improbable possibility of a second ballot, which would have taken place only with equality of votes of the two candidates in the first ballot, is considered. Nevertheless, 18 per cent evaluate the clarity of voter notification as 'very good' and 35 per cent as 'good'. About 15 per cent are dissatisfied. In particular the elderly criticize voter notification.

The qualitative interviews show that online voting is regarded as an alternative to postal voting. In relation to voting at a polling station, there is a higher possibility of manipulation of the results in postal voting, but many voters do not want to miss this option. Within postal voting voters try to ensure their intimacy and privacy. In principle there is a chance to influence postal voters and manipulate the vote, but so far from their own experience, no serious offences could be reported. At home, no individual manipulation was reported. The participants of the focus group reported on problems and a distrust of using e-mail, but confidence and trust in the German postal system

Table 15.2   Evolution of Internet voting and voting by mail

	Very good	*Good*	*Indifferent*	*Bad*	*Very bad*
Vote by mail	57	37	6	1	0
Voter notification (clarity)	18	52	14	10	5
Internet voting	66	24	7	1	1
Internet voting (with PIN and TAN)	33	48	14	4	2
Trustworthiness of Internet voting (with PIN and TAN)	28	40	23	7	2

was very high. Only in some cases did interviewees distrust post offices and deliver their ballot documents directly to the city hall.

At the same time, organized manipulation of postal voting, similar to some cases in Bavaria in 2002, was not experienced. Also, speculations on the possibility of political parties or other interest groups manipulating voting behaviour or selling votes was not expected. For most respondents, casting their vote and meeting other citizens in the polling station was an important symbol of democratic identity and gave a feeling of inclusion in the political community. But according to the participants of the focus groups, this social capital can also be developed by other social contacts. The option of postal voting, which some participants of the focus groups regularly used, prevented the common experience of voting on the election Sunday, but with this method voters don't forget to vote and postal voting from home is regarded as a fast and comfortable option.

Nevertheless, many assumed that older voters do not fill out the ballot independently. Postal voting is assumed as a good alternative in order to reach a higher election turnout, and to reach this goal compromises regarding secrecy and a possibility of manipulation are allowed. Often in the focus-group interviews the old-folks' homes are mentioned, where relatives and caretakers could probably have a high influence on the habitants.

Technical security and confidence

In Marburg, the Internet voting project used a special procedure which has already become generally accepted in e-banking. Together with the postal voting ballots, PIN and TAN numbers were sent to participants in sealed envelopes (see Table 15.2), to be used for the identification of the Internet voters. In principle, 81 per cent evaluated the procedure of the Marburg Internet voting simulation as 'very good' or 'good'. Almost one-third responded 'very good' and 50 per cent 'good'. Four per cent evaluated the Marburg procedure as 'sufficient' and only 2 per cent as 'unsatisfactory'. Criticisms aimed at the general procedure of the Marburg Internet voting experiment resulted particularly from fears of a lack of anonymity. The use of PIN and TAN numbers was evaluated by 83 per cent as 'very good' or 'well'. About 6 per cent criticized the procedure. The groups which fear manipulation and a lack of secrecy evaluated the instrument more critically. In principle, 68 per cent considered the procedure very trustworthy; only 9 per cent regarded the trustworthiness of the procedure as 'very bad' or 'bad'. This evaluation depended both on estimates regarding the anonymity of the electoral process and concerns about the secrecy of votes.

Qualitative interviews showed that the technical security of the Internet and confidence in Online elections are seen as very controversial. One rather techno-optimistic group had high confidence in the Internet services, for example online shopping and home banking, whereas a techno-pessimistic group, which also consisted of trained computer experts, stated a distrust because of fundamental security problems regarding the Internet. Thus, these groups refused to submit personal data to the Internet; on the one hand fearing that e-mail addresses and so on are abused for advertising purposes or passed on to commercial organizations, or on the other hand that someone could decode the password and misuse their credit card and other personal details:

> Addresses are passed on ... One shouldn't give away their addresses or bank account numbers so easily. I am very skeptical. With on-line booksellers I don't order, if one cannot order on invoice. It is rare that I indicate my correct Internet address, in order to avoid my mailbox being 'spammed'.

The techno-optimistic group used technical options to delimit possible damage. For example, implementing online banking only with a daily limit. However, Internet shopping is often seen as a calculated risk:

> Here [in e-commerce] I am completely different and sometimes, perfectly disinhibited. I have been a kind of 'Internet junkie' for years. I also have used Internet banking for many years and it is very practical.

Within the economic sector a certain range of risk-taking becomes obvious, but within the political sector higher standards are expected. So here the techno-optimistic group also postulates that all technical measures must be seized in order to protect the individual against attacks from others, such as hackers. There is a consciousness that in the long term all codes can be decoded. However, hardly any individuals or private organizations might be interested in such decoding, and the danger that decoding by state agencies where the majority of the electoral data records are stored is estimated as very small. State intervention into the privacy of voters is regarded as only a small problem in the possible introduction of Internet voting. Possible manipulation on the part of the state is hardly seen in Germany, and there is a high degree of confidence and trust in national organizations and existing safety precautions, which will also ensure data security. But the comprehensiveness and the transparency of the electoral procedure in Internet voting is assumed as a fundamental weak point. In online elections the counting of the ballots is not transparent, recount is not possible and the process works as though in a 'black-box'. So in principle the possibility of electoral manipulation by hackers or the public administration is there. Interviewees assumed, however, that their individual votes would be counted correctly. Participation in Internet elections presupposes a basic confidence in relation to the medium:

> It [the Marburg online election] was this time only a test election, i.e. it was not very interesting for hackers. As soon as it will be serious, some hacker may manipulate it and a change of only 2 per cent of the votes ... would have terrible consequences ... An election of a county head of administration (Landrat) may be still uninteresting for a hacker, but if it is an election at the federal level, that is terrible.

Confidence in the traditional casting of the vote is also based on the fact that the voter's envelope is put into a locked ballot box in front of the voter's eyes and symbolically the ballot box is locked and sealed: 'Easily one can be sure: here abuse is not possible and if all this is in the ballot box, no one can assign who belongs to which ballot paper.'

With the introduction of smart cards in the private sector the confidence in these cards and in safeguarding methods could increase. According to the interviewees, these procedures, however, could have the disadvantage that the totally transparent citizen could become reality. Trust in the electoral offices and organization, though, is based on a basic confidence in German thoroughness in the public sector.

Secrecy and privacy of the vote

Postal voting and Internet voting move away from the mandatory principle of the secret vote and therefore the German Federal Constitutional Court recognized this as a supplementary way of voting. The secrecy of the vote is the responsibility of the citizen, but there are fears that in certain spatial and social contexts the secrecy of the vote is not protected. These are the major concerns regarding online elections.

Of the participants in the Internet voting project, 81 per cent believed that the secrecy of the vote was protected sufficiently (Table 15.3), but 19 per cent criticized a lack of secrecy. Analysis of the spatial and social context of Internet voting gives further information about the secrecy of the vote. It must be noted that the Internet voting procedure in Marburg was only a simulation, because citizens were required to use the traditional electoral procedures as well. Nevertheless 90 per cent accomplished the act of voting through the Internet without observation and assistance. This means that there were no manipulations or other people trying to influence the electorate or to injure the secrecy of the vote. Five per cent voted by Internet under observation but without assistance of others, and a further 5 per cent voted by Internet under observation and with technical assistance. However, the theoretical risk of influence and manipulation from the outside cannot be totally disregarded. Furthermore, voluntary or involuntary disclosure of the vote by the voter is also always possible. There are many people with little knowledge of the Internet; predominantly the older part of the population, women, and people with a lower level of education.

Table 15.3　Secrecy, place, context and motivational factors of voting (percentages)

Where did you vote by Internet?		Did you cast your ballot via the Internet alone, or not?	
At home	83	Alone	90
Other	3	Under observation, but without assistance	5
At work	9	Under observation, with assistance	5
At town hall	5		
When did you vote by Internet?		Do you think that the secrecy of the vote is sufficiently protected within Internet voting?	
About 1 week before the election	37	Yes	81
About 2 weeks before the election	31	No	19
About 3 weeks before the election	18		
About 4 weeks before the election	15		
Would you have voted, if no Internet election had been offered?			
Yes, via ballot	8		
Yes, vote by mail	90		
No	2		

N = 212.

According to the qualitative interviews in many households with members from older generations, the secrecy of the vote was and still is very important. Some family members suspect or believe they know which party parents or children have voted for, but inquiries often do not occur or get no clear answers. In younger families, voting behavi- our is much more open and often controversially discussed. Sometimes parents try to influence their children, but for the most part not very successfully.

Locality of the vote and symbolism of elections

Internet voting offered different voting possibilities, and the spatial context is particularly important in an analysis of the voting pattern. Eighty-three per cent used the domestic PCs for Internet voting (Table 15.3), 9 per cent voted at work, and 5 per cent used the option of voting in the city hall, that is in a polling station which was opened about four weeks before election day.

The difference between online elections and traditional ways of casting the ballot may be analysed more deeply through the qualitative interviews. In rural areas in particular a high level of ritualization in voting procedures can be seen. Polling stations in villages, school buildings and so on seem to have a sacred atmosphere and voting is strongly ritualized. With online voting the importance of these ritual- ized procedures may possibly decrease. One interviewee commented:

> It's fascinating. They go to the polling station like they go to church and deliver their vote. In the city this already is less obvious, but in the countryside it still plays a large role.

On the other hand, the atmosphere in the polling station is often described as very rigid and too official. The formalization of the voting procedure, including processes of identification and so forth is rather deterring. In particular, younger voters show a certain uneasiness:

> Each election you got the impression that you were always somehow being observed by the electoral officers in the polling station. As soon as you left the polling station, you got the impres- sion that they were whispering about who you voted for. Therefore, I did not trust the whole procedure. I thought they even checked, who I voted for. This feeling continued until I first worked as a electoral officer on my own.

The environment in the polling station also works rather discourag- ingly, in particular for the younger generation. On the other hand, older as well as younger voters demand an appropriate framework for this important sovereign act of voting:

> there [in the polling station] is no atmosphere. It's terrible. Especially now within the local election they used blue garbage cans as ballot boxes. Thus, I had the feeling I was throwing my ballot in the recycling bin. That was a little bit tasteless.

In rural areas and with older people symbolism of the election and ritualization becomes obvious. After a church service and lunch, citizens follow their obligations to vote. Some stated that this should happen rapidly; the pressure on voters to cast their votes as soon as possible seems to result from the fact that nobody wants to forget or miss the election. Everyone prefers to keep the rest of day free for other activities. Here the oppressive character of voting as a citizen obligation and duty is obvious. Watching the TV electoral analyses at 18:00 seems to be another part of the ritual on election Sunday.

It is assumed that the loss of these rituals could deter and disorient many voters. In particular the older constituency regards the continuity of the polling station, which should represent a politically neutral, public place, as important. But the older generations are not against youth using the new procedures, for example Internet elections. However, for themselves voting is an important expression of representation of their rights as citizens. Nevertheless, older people also criticize the strong social control in polling stations; in smaller municipalities in particular and in rural areas it is important to vote since it is checked upon if one has participated or not, and there is thus a high level of social control. The polling station, frequently the old village school or the community centre, is accepted as a politically neutral public place. The younger generation assumes voting as a more negative duty of citizens. In families, social control by parents plays an important factor:

> I must say sometimes I wouldn't have been highly motivated to vote if there wasn't external pressure. My father insisted the whole Sunday, saying: What's up, you don't want to go to the polling station?

Family and democratic initiation

Frequently parents have to remind children to go to vote. In the older generation, parents and sometimes their children together would often go to the polling station. In multi-generation households with sometimes different party preferences, a very strained family atmosphere may be reported on election day. Parents often play a central role in political socialization and particulary for first-time voters. At their children's first election, parents not only literally take their children by the hand, but may also try to influence their child's vote.

First-time voters accept this 'initiation ritual', which gives a feeling of political efficacy and leads to democratic identity and legitimacy, but at their second or third elections this special status is already void:

> The first time I voted I felt unbelievably important like a part or an element of this state. Never before did I feel my political role as much as on election day.

> I was very nervous and fevered before the first election, and then it was actually a little boring to go there and cast the ballot. I had higher expectations, but it was still spectacular, because you can use your right to participate.

Place of election and identity

Direct contact in the polling station with other citizens is seen as precious and has an important democratic value, related to democratic identity. Symbolically, citizen build up their own democratic identity and their personal affiliation to the political system and democracy. For a lot of citizens the polling station as an official area seems to be very important for voting. The question might arise as to whether political discussion takes place at such sites or whether the official surroundings makes political discussion more difficult. In some countries political campaigning close to the polling station is even prohibited. The older generation in particular mentioned that using other places, such as a cinema for example, as polling stations would reduce the characteristic sovereign act of election. Younger citizens, however, are mostly attracted by the possibility of voting in different places. Furthermore, local binding can be reduced by the option of voting in other polling stations, which corresponds to higher mobility of citizens. The possibility of voting at a polling station during a visit to a parent's home, during holidays and so on, is regarded as an additional liberty

Time of the vote and rationality of electoral decision-making

Postal voting, if it is connected with Internet voting, offers the possibility of voting within a longer period before election day. However, the expansion of the voting period is criticized by some constitutionalists because of the negative effects of early voting. The survey showed that within the Internet voting project the voting rate rose with proximity to election day (Table 15.3); 37 per cent voted about 1 week before election day, about two-thirds had already voted during the three or four weeks period before election day.

How voters choose

The results of the focus groups show that the decision of who to vote for is usually made at least two days before the election Sunday. In the cabin the ballot paper is not studied properly, since voters already know where they want to make their cross. Mostly only the first three parties on the list are read superficially. With the introduction of the personal vote (cumulative voting, Panache), for example in the state of Hessen where different candidates from different lists may be voted for, many voters stated that for the first time they stayed in the cabin longer to study the ballot properly. They also mentioned that with Internet voting at home they would take more time for voting.

During local elections with personal votes (as cumulative voting), many voters prepared ahead of time with a sample of the ballot as printed in the newspaper, studying the lists of candidates at home:

> This [cumulative voting] is an aspect which would affect my voting pattern. I would take much more time for voting in the Internet election and I would look at all parties and candidates more exactly. I wouldn't do this in the cabin, because I would think, I cannot stay there for such a long time.

So the younger generation is conscious about the significance of the electoral procedure, but the chance to take more time for voting and the possibility of voting in advance could promote election turnout.

Irrational electoral decision?

The lack of information about parties and their programmes is not assumed to be the only factor responsible for low election turnout. A higher openness and responsiveness of parties is regarded positively and could be facilitated by use of the Internet. New election portals could make it possible to implement new ways of party campaigning, with some suggesting that such portals could have Internet links to parties and their programmes. A minority rejects the idea of building up official election portals with links to parties, homepages, because this could be an unlawful manipulation. In Germany political advertisement in and around the polling station is forbidden, so it should be forbidden in Internet elections as well. Nevertheless, another group demands such links within Internet elections and in election portals.

The danger of junk votes, that is a thoughtless casting of votes, is not expected. In contrast, Internet voting could provide a longer phase of reflection at the domestic PC and a more considered casting of votes:

> If someone votes, he doesn't decide the moment he sits in the cabin or in an Online election, if he has the mouse in his hand ... I think voting is not a last minute decision ... In real life there is plenty of time to think about your vote. At local elections there have been long queues in front of the polling station. The people then sat in the election cabins and felt under pressure because people were waiting outside and everyone wanted to be finished.

> ... and I believe many people don't vote, because they are comfortable and because they say simply: We have beautiful weather, we want to go walking, we go to the pool or to the Sauna and when it's six o'clock then the polling stations are closed and it's too late. There is unbelievably amount of people who do not vote simply because they are too lazy.

Increase of voter turnout

There has been much speculation about the influence of online elections on voter turnout (Buchstein 2000). Electoral apathy may be lowered and new sub-populations motivated to participate in elections. Because the Marburg Internet voting project was only a simulation, our survey cannot give final empirical testimony, and, furthermore, survey data about attitudes towards voting may often be characterized as lip-service of respondents.

The question as to whether participants in the Internet voting project would still have voted if no online voting possibilities were offered resulted in 8 per cent indicating that they would have voted in the polling station; and 90 per cent would have voted as postal voters anyway. Two per cent confessed that they wouldn't have voted in the local election. This shows that postal voting coupled with Internet voting focuses mainly on postal voters and raises their participation level. The increase of voter turnout by an introduction of such an instrument is, however, only very small.

Delegitimization and acceptance of intergenerational differences

According to the results of the focus groups, the older generation seems to grant the possibility of testing new election instruments to younger voters. They do not suggest a delegitimization of the political system, because from the view of the older generation online voting could be a modernization in favour of a higher election turnout:

> Perhaps today it is uncool to vote... Is it not the case that young people, if they spend election Sunday traditionally with people over 30, that they regard election as an old-fashion thing?

Fundamentally all groups believe that due to the sinking election turnout new modes of election must be developed. So safety problems are taken into account. The danger of a superficialness within the voting decision is evaluated differently; some interviewees forsee the possibility of junk votes.

While in the older generation the election committee and the polling station is regarded as a sovereign symbol, the younger generation looks upon these institutions as threatening and renounceable. Online election do not produce a public, but a private atmosphere. Here the possibility of being informed about party programmes and electoral procedures exists. However, electoral Internet portals and ballots should be arranged in as neutral a manner as possible. According to the opinions of the focus groups, in the long run new technical possibilities such as online elections will not waive the basic problem: that of depoliticization and a lack of political interest. Here other factors are responsible.

Conclusions

Electronic democracy and online voting offers a number of possibilities but also some threats (see Buchstein in this volume). Until now statements on online voting have not been based on fundamental research but mostly on techno-optimistic and techno-pessimistic prejudices. Some normative democratic theorists in Political Science have picked up the negative attitudes on new technologies and foresee an endangerment of the democratic principles. They mostly present empirically unproven scenarios in which the introduction of online voting as well as postal voting would lead to electoral fraud, rigging and broadly-based manipulation of the electorate. This could undermine the legitimacy of the political system to an extreme extent. Regarding postal voting there is no evidence of a broadly-based misuse of this instrument, but empirical research is necessary to prove these prejudices and reject or support the hypotheses. Empirical research also has to analyse the acceptance and other attitudes towards new electoral instruments (see Kersting and Vetter 2003; for empirical research projects see Solop 2000; Alvarez and Nagler 2000; Southwell and Burchett 2000).

The new information and communication technologies have changed the lives of a large majority of the population and also beliefs and attitudes on these issues (see Norris 2001). A neutral research approach can give a better insight into the preferences of citizens because theoretical and normative theories are probably overseeing relevant societal developments. Because of the implementation of pilot projects using online voting instruments, there is research on its consequences on electoral behaviour. Electoral studies can also use exit polls to get detailed information about voting behaviour. However, because of data protection in political elections postal voting is not adequately analysed, and regarding postal voting and online voting research is restricted because voters in these elections are highly protected by electoral supervisors and commissioners on data protection.

Research on these electoral instruments therefore normally has to use representative survey data. Here, research has not focuses on the attitudes and behaviour of postal voters, and in the research project presented here the electoral supervisor and the commissioner for data protection allowed us to contact the participants of an online voting project using classical quantitative research instruments. These data were enriched by qualitative data from focus-group interviews. The presented quantitative results were collected from a postal survey within the participants of the Internet voting project. During the direct election of the Landrat (the county's head of the administration) in the county Marburg-Biedenkopf in September 2001, voters had the opportunity to vote by Internet. This simulation was implemented in the binding voting process and coordinated by the state and local public administration and adjusted to the legal and organizational framework. Participation in Internet voting in Marburg depended highly on political interest, as well as general Internet use. Of the participants 87 per cent were frequent (most of them daily) Internet users, and more than 90 per cent were frequent voters. Citizens who prefered to vote by mail also prefered Internet voting. Nearly two-thirds usually voted by mail, whilst 10 per cent voted by mail for the first time.

The 'digital divide' is a counterargument against implementation of online voting. Empirical data show that with the proliferation of new information and communication technologies, public Internet access points, and so forth, the digital divide could become a minor problem (see for example Cap Gemini and Young 2003; Norris 20001; Grönlund in this volume). Although younger age groups are predominantly using the new media, the spread of the new modes of communication is also visible in the older generation. This development can also be seen in this socio-economic analysis that focuses on special user profiles. Internet voting is not restricted to young age cohorts; even those over 60 years old represent 15 per cent of participants. However, males are seen to predominate in Internet voting because knowledge of the Internet as well as political interest (65 per cent) is higher in that group. Internet voting is also found to depend on the level of education. Furthermore, employees and public officials are a predominant group because within this group there is a high level of political knowledge as well as a high understanding of the Internet. Students are, because of their low local political engagement, not represented; the self-employed are overrepresented.

The acceptance of new electoral instruments is very high in our survey, which is not a surprise because the participants of the pilot project have voluntarily chosen this opportunity. But this high acceptance still exists after the usage of the instrument. The possibility of Internet voting (90%) and the availability of postal voting (94%) are evaluated very positively. The group of critics (1–3%) is rather small. On this issue future research will need to use survey research to focus on representative samples and exit polls focusing on traditional voters at polling stations to compare results.

Distrust of the new instrument using computer technology, instruments for cryptization and computer networks is predicted as extremely high (see Buchstein 2000). Attacks by hackers and the rigging of electoral results may undermine the legitimacy of the political system to an extreme extent. The respondents accepted the procedure of the Internet voting project and evaluated it as positive. An even higher percentage was very content with the procedure of PIN and TAN numbers. A small group (6%) criticized the trustworthiness of the procedure, specifically the possibility of data manipulation and the possible lack of anonymity.

If the level of advanced voting is very high it could be argued that there is no equal vote. The number of online votes cast rises with the proximity to the election date, with over two-thirds voting two weeks before election day. But this is a voluntary decision by voters. The process of decision-making in online voting may lead to the privatization of politics and to spontaneous, hasty participation without a qualified process of reflection. The majority of online voters cast their votes at home (83%), with only a small portion voting from work (9%) and only 5 per cent at the city hall.

The qualitative interviews show that long queues at polling stations may have a negative effect on voters who feel under pressure and forced to make a hasty decision in the ballot cabin. At home there may be more time for a profound analysis of the ballot paper and candidates. Here it is often argued that the electorate on the way to polling stations has the necessary time for rethinking final decisions, but the empirical research on electoral behaviour analysing the time of voters' decision-making shows that this decision is already made some days before election day.

The context of voting and the atmosphere at the polling station seem to be important symbolic expressions of citizens' political rights. The electoral process is a positive factor for the development of social capital and for political community-building (see Putnam 2000). In introducing online voting this symbolism of identity and of citizen rights may be lost and individualization strengthened. This symbolism of elections has a high importance to the older generation in particular and in rural areas, where family voting is the predominant pattern. However, the qualitative interviews show that the older generation accepts that this is no longer an important aspect for youth, and indeed younger voters often claim that the polling station is characterized by a stiff atmosphere of social control.

The main critical point towards online voting seems to lie in the undermining of the legitimacy of modern democracies, which are based on the law of an obligatory secrecy of the vote. Here, online voting is seen as incompatible. In our study, 81 per cent believed that the secrecy of the vote is sufficiently protected in Internet elections, and 90 per cent claimed to have voted without observation or assistance. So, here, secrecy of the vote was not injured. The hypothesis that online voting could lead to a high number of cases of manipulation and coercion has to be rejected. Although there is a threat that manipulation of voters may occur, the empirical data show that citizens are able to protect their privacy and the secrecy of the vote. Here representative empirical research is needed as to whether the responsibility to protect this secrecy should be in the hands of each voter, or whether secrecy has to be controlled by the state administration in the polling station (mandatory secrecy) (see Buchstein in this volume).

In most OECD countries electoral turnout is decreasing (see for example IDEA 2002), and especially in the younger generation voter turnout is tremendously declining. The reason for this is not only political apathy, a lack of knowledge and a disinterest in politics, but also the political cynicism of interested citizens (Kersting and Sperberg 2003). The younger generation is the main target group of Internet voting strategies, with the aim of using the Internet as a door-opener to political participation (see Norris 2002). Changing habits and higher mobility are leading to the creation of a new instrument in electoral procedures, which may strengthen the motivation of younger voters. So mobilizing young voters, bringing in a new motivation to overcome the political divide and enhancing the low voter turnout among young voters are important aspects.

Online voting does not seem to repair voting apathy inevitably, since 90 per cent of the online voters would have voted anyway as postal voters, and about 8 per cent were motivated by the opportunity of online voting to abstain from voting at the polling station or to use postal voting. Only 2 per cent were attracted to vote who would not otherwise have voted by the possibility to vote online. Although this was only a pilot project, it can be argued that the new instrument will not lead to a sustainable boost of voter turnout.

Even when because of new technologies, public Internet access points and other developments the digital divide could become reduced, there may be still the question as to whether the Internet could be better used as a tool for information and as a record of organizations or communities than an interactive instrument for participation (see Kersting 2003a). The attractiveness of online voting may then lie in the possibility of combining participation, communication and information. The main goals and prospects of future strategies should focus on higher political inclusion, that is increased voter turnout and better information and discourse before the ballot (Kersting 2003b). Apart from a probably small, short-term and not sustainable enhancement of voter turnout, online elections may lead to an empowerment of voters. Internet users are already getting more and better political information using the web and are part of an information elite. So the implementation of online voting portals with information on parties' programmes and so forth, and forums with a deliberative discourse could introduce a higher rationality into the electoral process and strengthen democracy (see Kriesi 2002).

This research had contradicted some existing prejudices, and introduced evidence on some major questions on online voting. If we expect a radical proliferation of new information and communication technologies, these will undoubtedly dominate political discourse over the next decades. I expect that within this development, online voting procedures will be implemented. Economic reasons, administrative efficiency and a fast and efficient way of counting votes are seen as other positive effects. Normative political theory will not be a barrier if there is a high acceptance of these instruments by the majority of the population. Similar to the introduction of postal voting, once introduced, online voting will gain a broad acceptance and will be difficult to stop, although some democratic principles (secrecy) may be endangered. It seems that only on the basis of profound future research will an implementation of e-democratic and online voting instruments according to democratic principles be possible.

References

Alvarez, M. and Nagler, J. (2000) *The Likely Consequences of Internet Voting for Political Representation*. Los Angeles: Loyola Law School.

Buchstein, H. (2000) 'Präsenzwahl, Briefwahl, Online-Wahl und der Grundsatz der geheimen Stimmabgabe', *Zeitschrift für Parlamentsfragen*, 4(S): 886–902.

Cap Gemini and Young (2003) *Online Availability of Public Services*. Berlin, <http://www.de.cgey.com/ servlet/PB/show/1005708/eEurope.pdf>

Coleman, S. (2001) 'What Was New? Online Innovations in the 2000 US Elections', in S. Coleman,(ed.), *Elections in the Age of Internet. Lessons from the United States*. London: Hansard Society, 48–64.

Gibson, R. (2001) 'Elections Online: Assessing Internet Voting in Light of the Arizona Democratic Primary', *Political Science Quarterly*, 116(4): 561–83.

IDEA (International Institute for Democracy and Electoral Assistance) (2002) *Voter Turnout from 1945 To 1997. A Global Report on Participation*. Stockholm: IDEA.

Kersting, N. (2003) 'Internet-Wahlen im Vergleich. Deutschland, USA und Schweiz', in A. Siedschlag *et al.* (eds), *Kursbuch Internet und Politik 2/2002*. Opladen: Leske.

Kersting, N. (2003a) 'New Information and Communication Technologies and the Future of Local Democracy', IPSA Conference 2003, Durban.

Kersting, N. (2003b) 'Electronic Voting and Local Democracy in Europe', ECPR Conference 2003, Marburg.

Kersting, N. and Sperberg, J. (2003) 'Political Participation', in D. Berg-Schlosser and N. Kersting (eds), *Poverty and Democracy. Political Participation and Self-Help in Third World Cities*. London: ZED Books, 153–80.

Kersting, N. and Vetter, A. (eds) (2003) *Reforming Local Government in Europe. Closing the Gap between Democracy and Efficiency*. Opladen: Leske and Budrich.

Kriesi, H. (2002) 'E-voting. Motivation and Information Issues', workshop on E-voting and the European Parliamentary Elections. Florence: European University Institute, May 2002.

Norris, P. (2001) *A Digital Divide: Civic Engagement, Information Poverty and the Internet and in Democratic Societies*. New York: Cambridge University Press.

Norris, P. (2002) *Democratic Phoenix: Political Activism Worldwide*. New York: Cambridge University Press.

Putnam, R. D. (2000) *Bowling Alone. The Collapse and Revival of American Community*. New York: Simon & Schuster.

Southwell, P. and Burchett, J. (2000) 'The Effect of All-Mail Elections on Voter Turnout', *Social Science Quarterly*, 28: 72–9.

Solop, F. I. (2000) *Digital Democracy Comes of Age in Arizona: Participation and Politics in the First Binding Internet Election*. Paper presented at American Political Science Association National Conference in Washington, DC.

16
Conclusions: Adopting Electronic Voting – Context Matters

Norbert Kersting, Ronald Leenes and Jörgen Svensson

In the preceding chapters a variety of views and developments regarding electronic voting has been presented. On the one hand, the evidence makes it clear that in some places the opportunities offered by Internet voting are being keenly explored. In several countries the foundations for online voting are being put in place, experiments have been carried out or policies are being drafted. On the other hand, critical analyses that warn against fundamental problems of Internet voting have been presented, suggesting that Internet voting is not really a viable option for serious democracies. A number of countries otherwise deeply committed to democratic practices hesitate to pursue online democracy. What can be made of these seemingly contradictory trends? Is there a future for Internet voting? Are the critics right in their claim that online election is a dead-end street? Or should we trust the proponents' belief that technical and social problems will be overcome, and go for the advantages promised by electronic channels of voting?

Interesting as these issues of the feasibility and desirability of online elections may be, we wish to develop a somewhat different line of reasoning by asking *why* some countries decide to move faster along the path of Internet elections than others. In our opinion, it is impossible to make definite claims about the appropriate stance to be taken, irrespective of the particular context in which voting takes place. In this chapter we will argue that variations in social and political context influence the adoption of Internet voting. Countries, populations, electoral systems, public attitudes, political and administrative arrangements differ widely, and all these factors play a role with regard to how Internet voting may be adopted. This means that in different countries with different circumstances the decisions on whether or not to introduce a particular kind of Internet voting may, and indeed do, differ.

The first part of the chapter reviews opportunities and threats associated with Internet voting: what are the possibilities, what is to be gained, and what could be lost? At the end of this book we find it not too difficult to compile such a list, but it is still not easy to make definite claims about the desirability of Internet voting. Not only is there much uncertainty with respect to the precise outcomes of Internet voting in a certain context, but interests and opinions may vary as to whether a specific outcome is to be regarded as a serious threat, an acceptable risk or, indeed, an opportunity. This in turn suggests that the evaluation of Internet voting in different countries is likely to differ. In the second section, current practices of voting in general and Internet voting in particular are outlined. What are the trends that emerge in a broad overview of the countries covered by this book? Are these countries all more or less on the same track, or are we witnessing the beginnings of diverging trends in Internet voting? As we look at the evidence, we will argue that the latter is the case. So, our next step is to spell out what we think are the main factors impinging upon the implementation of Internet voting and to analyse the country-specific discourses. These analyses lead to some further reflections but, more important, they help us in formulating an agenda for future research.

Prospects and threats of Internet voting

Electronic voting is generally seen as any type of voting that involves electronic means (see for example IPI 2001; Pratchett 2002). Although electronic voting can be conceived in many different ways, a crucial distinction may be made between voting by electronic polling machine and Internet voting. *Voting by polling machine* simply refers to the use of any electronic apparatus to record and count votes in a fixed public place. This may be a specialized voting machine in a voting booth or a standalone PC specially installed for this purpose in a voting kiosk. Polling machines may be especially helpful for a reliable, objective, efficient and expeditious counting of votes and may also offer some possibilities for electronic verification (for example verification of whether the user is indeed entitled to vote and whether the vote is cast correctly).

Internet voting goes a step further in the sense that it implies electronic registration, culling and counting of votes cast from different locations. It typically allows voters to use a more generic technology such as the Internet, to cast their votes from any preferred place – be it from the home, from the office or even from an Internet café while travelling abroad – and, as Buchstein observes, in many new forms such as 'on-the-run voting' or 'vote in your underwear'. In this section we will discuss the main opportunities and threats that seem to be connected to Internet voting. What are those threats and opportunities? How real are they? How should we weigh the various arguments in a comparative evaluation? As we will explain, there are three arguments in favour of not giving definite answers to these questions as yet:

- There is still much uncertainty about the validity of claims of both proponents and opponents.
- The validity of claims and their relative weights depend on the specific context in which they are evaluated.
- Even if we could know the actual consequences of Internet voting, different actors would have different opinions and different interests.

The main arguments of proponents and opponents of Internet voting often only reflect initial beliefs and fears and lack an empirical basis for a more thorough evaluation. Therefore, we focus on whatever empirical support is available with regard to the claims being made. As we write this chapter, we find that the empirical evidence on Internet voting is still scarce and generally inconclusive, and that, apart from the evidence in this volume, we can rely on only a few other serious studies available to us of which the most important are:

- The use of Internet voting during the 2000 Arizona democratic primary (Mohen and Glidden 2001; Philips and Spakovsky 2002; Solop 2000).
- The Internet pilot voting project of the US Department of Defense during the 2000 US presidential elections (FVAP 2001).
- The use of Internet voting during a referendum in Bristol and Croydon in the United Kingdom (Thomas 2001).
- The 2002 local election pilots in the United Kingdom (Electoral Commission 2002).

There are, furthermore, some relevant research projects on non-binding simulations of Internet voting, for example the 2001 local election pilot project in Germany (see Kersting 2002b, and Kersting in this volume). Besides this research on pilot projects there is also some research on attitudes to ICT and Internet voting acceptance.

Prospects

Internet voting is often considered to provide new opportunities in the organization of elections. As proponents of electronic voting point out, these possibilities may help to make voting easier and more cost-effective, and may also help to increase voter turnout, facilitate direct democracy and enhance voter information.

Costs and effectiveness

Internet voting may be expected to offer benefits regarding the cost-effectiveness of elections. The costs of introducing this type of voting are relatively high, but costs may be reduced with large-scale proliferation over a longer period of time. The argument of cost-effectiveness received some support in the experiments in the UK, where the elections were outsourced to a contractor who charged 30 pence per telephone vote and 60 pence per Internet vote. However, we should keep in mind that in this case there was also an additional fee for general services, that the costs of the freephone number were met by the authorities, and that the Internet voters, of course, had to provide their own equipment and Internet access.

However, the cost-effectiveness argument looks ridiculous if the Internet voting project of the US military (FVAP 2001) is considered. Here each vote (in total 84 votes) cost the US taxpayer US$73,809 (<http://www.public-i.org/story_01_080901.htm>), although this was, of course, the result of very high initial costs. In Switzerland and the Netherlands, the costs of introducing electronic voting have been found to be much higher than expected because of the necessary security measures (Ministerie van Binnenlandse Zaken en Koninkrijkrelaties 2002; Schweizerischen Bundesrat 2002).

Turnout

The particular strength of Internet voting is that it enables people to vote without having to go to a special polling station. It thus provides the prospect of reducing the effort needed to vote, especially for people who find it difficult to visit a polling station on election day, such as the physically challenged or people living in remote areas. Especially when electronic voting is used as part of a multi-channel approach (Internet, TV, telephone, cell phone) and a combination of different forms of voting is offered, there is the prospect of people being able to vote by the means they prefer. Electronic voting is considered as a way to modernize the voting process and to give voting a new, modern image. According to some commentators, modern people and especially young voters are used to the idea of electronic transactions and simply expect the government to provide the possibility of electronic voting.

However, serious doubts arise with respect to increased voter turnout as a result of the introduction of Internet voting. Philips and Spakovsky (2002) and IPI (2001) conclude that previous reforms designed to make the voting process more convenient – simpler voter registration, extended voting times, voting by mail – have had little, if any, effect on voter turnout. Pratchett *et al.* (2002) also conclude that an increase in voter turnout is not likely because factors such as 'time poverty', inconvenience and inaccessible polling procedures are relatively unimportant in explaining turnout decline.

The fact that the Arizona primary of 2000 saw an increase in voter turnout as compared to the 1996 primary, is considered to be a result of very different circumstances. In 1996 there was only one candidate, there were significantly less physical polling places, far less media attention and few get-people-out-to-vote initiatives (Philips and Spakovsky 2002). In Bristol and Croydon, the percentages of Internet voters were 2.7 and 3.4 per cent (Thomas 2001), hence the UK Electoral Commission (2002) concluded that the these pilot projects appeared to have no significant impact on turnout. This argument is substantiated by the findings in Marburg where 95 per cent of the online voters argued that they would also have voted if Internet voting had not been an option (see Kersting in this volume).

Direct democracy

If elections can be handled more easily, mobilization for initiatives and referenda could be enhanced as well. This is what advocates of direct democracy maintain. In contrast, some opponents of Internet voting argue that its introduction may lead to fundamental and undesired changes in the nature of representative democratic systems. As some observers notice, once electronic voting systems are implemented, the marginal costs of organizing new elections and citizen consultations may be so low that there will be pressure to organize them more often, perhaps even on a daily basis (Instant Democracy). This would certainly undermine the idea of representative democracy and may be considered a threat. Or, as the IPI report put it: 'In the long run e-voting could lead to more referenda and threaten the deliberative nature of the political system and the protection of the minority' (IPI 2001).

The Swiss example, however, shows that distant voting may also have a negative influence on direct democracy. The organizers of citizen initiatives in Switzerland predominantly collect the necessary signatures in front of the polling stations. This is no longer effective if many people rely on postal voting or Internet voting. Without direct contact with citizens on election day, citizens' initiatives may have problems collecting the required number of signatures to start a referendum.

Voter information

Democracy may be enhanced through various strategies. One may be to simplify the act of voting and another to facilitate access to useful information (see Kriesi 2002). Converse (1964) assumed that the majority of voters were characterized by a low interest in politics. In order to reduce information costs to a minimum, voters try to simplify their decision-making process, which is fostered by low political attention and a low competence level caused by a lack of interest, resulting in limited cognitive investment. Downs (1957: 230) argues that voters use cognitive shortcuts by delegating their decisions to other actors, whom they trust, and whom they regard as reliable and competent. Here, the political elite and the political parties play an important role.

In traditional societies, the public sphere is constituted by public assemblies, that is to say by speaking in small groups. This kind of micro-public was replaced by a more or less homogeneous setting of mass-media which was controlled at the national level by some dominant newspapers and mostly state controlled electronic media (television and radio). The development of private radio and television channels led to fragmentation and segmentation of the public sphere. Reinforced by the introduction of the Internet, a 'Balkanization' of the public sphere is taking place (Kriesi 2002).

Kriesi argues, furthermore, that the introduction of Internet voting could contribute to rehomogenization if the voter gets special information on elections and referenda through state-controlled and moderated Internet portals which provide different forms of information and communication. This model refers to the Swiss referenda where each voter is provided with a ballot and special information, which gives him/her a brief introduction to the issues. This not only includes the government's argument, but also a brief overview of the opponent's position, which means the voter is provided with both pro and contra arguments. This could be easily organized in Internet voting. Furthermore, voters need an overview of the relevant partisan cues

(Kriesi 2002: 20), and such party cues could be included in Internet elections. If independent regulatory agencies were to supervise voting devices as well as the information presented, more reasoned voting behaviour by informed citizens might come about.

Threats

As we have seen, some of the promises of online voting can also be seen as threats. Critiques of online elections often refer to normative democratic theory (see Buchstein in this book). The digital divide and the possibilities of external and internal attacks and manipulation create legal problems and can affect the legitimacy of elections and, in the long run, destabilize the political system.

Digital divide

With respect to the problem of user proficiency, Internet voting may strongly increase this problem and lead to a digital divide in voting. ICT is not distributed equally in the electorate, nor are electors from various socio-ethnic and socio-demographic backgrounds equally likely to be able and willing to use the technology (see for example IPI 2001; Pratchett 2002). Widespread electronic voting can thus lead to some voters having far more difficulty in voting than others, and even to stigmatization of traditional voters as either Luddites or lacking the technical means or skills to vote electronically (Pratchett 2002).

As far as the digital divide argument is concerned, this threat is also reflected in the available material. In the Arizona primary, the fears of digital division were substantiated. Large urban counties with predominantly white voter populations voted via the Internet in much greater numbers than their counterparts in rural counties with large populations of minority voters (Philips and Spakovsky 2002).

Pratchett and others conclude that Internet voting turnout will most likely mirror conventional voting patterns:

> Indeed, the evidence appears to suggest that Internet voting will perpetuate the existing socio-economic and demographic differences between those who vote and who does not, regardless of how widely available the relevant technologies are within society. (Pratchett 2002)

Technical problems and trust

The operation of Internet voting (and this also is the case for all electronic devices and voting machines) by individual voters may be considered a relatively new risk. As we know from numerous studies, many people have difficulty with operating modern technical artifacts (see for example Wyatt 2001), and with the introduction of machines in the voting process there is a risk of complicating this process for the average voter. Although designers may claim that a certain system is user-friendly and 'foolproof', experience often proves otherwise. The recent experience with (mechanical) voting machines during the presidential election in the USA is just one extreme example.

There are, furthermore, problems related to the reliability and robustness of technical systems. Any complex technology, and especially computerized machines, may break down and cause problems which may be hard to correct. In the case of e-voting machines, risks of disturbances of power supplies and failures in the electronic storage of the votes certainly require special measures in the form of verification and backup facilities, to identify errors and correct them.

All of the Internet voting experiments show that the new technology comes with serious problems which voters often find difficult to solve. In all projects reviewed, there were problems related to the hardware and software needed for casting Internet votes (FVAP 2001; Philips and Spakovsky 2002; Solop 2000; Thomas 2001). In the Arizona Democratic primary, 4 per cent of non-Internet voters, amounting to roughly 1,800 voters, unsuccessfully tried to cast their vote via the Internet first (Solop 2000). In the US military experiment there were 128 motivated potential voters, of which only 91 actually registered online, and of which only 84 managed to cast their vote. Meanwhile, the help desk was contacted 71 times for many different problems relating to the use of digital certificates, installing required software, and access problems (FVAP 2001).

As critics point out, Internet voting may also be vulnerable to insider attacks on the integrity of technology and procedures. Computerized machines especially are essentially opaque and therefore allow for manipulations that are not recognizable to the user or even to supervisors present at the elections (for example computer programs which during voting switch one in 10 votes to a preferred party and which erase themselves at the end of the voting process, without leaving a trace). Although people involved in the manufacturing of voting machines could be capable of such fraud, the more serious danger here would be that of organized manipulation by authorities. In weak democracies or under circumstances of political turmoil, it would be impossible to guarantee the trustworthiness of voting machines, and even in the absence of actual fraud, this could seriously undermine the legitimacy of the voting process (see for example Brunazo 2000). However, these threats also exist to some extent with polling machines and even the traditional polling booth.

Vulnerability is also increased since practical implementations of online voting relies on open networks of PCs and servers, which are therefore more vulnerable to accidental failure and intentional attacks. Servers are exposed to intrusion and denial of service attacks rendering election services unavailable. Client PCs used by voters can be attacked by Trojan horses and viruses aimed to spy on ballots, or to modify them. Communications between clients and servers can be intercepted and clients lured to imposter sites (spoofing) which can cause unde-tected loss of votes or act as a 'man-in-the-middle' between voters and the real vote site (IPI 2001). In short, the risk of undetectable fraud by insiders and corrupt regimes is extended to attacks by outsiders, such as bored wizzkids, radical groups or even foreign powers.

The symbolism of voting

Internet voting also introduces some new risks, which are especially connected to the fact that it may lead to a fundamental change in the social conditions under which the vote is cast. Internet voting does not take place in a public locale in a controlled environment, and this removal of voting from the public to the private sphere is considered to be of symbolic importance. To some people voting is just a form of public-service delivery, to many it is much more:

> It is a constituent element of representative democracy and a ritual of coming together of concerned citizens. At this one time, all citizens who enter the voting booth are of equal stature – each casts one vote notwithstanding their differences in race, education, occupation, or net worth. (IPI 2001)

There is concern that with an introduction of Internet voting, elections may lose their visible, public and symbolic character.

The German research showed that among the older generation the electoral norm, that is the duty to vote, is a very important and wide-spread attitude. In this group voting behaviour is highly ritualized and important for personal identity and social cohesion (see Kersting in this volume; Kersting 2002b). However, the social and symbolic threats attributed to Internet voting may be somewhat overstated. For instance, the idea of a diminishing symbolic importance of the electronic vote is certainly debatable when it comes to the younger generation.

Secrecy

The reduction of supervision and the concomitant threat to the secrecy of the ballot may be the most crucial issue, however. Secrecy of the ballot is considered essential in most modern states, and is adopted in a wide range of conventions and declarations to which many western democracies are signatory, such as:

- The Universal Declaration on Human Rights – Article 21 (3).
- The International Covenant on Civil and Political Rights – Article 25.
- The European Convention on Human Rights – Protocol 1, Article 3 (Watt 2002).

Paradoxically, the secrecy of the ballot in traditional voting is brought about by supervision. The election officers in the polling station see to it that voters enter the voting booth alone and that they can cast their vote free from undue influence and in secret. Supervision, furthermore, reduces the risk of impersonation. With the introduction of Internet voting, this type of supervision will be lost, which clearly compromises the secrecy of the ballot. With voting moving into the private sphere, threats run from social pressure in the family ('honour your father', 'obey your spouse') to actual physical intimidation and coercion in other uncontrolled environments.

As Buchstein (2002) shows, the question of a secret ballot goes a lot further than the idea that people who want to vote in secret must be able to do so. As he argues, there is a strong case for 'mandated secrecy', that is that people should never be able to prove to others how they voted. This mandated secrecy is not only desirable because a possibility to prove, in some circumstances, may turn into an obligation to prove, it also prevents people from selling their votes, which is widely seen as undesirable.

Although the available experiments tell us far less about the validity of the arguments of the critics, additional analysis suggests that some of their claims may be toned down. On the one hand, as experience with Internet voting increases, some developers of Internet voting systems have come up with interesting ideas on how to counter certain threats. The threats of coercion, for instance, might be addressed by providing voters with a so called 'distress pin': an identification code which the user could enter instead of the real one and which would allow casting the vote in a normal manner, with the exception that the vote does not count. Similarly, there may be an option of reserving the last day of an election for on-paper voting in polling stations only, and to allow voters to replace any earlier vote by a final vote.

Furthermore, research has shown that in actual practice most Internet voters vote without observation and/or assistance (see Kersting 2002b). In Marburg only 5 per cent of the voters reported being observed and receiving some technical assistance during the voting process.

Validity of claims, context and interests

As we discuss the possible promises and threats of Internet voting, it becomes clear that, although we have to seriously consider each argument, we may very well doubt the certainty and absoluteness of some of the claims. With regard to the main arguments of proponents of electronic voting, we find that the central claims of cost-effectiveness, ease of use and higher turnout are not yet substantiated by facts. But the same holds for arguments against electronic voting. The introduction of Internet voting may be associated with problems concerning user proficiency, system reliability and inside manipulation, but actual proof is lacking. Further research and the development of a research agenda which allows comparative studies is necessary (see below).

The second reason why we think it is not possible to present a final evaluation of Internet voting has to do with the importance of the context of the election, which may vary considerably. In the case of the Arizona primary, for example, it is clear that this election took place under conditions which were quite unique. Not only was it a very specific type of election, it was also held in a huge, sparsely populated state, with a limited number of polling stations available and with a record of very low voter turnout. The specificity of the Arizona context makes it difficult to compare this election to the ones in Germany or the Netherlands, where people live much closer together, polling stations are always near and turnout is around 80 per cent.

Differences in context seem especially important when we want to discuss the possible risks of Internet voting. As we already indicated, the risk of large-scale inside manipulation would probably receive much more attention in a young, vulnerable democracy than in a vested democracy with strong democratic institutions. The same argument may apply to fears about the secrecy of the ballot. There are even some circumstances in which such fears may indeed be turned around. In countries and places where elections are surrounded by violence and intimidation, Internet voting could even support the free and secret vote.

Finally, we have to acknowledge that even if electronic voting was guaranteed to have certain consequences, this would not oblige different actors to come to the same conclusions about this instrument. The clearest example is the idea that Internet voting may lead to more frequent elections and to more direct democracy. Even if this was proven, which it is not, different people might assess these facts in different ways. Some would see this as undermining the valued (representative) democracy, whereas others would judge it as a welcome strengthening of democracy. The same holds for the fear of a digital divide in voting: where parties with a less-educated, poorer electorate may be expected to really embrace this issue, parties with a more-educated, richer and predominantly male electorate will probably not worry much about it.

Internet voting: present forms

So, we have to accept that different actors in different circumstances may come to very different conclusions regarding Internet voting. What does this mean in practice, and what does it mean for the actual adoption of Internet voting? Do different countries in different circumstances actually reach different conclusions? Or, are differences in circumstances, beliefs and interests relatively small, with consensus, either in favour of or against Internet voting, and a convergence in policy as the result?

As we compile the information from this volume, together with additional research (Svensson and Leenes 2003), we find that there are clear indications for our thesis that due to differences in context, countries will diverge with respect to Internet voting. There seem to be different strategies towards the implementation of Internet voting. The first route starts with differentiating between political spheres, where a local election is seen as a testing ground for new instruments of voting. The second path involves differentiating the steps towards electronic voting. This begins with the introduction of electronic registration, which seems to be more of a problem than the introduction of polling machines. The next step, kiosk voting, is leading towards less control oven the electoral process. The last step, the implementation of remote Internet voting, makes the state-controlled electoral supervision of the secrecy and the privacy of the vote impossible. Here the citizen is responsible for respecting and protecting his/her rights. Table 16.1 provides an overview of the ICT context, the political context, the use of different voting technologies and policy plans in national and federal elections. (The data on the policy plans are based on a survey

Table 16.1 Voting technology and voting policy in Western Europe

Technology/policy	Austria	Belgium	Germany	Finland	France	Ireland	Italy	Netherlands
Elections								
Low turnout								
High number of elections and referenda								
ICT								
High use of ICT				x			x	x
Introduction of private online elections	x	x	x					x
Paper technology								
Early vote	x		x	x		x		
Postal vote			x			x		
Proxy vote					x			x
Current electronic voting strategy								
Polling machines		x	x^a		P	x^b	P	x
Kiosks						P	P	P
Internet voting			L					L

Notes: x = implemented; P = planned; L = long-term planning; ^a Electronic polling machines were introduced in Cologne and some other cities; ^b Pilots in England during the 2002 local elections with all-postal voting, Internet voting, SMS voting and telephone voting.

Table 16.1 Voting technology and voting policy in Western Europe   *continued*

Technology /policy	Norway	Portugal	Spain	Sweden	United Kingdom	Switzerland	Estonia	United States
Elections								
Low turnout					x	x	x	x
High number of elections and referenda						x		x
ICT								
High use of ICT	x			x	x		x	x
Introduction of private online elections	x							x
Paper technology								
Early vote	x	x	x	x	x[b]	x		x
Postal vote	x	x	x		x[b]	x		x
Proxy vote								x
Current electronic voting strategy								
Polling machines		P			P	P		x
Kiosks		P			x	P		x
Internet voting					x[b]	P	P	

Notes: x = implemented; P = planned; L = long-term planning; [a] Electronic polling machines were introduced in Cologne and some other cities; [b] Pilots in England during the 2002 local elections with all-postal voting, Internet voting, SMS voting and telephone voting.

commissioned by the Dutch Ministry of the Interior and Kingdom Relations, project number DIOS/IC2000/U66759.) When we look at this table, important variations emerge.

Although voter turnout seems to be a problem at all lower levels in all the political systems analysed, turnout is extremely low in national elections in the UK, Estonia, Switzerland and in the USA (see Kersting 2002a). The number of elections and referenda in Switzerland and in the USA, however, is high. We argue that there must be a high pressure on the administration to implement efficient electoral systems.

The penetration and proliferation of the Internet is quite high in the Scandinavian countries, Estonia and the USA, and this level may in due course be expected in all OECD countries. The introduction of smart cards as identity cards, which could also be used as a digital signature for verification in online elections, is well on its way in Estonia and Italy. In Germany, the legal framework needed to implement the digital signature exists. Furthermore, the USA, Germany and some Scandinavian countries have experience with private-sector online elections.

With respect to 'paper technologies', all countries still use the traditional polling booth but many also offer the possibility of postal voting and/or proxy voting. Advance voting is also possible in most of the countries. The Netherlands and France allow proxy voting, while postal voting is lacking. Four countries, Belgium, the Netherlands, Germany and some parts of the USA have adopted polling machines. The Netherlands have had them for well over 20 years and 90 per cent of the votes are cast electronically. Belgium is expanding the number of these machines steadily. In Germany and the USA, polling machines are only used marginally. Internet voting is not yet an accepted method of voting in any European country, or elsewhere for that matter.

With respect to the explicit Internet voting targets in our sample, we find that there are clear differences and that we may distinguish between three groups of countries. The first group consists of Austria and Spain, together with the Scandinavian countries. These countries rely on the traditional 'paper-and-pencil' voting schemes and seem quite happy with the status quo, which is reflected in the fact that there are no policy plans with respect to Internet voting.

France, Ireland, Italy and Portugal make up a second group. These countries have traditional voting schemes and plan to introduce polling machines, like the Netherlands, but have no plans to convert all the way to Internet voting. However, Portugal will carry electronic voting a little further than the others by introducing voting from kiosks. Ireland has taken the first step to the implementation of polling machines this year by allowing voters in three polling districts to use electronic voting machines during the local elections.

The third group of countries consists of Estonia, Switzerland, the UK, Germany, the USA and the Netherlands. They are planning to go all the way. The Netherlands, Germany and the USA are thinking of extending, step by step, the already existing polling machines to voting from kiosks (existing in the USA) and then to Internet voting. Here, the US and German governments are even more cautious about the final introduction of Internet voting. Estonia, the UK and Switzerland plan to take a larger leap. The UK has ambitious Internet voting plans which it aims to introduce after 2006 (e-Envoy 2002), and there have already been a number of experiments (with legally binding results) with various types of Internet voting during the 2002 local elections. Switzerland has established a policy outlining the experimentation and introduction of ICT in the voting process to facilitate voting and ease the organization of referendums and elections (Schweizerischen Bundesrat 2002). Estonia will implement Internet election in national elections in 2005.

Diverging democracies?

The observations from these data may be interpreted as nothing more than the result of differences in the speed of development of Internet voting, and they may suggest that in the near future all countries will take the road to electronic and Internet voting. Given our analyses in the previous sections and information about the background of the differences in policy plans, we think this is not the case. In our opinion, the difference is not one of speed, but a reflection of the position countries take with respect to the desirability or necessity of introducing Internet voting.

In other words, the plans reflect the assessment of the promises and threats of electronic voting. Estonia, the United Kingdom and Switzerland seem to be on the brink of deciding in favour of Internet voting; the Netherlands, Germany and the USA are planning online voting in the long run and seem to rely on a stepwise approach. In some countries there is high pressure on the government to facilitate the voting process. In Belgium, polling machines have been introduced and in Italy an implementation is planned. Italy has, because of its advanced discussion of an electronic identity card, a positive framework for implementing Internet voting, but has, however, no experience with postal voting, and the secrecy and privacy of the vote is highly valued. Other countries, in particular Spain, France and the Scandinavian countries, are not lagging behind, but have simply drawn a different conclusion with respect to the need to introduce online voting.

Looking at the reasons why various countries are not opting for Internet voting we find that, together with more formal legal arguments, Internet voting is currently dismissed as an option because of its threats to the integrity of the voting process. As Olsson and Åstrom (see their chapter in this volume) argue, Sweden, although advanced in electronic service delivery, is not taking any serious steps towards Internet voting because of its strong democratic tradition and its emphasis on security. In France, a parliamentary bill to introduce Internet voting was not passed, and some experiments were even prevented by a ruling of the Commission Nationale de l'Informatique et des Libertés (<http://www.cnil.fr/thematic/docs/internet/d02_022.pdf>).

Given these strong conclusions against the implementation of Internet voting, the question is, of course, why other countries are aiming to become electronic voting champions. Can we explain why Internet voting is implemented in countries such as Estonia, the UK and Switzerland? As suggested, such an explanation may be found in the specific circumstances and in the beliefs and interests of groups promoting Internet voting. We will now take a more specific look at some of the countries in Table 16.1, starting with the prospective e-voting champions – the UK, Switzerland, Estonia, the Netherlands and the USA – followed by a group of more cautious countries – Austria, Finland, Sweden and France.

The United Kingdom

In order to explain Internet voting ambitions in the United Kingdom, we find that we can point to several reasons why this country is more eager to adopt online voting than others. First of all, an important factor is the strong modernization drive within the British government. Many policy documents all over the world express the desire to modernize government and to invest in an e-society, with of course an 'e-government'. However, where most of them mainly produce e-government rhetoric, the UK seems to take e-government seriously by establishing agencies such as the office of the e-Envoy and making e-government the responsibility of a senior cabinet member. Modernizing the voting process in order to make it fit a twenty-first century lifestyle is an endeavour that follows the e-government's general aims.

A second important factor is the serious decline in voter turnout in the UK, which is seen as a major cause of concern (e-Envoy 2002). Related to this problem, the Political Parties, Elections and Referendums Act 2000 (PPERA) was passed. This Act established the Electoral Commission, whose principal aims include the encouragement of participation in the democratic process and the promotion of electoral registration and voting. Where concerns about low turnout have already led to the introduction of postal ballots, we may see the introduction of ICT as an additional measure along this line. Although both the e-Envoy and the Electoral Commission stress that the introduction of postal ballots and ICT in itself will not increase voter turnout (e-Envoy 2002; Electoral Commission 2002), decreasing turnout is still an important factor driving Internet voting enthusiasm.

Moreover, as the PPERA allows local authorities to conduct pilots with new voting techniques under supervision of the Electoral Commission, it has opened the door for many local entrepreneurs who for many different reasons may be eager to have a go at electronic voting. Not only are the local experiments seen as an excellent chance for local authorities to promote themselves as modern and efficient, but several local managers seem to regard electronic voting as an excellent career opportunity as well. In this enthusiasm local authorities and their managers find themselves backed by international 'election service providers', who according to Ledbetter (2000) 'spend like mad' to ensure that such elections work and that the whole world will hear about them. The evaluation of the pilot projects shows that introduction of postal voting could enhance voter turnout, but that electronic voting instruments were not successful in the same way (see Norris in this volume).

Switzerland

Switzerland also has a relatively low turnout in national elections. In the 1990s postal voting was introduced, in part to reverse the trend of decreasing voter turnout, but it has not succeeded in this respect. This was one reason why, in 2001, Switzerland introduced plans for online voting. Electronic voting will be developed through three separate projects: an electronic voter registration is to be established; a digital signature as a base for national and local referenda will be introduced; and, in Geneva, online voting is to be tested. In the latter case, the administration takes a practical view by not using the digital signature, which is not yet well-known or accepted by citizens.

Online voting is a feasible option for Switzerland for several reasons. For one, the large number of polling procedures (elections as well as issue voting) on the federal, cantonal and communal levels each year suggests that Internet voting may entail considerable economic and organizational advantages. Secondly, the Swiss norms concerning the secrecy of votes are less pronounced than in other countries. Switzerland has a long tradition of open voting in public assemblies, and with the postal-vote legislation of the 1990s Switzerland has already gone a long way towards 'distant polling'. Thirdly, the proliferation of elections and referenda has led to a deritualization and desacralization of elections, which means that the acceptance of online voting in Switzerland is probably quite high.

Although there are clearly reasons why Internet voting in Switzerland might take off, there are also concerns. The project is thought to include a special portal as a 'one-stop homepage' for elections, where, beside the possibility to vote, information on political parties and referenda will be found. This seems convenient for the voter, but it is also a cause for concern. An online voting system lacks a cooling-down phase, which introduces or enhances the possibility of casting ill-considered, spontaneous or last-minute votes. This could lead to much 'junk voting' despite the amount of electoral information on the Internet. Also, the gap between modern online voting at home and the traditional voting system often in the form of an open ballot is seen as problematic Finally, the moderation and the selection of the Internet portals are seen as problematic. The mobilization of weakly informed citizens is feared.

All in all, the balance seems to tip towards experimentation and, finally, the introduction of online voting in Switzerland. In January 2003 in Geneva's suburb Aniere, the first online referendum took place.

Estonia

Estonia is a new democracy that wants to catch up with modern democracies and is prepared to live with the uncertainty involved in new electoral instruments. The conditions for the implementation of electronic voting are right: new electronic technology is widespread and so is the use of the Internet. It is therefore not surprising that plans to implement online voting already existed prior to the national elections of 2003. However, because of political calculations, amendments of the electoral legislation have postponed the introduction of online voting until 2005. The identity card, which already contains facilities for a digital signature, will be used for verification. It is planned that the online voting process should stop one day before election day, and that the voter may revise his/her Internet vote by voting at the polling station. Diminishing the secrecy of the vote is not considered to be a reason to abstain from introducing electronic voting. The Estonian electoral legislation gives full responsibility for the secrecy of the vote to the individual citizen.

The Netherlands

When we look at the general pro and contra arguments concerning Internet voting, we would not expect the Netherlands to be one of the forerunners in this field. The weight of the most crucial arguments in favour of introducing Internet voting seems limited here. Voter turnout has decreased over recent decades, but not as dramatically as in the UK or Switzerland (in the turbulent elections of 2002 and 2003 there was in fact a slight increase). As the Netherlands is the most densely populated country in Europe, organizing access to polling stations has never been a major problem. In most municipalities polling machines are in place, which means that elections are run very efficiently, with some of the smaller municipalities capable of offering vote counts seconds after the polls close.

Furthermore, the Netherlands has a history of being prudent in protecting the individual and promoting the secret character of voting. For this reason, postal voting never made it in the Netherlands and proxy voting is limited (a voter may cast a maximum of two proxy votes). So, when we look at the arguments that apply to the UK and Switzerland, the Netherlands really seems the odd one out.

When seeking to explain why the Dutch seem to be taking the road towards Internet voting, we are left with two possible reasons. The first is their very extensive and positive experience with polling machines. The Dutch are quite used to the application of this technology in the voting process, and this may be a reason why policy-makers in the Netherlands are less fearful of Internet voting than policy-makers in other countries.

The second reason has to do with political ambitions and political lobbying. Just like the British, the Dutch government strives to be at the forefront of e-government and government reform and, just like in Britain, there are links between the development of e-government and the development of electronic voting, both coming from the same ministry. Moreover, the former Minister responsible for e-Government, who was one of the driving forces behind electronic voting, is a member of D66. This party has, since its inception in 1966, campaigned for the introduction of referenda and elected mayors, aims that are quite consistent with the visions of electronic voting. In addition, there is an active Internet voting lobby consisting of organizations such as PELS (Platform Electronic Voting) and EPN (Electronic Highway Platform NL), which have been successful in mobilizing politicians to back electronic voting. This has resulted in persistent demands from members of parliament to continue with the introduction of electronic voting.

Having said this, we also have the impression that the responsible ministers may have started to back down in 2002 (Ministerie van Binnenlandse Zaken en Koninkrijkrelaties, 2002), and despite the responses to the survey carried out by Svensson and Leenes (Svensson and Leenes 2003), we are not certain that the Netherlands will really be one of the first to introduce Internet voting in local or national elections.

Germany

In Germany the expectation is that by implementing online voting, the time needed for counting and recounting votes can be reduced, the number of invalid votes minimized and new technologies for the handicapped can be developed. Electronic voting would also contribute to a higher mobility of voters. The existence of postal voting in the national elections (used by 18% of the electorate in 2002) paved the way towards electronic voting, just like in Switzerland. A number of simulations and binding pilot projects using online voting have also taken place.

Germany foresees a stepwise implementation of electronic voting. At the beginning, all polling stations are to be connected and a central voter register established. With the introduction of Internet and Intranet networks any voter has the possibility of voting in any polling station in Germany. In the following stages kiosk-voting and further online elections are to be implemented, with the possibility of remote online voting at home. Pilot projects are to be tested at the local level before implementation on regional and national levels.

There are also concerns. The constitutional framework emphasizes that external manipulation must be prevented, and that the secrecy of the vote during the voting process must be preserved. The principle of the one-man-one-vote idea should be ensured by special instruments for voter verification, such as electronic signatures, which receive a lot of attention in Germany. Furthermore, the anonymity of the vote should be protected for a long time.

USA

At the outset, the United States held a leading position regarding electronic voting (Solop 2002). The Clinton and Gore administration saw electronic government and electronic democracy as one of their main political goals. There is also an extensive lobby of electronic voting software and hardware vendors that keenly try to jump the e-government bandwagon. Before the presidential elections in 2000, a series of pilot projects with electronic and online devices was tested. Furthermore, trade union elections and elections of shareholder assemblies were organized via the Internet. Nevertheless, the primary of the democratic party in Arizona in the spring of 2000 is widely seen as the first binding and quite successful Internet voting experiment.

The problems of the presidential elections in 2000 have further sharpened discussions on standardizing elections and reforming electoral legislation, and concerns with respect to software integrity, loss of secrecy of the vote and other issues have somewhat dampened the initial enthusiams. Nevertheless, the decentralist US structure, which places the responsibility for organizing elections in the hands of county administrations, was maintained, and skepticism, and also optimism, about the introduction of online voting persists.

* * *

Apart from the countries above with a very positive stance towards the introduction of electronic voting, there are also more cautious countries who value the opportunities and risks of electronic voting differently and hence reach different conclusions. We will discuss four countries in this group, Austria, Finland, Sweden and France, in more detail.

Austria

In Austria, voter turnout at the election of the national parliament has been high. Nevertheless, at second-order, less important elections, as for example for the social partnership (*Sozialpartnerschaft*) and the Austrian student-union elections, turnout is low and even decreasing. Here, the Austrian student union and the Federal Chamber of Commerce plan to implement remote Internet voting by developing a technical and organizational concept, by changing the legal structure and by planning pilot projects in the 2005 elections. With the new laws on data protection and digital signatures and the introduction of the national ID card, the possibility of an implementation of online voting within these 'social elections' is enhanced. In national elections the principles of voting (universal, equal, immediate, personal and secret vote) are highly protected, and postal voting is restricted to the group of citizens abroad. So, an introduction of online voting is not on the political agenda for the near future.

Finland

A relatively high level of Internet use is characteristic of Finland, but the existence of a digital divide is still conspicuous (Grönlund and Setala 2002). Two-thirds of the population are Internet users, although the percentage of women users is lower, especially in the age group over 55 years. Students and middle and upper-management employees are somewhat above the national average, while the unemployed are below. The Internet is also widespread in rural areas. Electronic government and electronic administration are accepted by three-quarters of the population.

The possibility of advance voting also exists. Voter turnout in Finnish parliamentary and local government elections is decreasing, and in rural areas nearly 50 per cent of the electorate uses the option of voting in advance (the advance vote is organized mainly at post offices). In the cities, 36 per cent make use of this option. Internet campaigning is more and more becoming a feature of political discussions, and opinion polls are also organized via the Internet. There is a pilot project on the Åland Islands involving electronic voting: this small group of islands with around 25,000 inhabitants has its own parliament with legislative competencies and its own budget. Here, mail-in voting also exists and 1 to 2 per cent of the voters make use of this channel.

The high level of interest in communication technologies in Finland does not seem to result in strong pressure with regard to implementation of Internet voting. Social pressure on voters within families and the danger of vote-selling are perceived as factors to take seriously, and political and technical barriers also receive much attention in public discussions. Other reasons may be that in Finland elections are not as frequent as in many other countries, and that the electoral system has a good reputation. In the discussion on online voting the introduction of electronic identity cards came up: for the local election of 2003, online registration was planned, but the introduction of online voting is consciously postponed.

Sweden

In Sweden, societal impacts of the new Information and Communication Technologies are, just as in other Scandinavian countries, extensive. Still, only moderate steps have been taken towards online voting. According to

Swedish electoral legislation, the casting of the ballot is to take place on election day inside the polling station. However, there is the possibility of voting in advance in special public rooms, and, as in Finland, the post offices function as polling stations for advance voting. Postal voting in the Swedish sense is not voting by mail, but consists of advance voting in a post office. This kind of voting has existed since 1942, but has recently been taken up more and more by voters. In 1988, 37 per cent of the voters cast their votes in a post office. Mail-in voting only existed for citizens visiting or residing in foreign countries, because the embassies in those countries are not authorized to act as polling stations. Skepticism regarding online voting is widespread; the traditional voting process is seen as trustworthy and simple, unlike online voting. These views are dominant among the older generations, but nevertheless opinion polls show that 55 per cent of the Swedish population would prefer voting through the Internet. Also in Sweden the social aspects of traditional voting (going in person to the polling station, etc.) carry much weight.

The Swedish case demonstrates that the barrier to online elections is not necessarily widespread distrust of new technology, but rather a deep-seated satisfaction and conservatism regarding existing electoral institutions.

Notwithstanding the general reservation towards electronic voting, there are some experiments in which the government takes an active interest. All experiments concern hybrid elections, that is in elections with a more private and less public character. In an election of the student parliament of Umeå University, 90 per cent of the voters voted alone without any influence from other people. Further experience with Internet voting was gained in elections within political parties. The Swedish conservative party (*Moderaterna*) recruited their candidates in September 2001 by Internet voting. This was, however, only a pre-election, which had no binding consequences for the party. The first actual steps towards electronic voting are plans to install electronic polling machines in polling stations, because here the electoral process and the secrecy of the vote can be controlled by the state administration.

France

France has taken a special route to the information and communication era, including steps towards online elections. The adoption of the Internet in France is, compared to the other countries in this overview, fairly low (20%). This may in part explain the low level of support electronic voting receives from politicians; only 5 per cent of them favour electronic voting. Another explanation for the lack of support is the fact that France has negative experiences with postal voting. Postal voting was strictly regulated until the 1970s and was partly abolished because a massive wave of rigging had taken place.

On the local level there are experiments and proponents of electronic voting. In Corsica, for instance, electronic voting devices have been in use quite successfully since 1977. The city of Issy-Les-Moulinaux has taken electronic government quite seriously, and Internet coverage there is high compared to the rest of France. Some 35 per cent of Issy-Les-Moulineaux residents use the Internet. Official documents are online, the city council discussions can be followed via the Internet, and many municipal services are delivered online. It is not surprising that this city, and some others, opted to experiment with online voting during the presidential and parliamentary elections in 2002. The experiments provided an option to vote via the Internet parallel to the traditional way of voting. Other pilots were also proposed, but needed approval of the Commission National de l'Informatique et des Libertés (CNIL). This organization disapproved of some of the pilots, arguing that verification was handled only by a special code and a password, social pressure during the electoral process could not be controlled, and finally that the server handling the Internet voting process was situated in New York and thus outside of control by the national authorities. Two pilot projects (in Paris and in Merginac) got a better evaluation from the CNIL because they were using smart cards, and another pilot, in the Parisian suburb of Voisy-les-Bretonneaux, also received CNIL approval. The Ministry of the Interior, however, criticized the concept.

Whereas in the public sector there is little support from politicians, and regulatory bodies such as the CNIL are careful in assessing pilots, online voting is becoming more and more attractive in the socio-economic sector. Shareholder legislation and electoral legislation for universities have changed in favour of online voting.

Conclusions

Looking at the ongoing debate about Internet voting and its current status as a policy option in many different countries, a number of conclusions can be made:

- First, we have to acknowledge that Internet voting clearly involves some enticing promises as well as serious threats. On the one hand we may hope for the mobilization of young voters, the overcoming of existing political divides, the increase of voter turnout and improved administrative efficiency. On the other hand we may fear new digital divides, more individualized decision-making, superficial democratic participation, the loss of secrecy and large-scale election fraud.

- Second, we find that the expressions of such promises and threats are mainly just what they suggest: preliminary expressions of uncertainty about what the future may bring, formulated in order to influence decisions, to bring about or to prevent the very development that is hoped for or feared.
- Third, as noticed in cross-country comparisons, the various countries are now reacting quite differently to these promises and threats, with interpretations and policy plans clearly related to the institutional context of each country.

    In countries such as Switzerland, Estonia, the Netherlands and the UK most attention seems to be focused on the promises of Internet Voting, while in Scandinavia the promises seem to be largely disregarded because of satisfaction with existing electoral procedures.

Research agenda

That different countries reach different conclusions with respect to prospective changes in one of the central processes in democracy is, of course, not surprising. In fact, it might be a worrying sign if every country adopted exactly the same type of procedure and processes. The socio-cultural contexts differ between countries and this indeed should have its impact on institutional processes. However, the choices countries make should be made on the basis of knowledge about real opportunities and threats and, as this chapter has sought to demonstrate, more experience may be needed before a definite assessment can be made in this respect. To collect the necessary empirical data to make well-considered choices, we propose that a systematic research agenda be developed, of which we present a first outline below. As we have argued in this chapter, comparative research and attention to the context should be key features of research on electronic elections.

- A *digital divide and voter turnout*. This is probably the most crucial issue. Is the divide likely to persist, and perhaps even widen, or will it diminish as ICT equipment becomes more and more widespread? This is not only a question of further spread of technology and reductions in the price of equipment, but also a question of making the technology really user-friendly. But even then, there may be people who decide to opt out, for instance because ICT does not benefit them. It is also a question of public policies and efforts with regard to the training of users. And or course, the core question here is whether or not online voting will affect voter turnout. Will it, or will it not? What are the impacts, and under what circumstances? Perhaps turnout of certain groups will be affected (the educated and well-to-do?) while others remain untouched by the new opportunities? In the latter case, the digital divide may actually widen.

- *Trust in online voting.* This issue is related to the general legitimacy of, and trust in, political systems and governments. Research may focus on two sets of questions: How do factors that generate (or weaken) trust in voting procedures, including online voting, compare to factors that generally generate trust in political institutions? Under what conditions are voters and electoral authorities willing to face some measure of risk in voting procedures (as they are in for example Estonia)? Will online voting actually increase the level of trust in elections and institutions in some segments of the electorate?

- *Secrecy.* Secrecy is meant to guarantee anonymity in relation to the state administration and also to help keep one's vote to oneself and not have to share it with other social groups, such as the family or employers (privacy). Because the question of secrecy and privacy is important in mail-in voting, an analysis of existing postal voting habits can be used as an indicator of the effects of online voting. The problem of early voting is also relevant in Internet voting, so advance voting in general should be evaluated.

- *Voting and social capital.* This issue deals with the context and the situation in which the ballot is cast. As mentioned above, to many voters the traditional way of voting is an opportunity to express identity and to confirm social and political status. Related to this issue is the question of the extent to which voters prefer to involve others in their decisions – including technical help – or desire full privacy throughout the process of choice and reflection. Voters may be more varied in their habits and preferences than is conventionally recognized.

- *Internet politics and policies.* The decision-making process surrounding the initiation and implementation of Internet voting often bears the imprints of strong economic and political forces. The actors in these processes include not only bureaucrats, ministers and their advisers, but also lobbyists who work on behalf of the ICT industries. How decisions on Internet voting and related issues are reached, and how the processes may vary, should form the subject of comparative cross-country research.

- *Internet voting practices and procedures.* The issue here is how Internet voting is actually organized and carried out. This may vary from country to country, and also within countries, for example in comparing local and national elections. What are the experiences of different countries and levels of government? What are the typical problems in arranging such elections? Are there some ways that are better than others? Is it possible to develop a set of best-practice criteria?
- *Citizen empowerment and political choice.* Online voting does not occur in isolation, its introduction is usually accompanied by a variety of electronic communication channels to enhance citizen access to relevant election and policy material. Political parties, furthermore, develop their own websites to have a presence on the net, especially during election campaigns. For those with access to the net these electronic channels are clearly a source of empowerment, as it reduces the cost of political communication and transactions, also for individual citizens. Other things being equal, one may assume that more and better information makes for more informed and rational political choices and thus an enhancement of democracy. Exactly how citizens make use of the net for political purposes and how it influences the choice process is, of course, a vital future research issue.
- *Varieties of e-democracy and trajectories of change.* Just as democracy is a multifaceted ideal of governance, it is also a dynamic form of governance evolving in response to crises, pressures, needs and interests. Consequently, democratic countries vary considerably in their institutional forms and procedures. ICTs may well add to this variation, helping to create new forms of governance and participation, as suggested in the introductory chapter. Not all forms may be seen as equally desirable by everybody. A destructive potential may also be inherent in some forms of ICT (for example e-mail bombardment). The essential feature of ICT – faster communications – is also likely to speed up the processes of political evolution. It was suggested in the introductory chapter that Internet voting is emerging as an element of wider trends of individualization, liberalization and automatization of electoral procedures. It has been pointed out above, however, that contextual configurations of individual countries influence the

spread of such trends. Some countries, and even some regions within countries, may experience faster change than others. The comparison of trajectories of change is, therefore, another focus of research that we wish to put on the agenda.

The plea we make at this end of this book is that research on Internet voting and online elections should be carried out in a framework that is capable of grasping the wider democratic implications of these developments.

References

Berg-Schlosser, D. and De Meur, G. (1994) 'Conditions of Democracy in Inter-War Europe. A Boolean Test of Major Hypothesis', *Comparative Politics*, 26: 253–79.

Brunazo, A. (2000) 'Atual sistema de votação pode ser fraudado, diz especialista (Current system of voting can be embezzled, says specialist)', <http://www.brunazo.eng.br/voto-e/noticias/congressonacional1.htm Vol. 2002>

Dahl, R. A. (1990) *Democracy and its Critics*. New Haven: Yale University Press.

e-Envoy (2002) *In the Service of Democracy; a Consultation Paper on Policy for Electronic Democracy*. London: Office of the e-Envoy, Cabinet Office.

Electoral Commission (2002) *Modernizing Elections: A Strategic Evaluation of the 2002 Electoral Pilot Schemes*. London: The Electoral Commission.

FVAP (2001) *Voting over the Internet*, Pilot Project Assessment Report. Department of Defence: Federal Voting Assistence Program.

IPI (2001) *Report of the National Workshop on Internet Voting: Issues and Research Agenda*. Washington, DC: Internet Policy Institute.

Kersting, N. (2002a) 'Internet-Wahlen im Vergleich. Deutschland, USA und Schweiz', in A. Siedschlag *et al.* (eds), *Kursbuch Internet und Politik 2/2002*. Opladen: Leske.

Kersting, N. (2002b) *Internet Voting Behaviour*. Workshop on Internet Voting, Institut für Politikwissenschaft/IPSA, Research Committee for Comparative Studies on Local Government and Politics, Marburg 14–15 June 2002.

Kriesi, H. (2002) *E-voting*. Motivation and Information Issues Workshop on E-voting and the European Parliamentary Elections. EUI Florence, May 2002.

Linder, W. (2001) *Gutachten zum e-Voting*. Berne: Institut für Politikwissenschaft, Universität Bern.

Ministerie van Binnenlandse Zaken en Koninkrijkrelaties (2002) *Brief aan de Tweede Kamer over heroverweging Kiezen op Afstand*. Den Haag: Ministerie van Binnenlandse Zaken en Koninkrijkrelaties.

Mohen, J. and Glidden, J. (2001) 'The Case for Internet Voting', *Communications of the ACM*, 44(1): 72–85.

Philips, D. M. and von Spakovsky, H. A. (2002) 'Gauging the Risks of Internet Elections', *Communications of the ACM*, 44(1): 73–85.

Pratchett, L. (2002) *The Implementation of Electronic Voting in the UK*. London: Local Government Association.

Schweizerischen Bundesrat (2002) 'Bericht über den Vote électronique; Chancen, Risiken und Machbarkeit elektronischer Ausübung politischer Rechte', Schweizerischen Bundesrat.

Solop, F. I. (2000) 'Digital Democracy Comes of Age in Arizona: Participation and Politics in the First Binding Internet Election', Paper presented at the American Political Science Association National Conference, Washington DC.

Svensson, J. S. and Leenes, R. E. (2003) 'E-Voting in Europe: A Case of Structuration', *Information Polity*, 7(4).

Thomas, O. (2001) Bristol and Croydon follow-up letter. London: Electoral Reform Services.

Watt, B. (2002) *Implementing Electronic Voting: A Report Addressing the Legal Issues Raised by the Implementation of Electronic Voting*. University of Essex.

Wyatt, S. (2001) *Technology and In/Equality: Questioning the Information Society*. New York: Routledge.

Index

GPSR Compliance

The European Union's (EU) General Product Safety Regulation (GPSR) is a set of rules that requires consumer products to be safe and our obligations to ensure this.

If you have any concerns about our products, you can contact us on

ProductSafety@springernature.com

In case Publisher is established outside the EU, the EU authorized representative is:

Springer Nature Customer Service Center GmbH
Europaplatz 3
69115 Heidelberg, Germany